SECURE PROVISION

Andrew Graham.
Sept. '85

SECURE PROVISION

A review of special services for
the mentally ill and mentally
handicapped in England and Wales

Edited by
LARRY GOSTIN

Tavistock Publications
London and New York

First published in 1985 by
Tavistock Publications Ltd
11 New Fetter Lane, London EC4P 4EE

Published in the USA by
Tavistock Publications
in association with Methuen, Inc.
733 Third Avenue, New York, NY 10017

Typeset by Activity Limited, Wilts.
Printed in Great Britain
at the University Press, Cambridge

British Library Cataloguing in Publication Data
Secure provision: a review of special services
for the mentally ill and mentally handicapped
in England and Wales.
1. Insane, Criminal and dangerous – England
I. Gostin, Larry
365'.46'0942   HV8742.G7

ISBN 0-422-78420-6
ISBN 0-422-78430-3 Pbk

Library of Congress Cataloging in Publication Data
Main entry under title:

Secure provision.

   Bibliography: p.
   Includes indexes.
   1. Insane, Criminal and dangerous—Mental health
services—England—Addresses, essays, lectures.
   2. Insane, Criminal and dangerous—Mental health
services—Wales—Addresses, essays, lectures.
   3. Insane, Criminal and dangerous—Legal status, laws,
etc.—England—Addresses, essays, lectures.   4. Insane,
Criminal and dangerous—Legal status, laws, etc.—Wales—
Addresses, essays, lectures.   I. Gostin, Larry O.
(Larry Ogalthorpe)

   RC451.4.P68S43   1985   362.2'0942   84-26809
   ISBN 0-422-78420-6
   ISBN 0-422-78430-3 (pbk.)

Contents

List of contributors

Larry Gostin is General Secretary of the National Council of Civil Liberties; Visiting Fellow at Oxford University, Centre for Criminological Research, 1982–83; Legal Director, MIND, 1974–82; Western European editor, *International Journal of Law and Psychiatry*, 1979–82. His advocacy before the European Commission Rights and book, *A Human Condition*, led to a new Mental Health Act in 1983.

Andrew Ashworth is a fellow of Worcester College, Oxford. He was acting director of the Oxford University Centre for Criminological Research until 1984. He is editor of the *Criminal Law Review*.

Philip Bean BSc (Soc), MSc (Econ), PhD, is Senior Lecturer, Department of Social Administration, University of Nottingham.

Robert Bluglass MD, FRC Psych., DPM, is Professor of Forensic Psychiatry, University of Birmingham; Vice President, Royal College of Psychiatrists; and member, Mental Health Act Commission.

Paul Bowden MPhil., MRCP, FRC Psych., is Consultant Forensic Psychiatrist, Bethlem Royal and Maudsley Hospitals; and Consultant Forensic Psychiatrist to the Home Office.

Malcolm Faulk MB, BS, MPhil., FRCP, FRC Psych., is Consultant Psychiatrist, Wessex Regional Medium Secure Unit.

John Gunn MD, FRC Psych., is Professor of Forensic Psychiatry, Institute of Psychiatry, University of London; Honorary Consultant, the Bethlem Royal and Maudsley Hospitals; Chairman of the South East Thames Standing Working Group in Forensic Psychiatry; and member, Home Office Advisory Committees.

John Hamilton MD, FRC Psych., DPM, is Medical Director of Broadmoor Hospital; and Honorary Senior Lecturer in Forensic Psychiatry, University of London.

Brenda Hoggett is Reader in Law, Manchester University; a Law Commissioner with responsibility in family law; previously joint general editor of the *Journal of Social Welfare Law*; previously a member of a Mental Health Review Tribunal and a member of the Council on Tribunals.

Elizabeth Parker is Assistant Director of Special Hospitals Research Unit, Department of Health and Social Security; and was Research Officer at the Home Office from 1964–70.

I. H. Treasaden is Regional Consultant Forensic Psychiatrist for the North West Thames Regional Health Authority; and Honorary Senior Lecturer in Forensic Psychiatry at St Mary's Hospital Medical School, London.

Preface

This series of essays is both timely and important. We are in a stage of transition in respect of the provision of secure treatment for mentally ill and mentally handicapped people. The European Commission of Human Rights has recently made a number of critical reports in respect of the treatment of mentally disordered offenders; the Mental Health Act 1983, with the introduction of a new Mental Health Act Commission, has substantially altered the legal framework in which security and detention is carried out. Most importantly, a new layer is being placed onto the mental health services with the establishment of fully operational regional secure units throughout the country.

This series of essays is intended for policy-makers, mental health professionals, and lawyers. Its purpose is to help inform the debate on policy and professional practice in providing treatment for mentally disordered people in conditions of security.

I would like to extend my gratitude to the Department of Health and Social Security and the Home Office for their assistance with the project, and to MIND for its enthusiastic encouragement. I want warmly to acknowledge the King Edward Hospital Fund whose generous support enabled me to carry out this project; in particular I want to extend my appreciation to Robert Maxwell, David Towell, and Tom McCausland for their encouragement throughout. A copy of the full project report is available from the King's Fund. My thanks go to the Oxford University Centre for Criminological Research, which housed the project, and particularly to Roger Hood and Andrew Ashworth. As ever, pride of place in my appreciation goes to my family – Jean, Bryn, and Kieran.

Larry Gostin
Visiting Fellow
Oxford University
Centre for Criminological Research
September 1984

Introduction: a policy overview
Larry Gostin

Any examination of social policy relating to the mental health services will show that, until comparatively recently, little attention has been given to the particular problems of mentally disordered people who exhibit difficult or dangerous behaviour. The Royal Commission (1957) and Mental Health Act 1959 provided a symbolic turning-point away from the legal and custodial aspects of the old lunacy laws (see further Chapter 10). Several policies very clearly emerged in the late 1950s and 1960s: patients, whenever possible, would receive treatment on an informal basis; they would be treated in the same way as physically ill patients in open wards and, increasingly, in district general hospitals; the ultimate goal of the treatment was to return the patient to the community. New and distinct terms arose from that era that still are put forward as enlightened concepts – the 'open-door' policy, the 'therapeutic community', and 'community care'. Not only was there new legislation in the form of the Mental Health Act 1959 which made this therapeutic revolution possible, but there was also the advent of the major tranquillizers which was to play a large part in opening the hospital doors.

These are concepts which still find favour in official and professional thinking. They have changed the whole nature of psychiatric services. In particular, the mental health services slowly began to lose the capability of caring for difficult or dangerous patients; it was also more likely that the patient with chronic mental illness would slip through the therapeutic net; and the concept of 'asylum' lost favour. In short, very little consideration had been given to the effect of the dangerous patient on himself, on his family, on the staff in hospital, or on society. The dangerous mentally ill person, once cared for on locked wards in the asylum, lost his home – he was to be found in prisons, special hospitals, youth custody, and in the streets – often passing from one institution of social control to another.

This collection of essays seeks to identify the problems and to discuss the developing laws and services intended to provide a solution. Evidence that there is a major developing problem is to be found in an analysis of the various places where mentally disordered offenders are cared for.

The prison system

It is sometimes not appreciated that judges do not have the power to compel a hospital to admit a mentally disordered offender. The hospital managers (whose powers are exercised through a consultant) have complete discretion whether to make a bed available in hospital. But prison governors have no choice whether or not to admit a person sentenced by the court to a term of imprisonment. If the offender poses a real danger to the public, courts will send him to prison if no therapeutic alternative is made available (see further Chapter 7).

Judges have expressed considerable frustration at the difficulties of finding a hospital bed for mentally disordered offenders (e.g. *R. v. McFarlane*, 1975; *R. v. Gordon*, 1981; *R. v. Brazil*, 1975; *R. v. Porter*, 1985). In *R. v. Officer* (1976) Lawton LJ said:

'From time to time in the past decade judges had been put in the position of having to sentence to prison for life, persons who clearly ought to have gone to mental hospital. Judges took the judicial oath of office to do justice by all men. When they had in the past to send persons to prison because no beds were available in a secure hospital, their judicial consciences were strained almost to breaking point.'

This kind of statement by the courts has been often repeated. In 1983 Lawton LJ in *R. v. Harding* suggested that in certain circumstances failure to make a bed available would be a contempt of court. Even though the sentiment is widely shared, as a matter of law it is doubtful whether Lawton LJ is correct (see Chapter 7).

In the parliamentary debates preceding the Mental Health (Amendment) Act 1982 the House of Commons Special Standing Committee tied in a vote to give courts the power to compel hospitals to admit patients given a hospital order. In the event Parliament struck a compromise and gave the court the power only to compel regional health authorities to give information about the availability of hospital beds (Mental Health Act 1983, s. 39). But the ultimate decision still rests with the managers to refuse admission to hospital. Other aspects of the Mental Health Act may make it more possible for the courts to make hospital orders in difficult cases by giving them the power to make interim hospital orders or remands to hospital for report or for treatment. These new powers allow the courts to try out a hospital for a limited period of time before making a more long-term sentence. This makes it more likely that hospitals may be prepared to take the patient at least for a period of assessment (see further Chapter 7).

Figures provided by prison medical officers consistently show that there are some 300 prisoners actually awaiting transfer to a NHS hospital (Elton 1983). Most observers regard this as a conservative figure for the number placed on the transfer list depends upon the prevailing philosophy of imprisonment, the attitudes of mental health professionals, and the facilities provided in the two systems. The fact is that many prison medical officers have stopped recommending that some mentally disordered people are transferred, because of the realization that they may not be accepted within the National Health Service. Indeed Professor Gunn suggests that fully 9 per cent of all remand prisoners are psychotic.

This poses a major problem for the mental health services. The Prison Medical Service is not part of the National Health Service and is largely unable to provide effective treatment and care for mentally disordered prisoners. Professor Gunn (Chapter 4) gives a number of reasons for this, including the difficulty with recruitment and insufficient training; the law which proscribes compulsory treatment; and the sheer number of prisoners. Mentally ill and mentally handicapped people, as a result, suffer in a prison regime which is often rigid and uncaring. (See e.g. *Cornwell*'s case (1976) where an 18-year-old woman with a mental age of 8 was forcibly tattooed by other prisoners.)

In sum, there has been ample evidence that mentally disordered offenders have been sentenced by the courts in cases where judges were convinced of the need for a hospital order; and while in prison mentally disordered offenders could not be transferred to the Health

Service. In both instances it is the inflexibility of the system itself which is acknowledged to be the cause of the problem. Prisons will not be better able to cope for the foreseeable future despite the continued existence of 'therapeutic' prisons such as Grendon – the fact is that prison populations are rising, the Prison Medical Service remains outside of the NHS, and there is to be no significant expansion of psychiatric services in prisons.

Special hospitals

By section 3 of the National Health Service Act 1977 the Secretary of State for Social Services has a duty to establish and maintain special hospitals for people who require treatment under conditions of special security on account of their dangerous, violent, or criminal propensities. The four special hospitals – Broadmoor, Rampton, Moss Side, and Park Lane – are described in greater detail by Dr John Hamilton in Chapter 3.

Reports from the Estimates Committee (1968), the Hospital Advisory Service (1975), the Butler Committee (1974), the All-Party Parliamentary Mental Health Group (1980), and the European Commission of Human Rights (1981) were all critical of patient care in many respects: lack of occupation for many patients unable to leave the ward; lack of motivation and increasing apathy; and inadequate facilities for personal hygiene and privacy. Particularly worrying was the Boynton report into Rampton Hospital (1980) and the police investigations following allegations of criminal offences made in the Yorkshire Television documentary, 'Secret Hospital'. The Boynton report was critical, *inter alia*, of the isolation of Rampton from the rest of the NHS, the absence of an effective complaints procedure, lack of therapeutic direction in the hospital, poor internal communication, staff tensions, and out-dated custodial attitudes. These criticisms only confirmed those made in earlier inquiries into the hospital in the Elliot Report (1973) and by the Hospital Advisory Service (1971).

These reports are not wholly representative of patient care in special hospitals today. Major improvements have been made: overcrowding has been relieved by the development of the new special hospital, Park Lane, and by the rebuilding and extension of Broadmoor and Rampton; community health councils and ethical committees have been introduced; exchanges with the NHS and universities in staffing and training have begun; and the occupational and recreational facilities (which have always been excellent) have been made more widely available to patients.

TRANSFERS

The special hospitals exist to treat patients who require maximum security on account of their 'dangerous, violent or criminal propensities' (see above). It is unlawful and harmful to a patient's prospects for treatment and rehabilitation for him to remain in conditions of security longer than is necessary. Yet, of the 1,673 patients resident in special hospitals as of 1 March, 1984, 16 per cent were waiting to go, their discharge or transfer having been agreed. In an important study Dell (1980) showed that in 1979 more than one in three patients awaiting transfer to local NHS hospitals had been waiting for over two years compared with less than one in ten three years previously. Recent figures show that – despite the direct intervention of the Secretary of State for Social Services in a plea to regional health authorities in 1981 – the percentage of patients and the time they are waiting to leave is slightly rising. Fourteen patients (most severely mentally impaired) have been waiting for a transfer for more than four years.

Ashingdane's case, which is currently before the European Court of Human Rights, is a neat illustration of the extent of the problem. Mr Ashingdane was recommended for transfer from Broadmoor Hospital by a formidable consensus of informed opinion: his responsible medical officer, the Secretary of State for Social Services, the Home Secretary, the consultant in the local hospital to which he was to be transferred, and a mental health review tribunal. Yet his transfer to Oakwood Hospital, Maidstone, Kent, was blocked by the Health Service union, the Confederation of Health Service Employees (COHSE), whose members had never even seen the patient. The fact that transfers between the various organs of the NHS remains so difficult and inflexible is the primary obstacle to overcome in order to achieve a more efficient and caring service for mentally disordered offenders.

REHABILITATION

The special hospital system concentrates some 1,600 patients, selected for their 'dangerousness', in four hospitals on just three sites. This concentration of people has produced large, relatively remote institutions with closed communities set apart from the mainstream of the NHS. As a result, both staff and patients suffer from a degree of isolation. Recruitment of staff with a wide range of therapeutic and rehabilitative experience is sometimes difficult and the insufficiency of contact with the rest of the NHS means that it is difficult fully to integrate the special hospitals into the mental health services. Much of the responsibility lies, not with the special hospitals themselves, but with local hospitals and local social services authorities which sometimes do not accept their fair share of responsibility for the rehabilitation of special-hospital patients.

There is only one realistic way out of a specific hospital, and that is by transfer. Special-hospital care means very strict control over the patient's behaviour; most ordinary association with family and friends is impossible, and most ordinary behaviour such as shopping, preparing a personal budget, and home-making cannot be practised. Thus there is no realistic opportunity for social rehabilitation until the patient is transferred to a more locally based therapeutic environment.

To the credit of the special hospitals, most have seen the need to improve their capacity to transfer patients. Rampton has a close relationship with the Eastdale Unit, while Broadmoor is considering similar arrangements with other units.

MANAGEMENT

The special hospitals are managed centrally by the DHSS, except Rampton Hospital, which is managed locally by a special health authority (the Rampton Review Board; see further Gostin 1985). Central management has proven to be too remote to be effective; it contributes to the isolation of the hospital by having it managed separately from the rest of the NHS; and it prevents a stronger medical and therapeutic element which would be more likely if the hospital were formally managed by a health authority, with day-to-day tasks delegated to the multi-disciplinary team. There is a strong case, therefore, for delegating the management of special hospitals to health authorities.

Local hospitals

Dr Malcolm Faulk (Chapter 2) gives us a thoughtful analysis of the problems of the modern-day hospital which has, quite properly, moved away from the concepts of custodial care and asylum, and towards active treatment in open conditions. He presents evidence showing that the locking of wards (so long as there is a therapeutic environment) does not necessarily have deleterious effects on patients. Yet a number of studies in different health regions continue to show a substantial unmet need for treatment under conditions of security. There are large numbers of people who would benefit from intensive care in a local mental hospital, but who are not currently being cared for in the NHS. These are the patients who are sentenced to prison, inappropriately placed in special hospitals, or simply left in the community – sometimes sleeping rough, neglected, suicidal, or dangerous.

The 'open-door' policy was undoubtedly correct, as the great majority of patients should continue to enjoy their freedom while receiving treatment in a local mental illness or mental handicap hospital or in a district general hospital. 'Open conditions' as a concept affords the patient his or her liberty and dignity, and also serves therapeutic objectives. But the pendulum has clearly swung too far so that district health authorities and local social services authorities have simply lost the capability of, or will for, helping mentally disordered people who are difficult or dangerous. There is a great deal of circumstantial evidence for this: the increasing reluctance of local hospitals and local authority accommodation to accept placements from the courts or transfers from special hospitals; the small number of facilities and the inadequate training and guidance given to nurses; and the alarming increase in the number of assaults on members of staff who clearly are not prepared to deal with violent or disruptive behaviour (COHSE 1976). (As to the legal position of patients and staff see Brenda Hoggett's comprehensive analysis in Chapter 8.)

The solution to this problem is to devote considerably more resources into local hospitals to help them attain the capability of caring for difficult patients – i.e. resources necessary for adapting wards for this purpose, higher staffing ratios, and additional training and guidance. In short, there needs to be a dramatic change in attitudes and shift in resources so that more intensive security arrangements are fully a part of an integrated service both inside the hospital and within the NHS.

Few people are 'always' or 'never' dangerous. As Professor Bowden (Chapter 9) shows, the concept of 'dangerousness' is situation-specific. Accordingly, a person may need an extra degree of security and staff supervision during occasional difficult periods for hours or days, but not usually months or years. The hospital must have the flexibility to remove a patient from his ordinary 'open' environment for a time and then return him to it as soon as the difficulty ends. The need for 'flexible response' calls for extra resourcing and training. At present nurses understandably feel reluctant to care for potentially dangerous patients, and an attitudinal change will not be possible until there are extra resources for staff.

Regional secure units

The evidence presented thus far points to an undoubted need for better provision for those people whose needs fall between the services offered by local hospitals and special hospitals. These people, because of their difficult and, at times, dangerous behaviour, require extra security which is not currently provided in local hospitals, but they do not require the degree of security found in special hospitals. The outward signs of the problem have just been discussed and manifest themselves in the number of inappropriately placed people in prisons and special hospitals.

There has been only one official solution suggested and that is for the establishment of regional secure units – i.e. units maintained within each health region which would provide treatment under medium-secure conditions. This was first proposed by a Ministry of Health working party in February, 1961. That was followed by a memorandum to regional hospital boards in July, 1961, but not a single secure unit was established. The idea was reintroduced in the Interim Butler Report in 1974 (Butler Committee 1974), which proposed secure units in each regional health authority as a matter of urgency. The revised report of the working part on security in the NHS (Glancy 1974) was published at the same time and made a similar recommendation. The Department of Health and Social Security agreed to fund these units from central government resources. (The development of regional secure units is set out in greater detail by Elizabeth Parker and Professor Robert Bluglass in Chapters 1 and 5.)

Progress in developing regional secure units has been agonizingly slow. From 1976/77 to 1981/82 the DHSS allocated £44,285,000 for the development of secure units. Of this amount only £17,902,000 was spent on security in psychiatric hospitals, and the majority of the rest of the money was spent on general medical services which had no connection to the mental health services (*Hansard* December 1982). As of 1981/82 there were no fully operational units. All regional health authorities now have some plans for permanent accommodation and seven regions have some unit in operation (see *Hansard* 1984, 1985).

Regional secure units were originally envisaged as relatively small, locally based, taking mentally ill patients for short periods of not more than eighteen months. I originally identified two principal measures of assessment to see if the units met their intended purpose. First, whether they admitted those who were inappropriately placed in prisons and special hospitals; it is important that they do not become a receptacle for difficult patients whom local hospitals would like to be rid of (Gostin 1977). The Butler Committee's overriding concern was that the units are needed for 'the early relief of the prisons and special hospitals'. Empirical research has shown that there are more than 2,000 patients in local hospitals whose staff wish to see them in more secure settings (Glancy 1974; see Chapter 2). There is little to prevent these patients from taking the majority of beds in regional secure units.

Regional secure units were intended to be an integral part of the Health Service, providing patients with an intensive period of treatment and rehabilitation for a short time; they are not intended to provide a solution for chronically ill and dangerous patients by providing asylum or a longer period of preventive detention. The second criterion, therefore, is whether patients actually remain in these hospitals for short periods of time. If patients are relatively easily transferred to local hospitals and discharged into community accommodation, with more patients from special hospitals and prisons taking their place, then the units will have achieved their main objectives.

According to the analysis of Dr Treasaden (see Chapter 6) there are reasonably encouraging signs under both of these criteria. The mean length of stay of patients in interim secure units was within the eighteen-month period suggested by the DHSS, although this masks the fact that some patients remained much longer (e.g. for over three years). On the second measure he shows that just more than half of the patients have been referred to the interim units from the courts, remand centres, prisons, or special hospitals. However, that leaves the balance who have been referred by local hospitals or community agencies. Clearly much more research is required to monitor the operation of secure units, particularly on these two standards. One of the major difficulties with the current research into interim secure units is that they may not be representative of the permanent secure units. Many interim units have smaller 'sub-regional' catchment areas, and they share grounds and facilities with local NHS hospitals. Such units provide models for the very best practice in treating difficult or dangerous patients.

Alternative policy

At best the building of regional secure units will simply add another, *albeit* important, layer of security onto the NHS. But that in itself will do nothing to solve the major problems: a lack of an integrated system where there should be few, if any, administrative barriers between the different layers of services; too little resources, staff training, and guidance in dealing with difficult or dangerous patients at a local hospital and community level; and the incapacity for a 'flexible response' to dangerous behaviour so that the person is contained only during difficult periods.

At worst, the regional secure unit programme will attract scarce financial and staffing resources from district health authorities, making it increasingly difficult to provide a local service for potentially dangerous patients.

The alternative vision of secure psychiatric services would have a reduced role for the special hospitals – i.e. they would come closer to the community by establishing a regional catchment area admissions policy and by management being delegated to regional health authorities or special health authorities. With the introduction of regional secure units the more radical vision would be towards phasing out the most remote and outdated of the special hospitals.

Ideally there would be several small and discrete secure units in each region attached to local mental illness or mental handicap hospitals or to district general hospitals; there should be very little, if any, administrative difference between the hospital and the secure unit. By minimizing the differences between secure units and the hospitals which they serve, it would help avoid the stigma of being admitted to a 'secure unit'. Clearly the less desirable form of secure unit is to have one very large, publicly visible unit in each region in which all of the 'difficult' or 'dangerous' people are detained.

District health authorities and local social services authorities must not lose the ability to deal with those who are difficult and disturbed. A far more extensive level of resources, training, and guidance must be provided locally. In many respects, it is to be regretted that so much money (a great deal of which was entirely lost to the psychiatric services) was diverted to specialist units rather than to local services. It is time for this resource imbalance to be redressed and provide more help to the local and non-specialist mental health services to enable them to cope with a wide range of troublesome patients. This will help to achieve a more integrated mental health service where patients who require a high level of security can receive it only for a short period of time; admission to a locked ward, a secure unit, or a special hospital would not be such a momentous event whereby the person is labelled as 'dangerous' and must reside there for months, years, or decades. There must also be substantial fluidity in enabling patients to be transferred to less secure places with the minimum of formality or encumbrance – i.e. from prisons and special hospitals to regional secure units, to local hospitals, and to the community.

References

All-Party Parliamentary Mental Health Group (1980)

Boynton (1980) *Report of the Review of Rampton Hospital.* Cmnd. 8073. London: HMSO. (Chairman, Sir John Boynton.)

Butler Committee (1974) *Interim Report of the Committee on Mentally Abnormal Offenders.* Cmnd. 5698. London: HMSO.

COHSE (1976) *The Management of Potentially Violent Patients.* London: COHSE.

Dell, S. (1980) *The Transfer of Special Hospital Patients to the NHS Hospitals,* Special Hospital Research Unit Report No. 16, London.

Elliot, J.L. (1973) Report on the Organisational Problems and Staff Management Relationships of Rampton Hospital. Unpublished.

Elton, Lord (1983) Letter, 8 July.

Estimates Committee (1968) of the House of Commons. *Second Report: The Special Hospitals and the State Hospital.* London: HMSO.

European Commission of Human Rights (1981) *Visit to Broadmoor Hospital in the Investigation of A. & B. v. the United Kingdom,* app. no. 6870/75, Report of the European Commission of Human Rights, adopted 7 October, 1981.

Glancy, J. (1974) *Revised Report of the Working Party on Security in NHS Psychiatric Hospitals.* London: DHSS.

Gostin, L. (1977) *A Human Condition,* vol. 2. London: MIND.

——(1985) *Mental Health Services: Law and Practice.* London: Shaw.

Hansard (1982) House of Commons, vol. 33, cols 293–96.

Hansard (1984) House of Commons Written Answer, vol. 483, 23 July.

Hansard (1985) House of Commons, vol. 185, cols 167–68.

Ministry of Health (1961) *Special Hospitals: Report of a Working Party.* London: HMSO.

NHS Hospital Advisory Service (1971) *Report on Broadmoor Hospital,* summarized in the report of the *Review of Rampton Hospital* (1980). Cmnd. 8073. London: HMSO.

NHS Hospital Advisory Service (1975) *Report on Broadmoor Hospital.*

Report of the Royal Commission on the Law Relating to Mental Illness and Mental Deficiency (1957) Cmnd. 169. London: HMSO.

CASES

Ashingdane v. *Secretary of State for Social Services and Others,* unpublished, Court of Appeal, 18 Feb., 1980. See *Ashingdane* v. *United Kingdom.* Report of the European Commission of Human Rights, 12 May, 1983.

R. v. *Brazil, The Times,* 29 Oct., 1975.

R. v. *Cornwell, The Guardian,* 7 Oct., 1976.

R. v. *Gordon* (1981) 3 Cr. App. R.(S.) 352.

R. v. *Harding, The Times,* 15 June, 1983.

R. v. *McFarlane* (1975) 61 Cr. App. R. 61.

R. v. *Officer, The Times,* 20 Feb., 1976.

R. v. *Porter, The Times,* 22 Jan., 1985. CA.

Part I History

1 The development of secure provision[1]

Elizabeth Parker

Early legislation

The practice of confining some of the insane stretches back more than 600 years in England. The type of patient detained has varied, always including those considered to be dangerous but extending in the eighteenth and nineteenth centuries to the majority of persons confined in madhouses, asylums, or workhouses and then diminishing to the present level of less than 5 per cent of the mentally disordered in hospital. The forms of security employed have changed little over the period; perimeter security, internal locks and bars, and individual restraint by both physical and chemical means have been in continuous use to a greater or lesser degree in various guises up to the present day. Secure provision as such is reserved for persons who are thought, according to the standards of the day, to require a greater degree of restraint than is usual for the ordinarily insane or the general run of psychiatric patients. It is normally applied to those considered to be dangerous.

By 1482 it had been established in English common law that it was lawful to incarcerate a dangerous lunatic, either in his own home or in the local Bridewell (Allderidge 1979). Specific statutory provision for lunatics was not achieved until more than two centuries later under the Vagrancy Act of 1714. This dealt, *inter alia*, with 'furiously mad and dangerous' wandering lunatics and empowered two or more justices of the peace to direct that they be 'kept safely locked up ... and [if such justices find it necessary] to be there chained'. The lunatics were only to be confined for as long as their lunacy or madness continued. A later Vagrancy Act of 1744 speaks of 'curing such person during such restraint'; no doubt an optimistic attempt to relieve the parish of the cost should the lunatic be unable to support himself whilst interned. Following from this the 1744 Act stipulated that nothing in the Act should prevent any friend or relative of the lunatic taking him into their own care or protection.[2]

It was implicit in both Acts that the justices were capable of identifying the dangerously insane, although it required at least two of them to do this. The Acts did not provide for any medical attention and it was presumably the justices or gaolers who decided when a detainee was fit to be released. This must have resulted in many a mad person being set free in a lucid or quiescent interval only to find himself reapprehended when his illness once more took a violent or disturbing form.

In the eighteenth century, apart from the specific provisions of the vagrancy laws, lunatics generally were confined in madhouses or singly in private residences, in both cases often with dubious legality, or, along with the sane, were liable to be detained under the Poor Laws or the criminal law. Wherever confined they were usually ill-treated, sometimes deliberately in an attempt to drive the madness out, or as an appropriate response to those who either could not or would not work, or as a result of indifference and neglect. In the latter half of the eighteenth century and throughout the nineteenth century there was a considerable amount of legislation devoted to lunacy reform. The main objectives of statutes passed during this period were to prevent ill-treatment of the insane and to ensure proper housing and care, preferably in special institutions, and to prevent sane persons being detained as lunatics.

Nevertheless, the improved conditions occurring in the nineteenth century were paralleled by an increased liability for lunatics to be lawfully deprived of their liberty. Following the Vagrancy Act of 1744 the next legislation providing for compulsory detention was the Criminal Lunatics Act 1800 (39 and 40 Geo. III, c. 94). On 15 May of that year James Hadfield fired a pistol at King George III as he entered the royal box at Drury Lane theatre. Hadfield was subsequently found 'not guilty by reason of insanity' on a charge of treason. He would normally have been released but for the fact he was considered to be dangerous, and 'for his own sake and the sake of society at large' he was returned to Newgate.

Meanwhile, legislation had been hastily drafted 'for the safe custody of insane persons charged with offences'. This allowed for the detention under His Majesty's Pleasure of those 'acquitted, on the ground of insanity, of treason, murder, or felony'; or persons 'indicted and found insane on arraignment' and those 'brought before any criminal court to be discharged for want of prosecution, appearing insane' (HMP cases). The justices were empowered to confine 'any person discovered or apprehended under circumstances that denote a derangement of mind and a purpose of committing some crime'.[3]

The Act of 1800 was retrospective as well as prospective in its scope but was vague as to where those falling under its provisions were to be housed, stipulating only 'strict custody in a place the court shall see fit'. Nor did it provide machinery for release. Under its powers Hadfield was admitted to Bethlem on 10 October, 1800.

The main point of interest is that if Hadfield had been more obviously mad he could probably have been detained under the 1744 Vagrancy Act as 'furiously mad and dangerous'. To the layman he seemed quite sane, as testified by the King's brother, the Duke of York, who questioned him in the theatre immediately after the shooting. Hadfield owed his acquittal to his defence counsel Erskine, who succeeded in imparting to the judge the recent medical knowledge of the nature and effects of paranoid delusions. The 1800 Act followed on directly from the Vagrancy Acts in that the main objective of all three was the protection of the sane from those considered to be dangerously insane by means of indeterminate detention.

An important omission in the Criminal Lunatics Act of 1800 was that it made no arrangements for payment for the care and maintenance of persons committed under its powers who had no means of their own. The result was that many criminal lunatics continued to be kept in gaols and houses of correction instead of being placed in more suitable establishments. In 1807 a parliamentary select committee was appointed 'to enquire into the state of the criminal and pauper lunatics in England and Wales'. It reported that there were at least thirty-seven[4] people in gaols under the 1800 Act and that they expected the number to increase, 'particularly if as at present no means are generally adopted for the cure of persons under such circumstances'. The committee members were fully agreed 'that to confine such persons in a common gaol is equally destructive of all possibility of the recovery of the insane and of the security and comfort of the other prisoners'.

The report recommended that all persons detained under the 1800 Act should be confined in a purpose-built asylum and as only one would be required it should be situated in or near London. The expenses of criminal lunatics who could not maintain themselves were to be met by their local parishes. The responsibility for the regulations concerning the care and management of the inmates was to be vested in the Secretary of State, who was also to ensure that the mental state of recovered patients was to be fully investigated by competent judges prior to discharge. For pauper lunatics the committee recommended the erection of asylums in various parts of the country. In the resulting legislation, the government economically combined the two proposals in the County Asylums Act of 1808 (48 Geo. III, c. 96), which permitted but did not oblige local justices to build public asylums for the admission of three types of lunatic: dangerous lunatics detained on a warrant from two justices under the Vagrancy Act of 1744; criminal lunatics detained during His Majesty's Pleasure under the Criminal Lunatics Act of 1800; and pauper lunatics who were kept at the expense of the local parishes. Arrangements could also be made for paying non-pauper patients.

Previous legislation had assumed that lunatics would be confined and had provided specific authority for the detention of dangerous and criminal lunatics in the Acts of 1744 and 1800 respectively. The County Asylums Act of 1808 authorized the detention of all patients admitted to the new institutions. The Act provided for a fine of between two and ten pounds for anyone who allowed the unauthorized departure of a patient. No mention was made of a state lunatic asylum.

However, at this time the governors of the Bethlehem Hospital in London (now the Bethlem Royal Hospital) were negotiating with the corporation of London about a site for a new hospital in St George's Fields, Southwark. On 25 August, 1810 an under-secretary at the Home Office wrote to enquire whether they would set aside part of the new site for a criminal asylum. He assured the governors that the erection of buildings and the maintenance of the prisoners, including their funeral expenses, would be paid for out of public funds. The governors agreed, only stipulating that the new department should be under their absolute control and not be subject to visits from the county magistrates. The two buildings, one accommodating forty-five males and the other for fifteen female prisoners, were completed and occupied by 31 October, 1816 (O'Donoghue 1914).

In 1835 a select committee of the House of Lords was appointed to inquire into the state of the gaols and houses of correction. Witnesses agreed that it was undesirable to keep in prison persons acquitted on grounds of insanity or found to be insane on arraignment (HMP cases) but there were often difficulties in transferring them to an asylum. Due to the permissive character of the County Asylums Act of 1808 many counties were still without such provision. Even when county asylums existed they were sometimes reluctant to receive insane prisoners, knowing that the cost would fall on the parishes, whereas the expense of maintaining prisoners in gaols was met by the counties. At other times a bed was not available because the asylum was full. The Middlesex Asylum (Hanwell) went so far as to write to the Home Office objecting to taking criminal lunatics on the ground that they did not have the security for that class of offender. The criminal blocks at Bedlam (i.e. Bethlem) were reported to be full, with two or three places being reserved for cases from the penitentiary (i.e. Millbank Prison). There was also the problem of HMP patients who subsequently recovered their sanity but who were considered to be too dangerous to be discharged. The county asylums were not empowered to detain the sane so this group languished in the prisons at great inconvenience to the administrators because as acquitted or untried men they were not subject to prison discipline, could not be put upon the treadmill, and were usually kept with the remanded prisoners.

The committee finally reported, rather baldly, 'that persons whose trials have been postponed [due to insanity], or who, having been tried, have been acquitted on the ground of insanity, shall not be confined in the gaols or houses of correction'. On 25 July, 1835, no doubt in anticipation of the report being published three days later on the 28th, an under-secretary at the Home Office again wrote to the governors of Bethlem, this time requesting that the male criminal department be enlarged to accommodate a further thirty occupants to be transferred from the gaols. This was agreed and the new wards were ready in 1838.

In 1844 the results were published of a two-year survey by the Metropolitan Commissioners in lunacy of all licensed houses and public and private asylums in England and Wales. It was found that there were only seventeen county asylums, and that there were twenty-one counties without asylums of any kind, either public or private. It is not surprising therefore that there were difficulties in transferring criminal lunatics. The commissioners reported that in April, 1843 there were 224 criminal patients confined in asylums, including 85 in Bethlem, and that there were a further 33 in the gaols. This increase in numbers confirmed the expectations of the 1807 select committee; the metropolitan commissioners, reiterating the conclusion of the 1835 select committee, strongly recommended that separate provision be made for criminal lunatics. The objections to their detention in the county asylums were that some of them were dangerous, had committed 'atrocious offences', and the security required infringed the liberty of the other patients, rendering the asylums more like prisons than hospitals.

The report by the metropolitan commissioners was followed by the Lunatics Act of 1845 (8 and 9 Vict., c. 100). This was a major reform as, by means of the newly founded lunacy commissioners, it established a country-wide system of inspection, licensing, and reporting of all institutions in which lunatics were kept. A further Act passed in the same year (8 and 9 Vict., c. 126) dealt with the erection and management of county asylums. Both Acts stipulated medical certificates as necessary for admission. Once again the assumption of confinement is explicit but it is significant that this now has the acquiescence of the medical signatory.

The Lunatics Act 1845 also authorized the continued detention of patients in hospitals and licensed houses who were considered by their medical attendant to be dangerous and unfit to be at large. The doctor was required to testify this in writing and to give the reasons for his opinion. Ultimate powers of discharge lay with the lunacy commissioner or the visitors, who could override the medical decision. This is directly comparable with the powers of the Mental Health Review Tribunals today. Patients in county asylums were not liable to be detained on the ground of dangerousness until similar provisions were enacted in 1853 (16 and 17 Vict., c. 97).

This involvement of the medical profession with statutory confinement was the start of a process which has continued up to the present day. Indefinite detention within the penal system has never been popular in England (Parker 1980) but indefinite detention in psychiatric hospitals of patients who are considered to be dangerous has remained a feature of mental health legislation up to and including the recent Mental Health Act 1983.

The 1845 County Asylums Act continued the authorization contained in the 1808 Act of fining staff who through wilful neglect or connivance allowed a patient to escape, the maximum fine rising to not more than twenty pounds. The metropolitan commissioners in their report on England and Wales in 1844 noted the penalties for permitting escapes from asylums in the 1808 Act and recommended that there should be similar provisions with regard to the staff of licensed houses. This was eventually achieved in the Lunacy Acts Amendment Act 1862 (25 and 26 Vict., c. 111).

The attitude of the metropolitan commissioners with regard to escapes is interesting. They disapproved of patients escaping not only 'on account of the hazard to others of permitting dangerous lunatics to be at large, but also for the excitement which they are apt to cause to the insane themselves'. But the commissioners also deplored the use of physical restraints. They considered that the 'proper means to keep inmates in safe custody' was by 'vigilance and care'. In practice this meant a general rise in standards. Released from physical restraint, as most patients were by this time, suitable day-rooms and spacious airing yards were required. Occupations, amusements, and exercise were introduced to prevent boredom and to promote interest and cure, and more attendants were needed, both for their own safety now that their charges were not physically restrained and to advance the new standards of care and vigilance.

Wide as their reforming scope was, the 1845 Acts were silent with regard to criminal lunatics, but the lunacy commissioners returned regularly to the subject in their annual reports. In 1848 the Home Office entered into a financial arrangement with the proprietor of a licensed house, Fisherton House near Salisbury, whereby a detached ward with its own yard was erected solely for criminal lunatics. This acted mainly as an overflow from Bethlem and the initial intake consisted of twenty-four male patients whose offences were neither 'atrocious or violent'. The lunacy commissioners continued to press for a separate asylum for criminal lunatics and in 1855 with reference to Bethlem expressed the opinion that it was 'highly objectionable' that such persons be detained in a 'general lunatic hospital'. The previous year the commissioners had attempted to engender a competitive spirit in the government and/or encourage them by pointing out that a state asylum had been established for criminal lunatics at Dumdrum, near Dublin, in Ireland and that after three years in operation it was reported to be successfully fulfilling its objectives. Eventually, in 1857, the commissioners triumphantly reported that the government had resolved to provide a new state asylum for 600 criminal lunatics. The bed estimate seems somewhat conservative as by this time there were already 581 criminal lunatics, of whom 99 were in Bethlem.

The building of Broadmoor

On 6 August, 1860 an Act was passed for the better provision for the custody and care of criminal lunatics (23 and 24 Vict., c. 75) and it was under its authority that the new state asylum was established. Control was by means of a council of supervision on which Sir Charles Hood, the late medical superintendent of Bethlem, represented the medical interest and Sir Joshua Jebb, the director of convict prisons, the penal interest. The site chosen was at Broadmoor on Bagshot Heath, about thirty-three miles from London. After further consideration it was decided to provide accommodation for only 400 men and 100 women, and to extend later if necessary. This decision was based on the finding that there were large numbers of criminal lunatics who had been many years in asylums and whom it would be unnecessary and in some cases a hardship to move. The lunacy commissioners were also hoping for a change in the Criminal Lunatics Acts that would subsequently reduce the numbers subject to their provisions.

Building began in March 1862; prison labour was used and 254 convicts, together with their officers, were transferred to the Broadmoor site from the public works prisons of Portland, Portsmouth, and Chatham. The new state asylum was completed in 1863, fifty-four years after it had been first recommended by the 1807 select committee. (For a discussion of Broadmoor and the other special hospitals, see Chapter 3).

Broadmoor experienced problems from the beginning; twelve months after opening, the lunacy commissioners reported that as the female accommodation was limited to 100 there was pressure for an immediate extension, which Dr Meyer, the medical superintendent, advised should be used exclusively for violent and refractory patients. The new block for fifty women was opened in May, 1867, but Dr Meyer's recommendation reflected the difficulties being experienced in the type of patient admitted. Three women sent from Millbank Prison had been transferred from Broadmoor to Fisherton House because of their troublesome and violent behaviour and a further three women due to be admitted from Brixton Prison were rejected because they were convicts. The lunacy commissioners disapproved of this undermining of the very reasons for which Broadmoor was established and they hoped that such practices would cease when the new asylum was fully completed. However, in 1867 the visiting commissioners were told that in future admissions would be limited to HMP cases and prisoners from the state prisons who had become insane subsequent to conviction. All prisoners in the county and borough gaols who became insane during sentence would have to be provided for by the county asylums from where they would not be admitted to Broadmoor 'however dangerous they may have become'. The commissioners' restrained comment was that such exclusion:

> 'would not be consistent with the intention of the legislation, or with one of the main objectives for which a criminal asylum was built, namely, to relieve County and Borough asylums by removing therefrom offensive and dangerous criminal lunatics, unfit for association with ordinary pauper patients by reason of their conduct and propensities, and requiring special custody and care.'

Broadmoor continued to experience difficulties in providing for both HMP cases and insane convicts. Dr Meyer, with the approval of the commissioners, separated the two groups as far as was practicable in order to facilitate different management and treatment regimes. The HMP cases were found to be ideal patients, tractable and well-behaved, whose crimes were a result of their insanity. In contrast the convicts were disruptive, many were dangerous, they required constant supervision, and their insanity was thought to result from their criminal life-styles. This classification had obvious social connotations; the HMP cases were comfortably accommodated with a separate reading-room and they did not mix with those admitted from penal servitude 'with the exception of a few lunatic convicts employed as ward assistants'.

By 9 December, 1873, out of a total population of 519 patients 163 were convicts, but during the previous thirteen months out of 62 admissions half had been of that class. The then medical superintendent, Dr Orange, considered that Broadmoor did not provide the proper security or means of treatment required by the convicted prisoners, and the Broadmoor authorities decided that the remedy lay in the complete separation of the two types of patient, to be achieved by the erection of new buildings specifically for the convicts.

By 1891 it was reported that Broadmoor was full and extensions were again being contemplated although the existing building had already been added to on several previous occasions. This situation reflected the shortage of provision generally with regard to the insane. Throughout the latter half of the nineteenth century the prisons and workhouses both contained substantial numbers of inmates who should properly have been in the county asylums.

The insane in the workhouses

The Poor Law Amendment Act of 1834 (4 and 5 Will. IV, c. 76) prohibited detention in a workhouse of 'any dangerous lunatic, insane person or idiot'[5] for more than fourteen days, during which time it was intended that arrangements would be made for transfer to a county asylum. This was taken to imply that it was lawful to detain those who were not dangerous – an interpretation of doubtful legality but practical in view of the few asylums in existence at this period. By 1859 over 40 per cent of all reported lunatics, idiots, and persons of unsound mind were in the county asylums, but over a fifth were still in the workhouses. The asylums were intended as curative institutions but the workhouses transferred not only their mentally ill but also their long-stay chronic mental defectives (Ayers 1971). The Lunacy Act of 1862 obliged the workhouse medical officers to transfer lunatics to the asylums unless a written opinion was given as to why placement in the workhouse was more suitable. On the other hand the Act authorized the removal of chronic lunatics from the asylums back to the workhouses.

By 1867 the position had worsened as the total number of reported lunatics had increased and there were over 10,000 pauper lunatics in the workhouses. In that year the Metropolitan Poor Act (30 and 31 Vict., c. 6) was passed which provided, *inter alia*, for the establishment of asylums (which were controlled by the Metropolitan Asylums Board (MAB)) for the harmless chronic insane in the metropolitan workhouses. Despite the provisions of 1834 against detaining the dangerous in workhouses there had been communications between the lunacy commissioners and the Poor Law Board as to the legality of detaining dangerous insane paupers. Later that year the Poor Law Amendment Act of 1867 (30 and 31 Vict., c. 106) regularized the position to some extent by legalizing the detention of persons suffering from 'mental disease' who in the opinion of the medical officer were 'not in a proper state to leave the workhouse without danger to themselves or others', provided 'that this enactment would not prevent the removal of the lunatic to a lunatic asylum, registered hospital or licensed house, when the removal is otherwise required by law'. The effect of this together with the provisions of the 1834 Act was to authorize the workhouses to detain in the long term dangerous mental defectives who fell short of idiocy. Despite the development of the metropolitan asylums and the increased accommodation in the county asylums, the growing absolute numbers of reported insane hampered progress. In 1890 the proportion of the insane in the workhouses (excluding the MAB asylums) had dropped to 14 per cent but the absolute number had risen to 12,126, many of whom were incurable mental defectives (Ayers 1971).

Insane convicts and prisoners

During this period the prisons experienced similar problems to the workhouses. The select committee of 1807 had reported on the undesirability of keeping the insane in gaols and the 1808 County Asylums Act was intended to effect the transfer of HMP cases from the prisons. In 1816 an Act (56 Geo. III, c. 117) was passed authorizing the transfer to asylums of prisoners who became insane after sentence. The Act cannot have been effective: there were very few county asylums in existence; the responsibility for identifying the insane prisoners, obtaining the necessary medical certificates, and sending them to the Home Office was not stated; there were no arrangements for maintenance costs to be met and there were no means of enforcement. Another attempt to relieve the prisons of the insane was made in 1840 (3 and 4 Vict., c. 54). The Act allowed the transfer to a county asylum of any insane prisoner, lunatic, or dangerous idiot either before or after trial, providing that any such transferred patient who recovered his sanity before the expiration of his sentence should be returned to prison. If the transferred prisoner had no means of his own, the maintenance charges were to be met by the prison.

The difficulties of effecting transfers to the county asylums have already been described but the prisons also contained large numbers of mental defectives who were not covered by the existing lunacy legislation. Like the workhouses the penal system was compelled to make its own arrangements for both the physically and mentally infirm. Certain prisons were designated 'invalid prisons'. Woking was opened in 1860 with the feeble-minded eventually being concentrated in Millbank from 1863 and in Parkhurst from 1869 (Walker and McCabe 1973). The Criminal Lunatics Act of 1867 (30 Vict., c. 12) extended the range of those who could be removed to the county asylums by authorizing the transfer of sentenced persons who 'were unfit from imbecility of mind for penal discipline'. Imbeciles were less severely defective than idiots and imbecility of mind would cover both imbeciles and idiots; the transfer of dangerous idiots had already been authorized in 1840.

Between 1855 and 1889, despite the rising population, the number of persons sentenced to penal servitude had fallen by nearly two-thirds. Also the courts were passing shorter sentences. The resulting smaller number of convicts rendered special invalid prisons unnecessary as the physically sick men could now be provided for in the ordinary prison hospitals. Consequently Woking Invalid Prison was closed in 1888, but Parkhurst survived to become the convict infirmary and received mentally abnormal, infirm, sick, and aged convicts.

In 1877 the prison commissioners became responsible for the local gaols, and insane sentenced prisoners, as opposed to convicts serving sentences of penal servitude, were once again eligible to be sent to Broadmoor, which admitted fifteen such men in that year. After that the numbers dropped to two or three per annum.

Broadmoor, Parkhurst, and Rampton Criminal Lunatic Asylums

Throughout the last decade of the century Broadmoor operated to capacity and in the Lunacy Commissioners' report on their visit on 19 May, 1899 they commented:

'The question of the provision of further accommodation for the criminal lunatics of the country is of pressing importance, and is, we are informed, receiving consideration. Of the various proposals we have heard, the suggestion that another asylum should be built in the north of England is one which appears to us to have some special advantages.'

The proposed asylum eventually materialized as Rampton but in the meantime the building at Broadmoor of a new block for eighty males was started in 1900. (For a discussion of Rampton and the other special hospitals, see Chapter 3.)

In November, 1903, the lunacy commissioners reported that 'the additional accommodation for men gained by the recently erected new wing has been practically entirely utilised and the question for yet further provision for the care of criminal lunatics becomes once more a pressing one.' Broadmoor could now provide accommodation for 566 males and 192 females but there were still 109 criminal lunatics in county asylums and 40 in a special wing at Parkhurst Prison waiting for vacancies at Broadmoor.

To alleviate the situation while a new state asylum was built, an outbuilding of Parkhurst Prison, formerly the printer's shop, was converted into Parkhurst Criminal Lunatic Asylum, opening in June 1908 with accommodation for fifty patients. This asylum, unlike Woking Invalid Prison, came within the purview of the lunacy commissioners and was not the responsibility of the director of convict prisons. It was intended that mentally abnormal prisoners would be sent to Parkhurst Prison for observation and those who came within the existing lunacy legislation would be transferred to Parkhurst Lunatic Asylum. Initially the lunacy commissioners' reports were favourable but after a few years disenchantment set in; the patients were too frequently secluded, there was insufficient employment, there was no remuneration or tobacco allowance as at Broadmoor, the patients wore convict uniform, and there was only a limited area for exercise. In short, the asylum was more like a prison and it closed in 1913 following the opening on 1 October, 1912 of the new state asylum at Rampton, Nottinghamshire.

In the first two months eighty-eight men and forty women were transferred to Rampton from Broadmoor, thus leaving space at Broadmoor for patients from Parkhurst. The transferred patients were carefully selected as non-refractory and preference was given to North Country people whose homes or friends were in the general vicinity of the asylum.[6] The medical superintendent, Dr Sullovan, was previously the medical officer at Holloway Prison, and the eighteen male attendants and thirteen nurses were drafted from Broadmoor.

The Mental Deficiency Act 1913 and the state institutions

The Mental Deficiency Act of 1913 (3 and 4 Geo. V, c. 28) provided a comprehensive legislative and administrative structure for mental defectives comparable to that provided for the insane by the Lunacy Act of 1890. The lunacy commissioners were to be replaced by the new Board of Control, which was to be additionally responsible for the 'supervision, protection and control' of all defectives. In particular, the Board of Control, subject to the approval of the Secretary of State, could 'establish and maintain institutions for defectives of dangerous or violent propensities'. Under this authority the Board acquired buildings at Maghull, near Liverpool, intending to use them as a state institution for mental defectives. Occupation was prevented by the outbreak of war and the buildings were transferred to the War Office as a hospital for soldiers returning from the front suffering from mental shock.

In the meantime there was a pressing need for a state institution for violent or dangerous female defectives. The Board managed to rent Farmfield in Surrey, a former reformatory for inebriates, from the London County Council, and this opened in December, 1914 with accommodation for ninety women. Farmfield was unique in two respects: it was the first state institution to provide for persons who were not certified under the Lunacy Acts and it admitted people who had not been before the courts. All the population were detained under the Mental Deficiency Act of 1913 and just over two-fifths had been dealt with under the civil sections. The women were found to be very difficult to control and manage, particularly those admitted via the courts or from prisons who realized that there was no prospect of immediate discharge when their sentences terminated. The Board of Control optimistically 'hoped that they may after a time come to understand that it is designed not to punish but to protect them'.

Meanwhile the Board were anxious to make similar provision for violent or dangerous defective men and had been discussing with the Home Office the possibility of obtaining a disused prison, although due to the war the Board were despondent about recruiting the required staff. Finally the prison commissioners loaned Warwick Prison, which, after modification, opened early in 1919 for female defectives who required greater security than was available at Farmfield.

At the end of the war, in August, 1919, Moss Side, the state institution near Liverpool, was handed back to the Board of Control by the military authorities and by the end of that year thirty-three dangerous male defectives were in residence. Paradoxically, after so urgently seeking a temporary alternative for Moss Side during the war years the building was returned at a time when the Board were making arrangements which would render it redundant. The populations of the county asylums and Broadmoor had dropped during the war[7] and it was suggested to the Board that it would be an economy to transfer to the county asylums all suitable patients from the two criminal lunatic asylums. The remaining Rampton patients could then be moved to Broadmoor and Rampton might then be transferred by the Home Office to the Board of Control as a state institution for defectives. This was formally agreed after the Board had visited Rampton and had been impressed by the comparatively new buildings and the scope for expansion. At this time there was a total of 290 beds in three blocks, two male and one female, and the Board considered that with additional female accommodation their requirements would be met for many years.

On 1 March, 1920 Rampton was taken over by the Board and in the same month admitted the patients from Moss Side Institution and Warwick Prison, the latter being handed back to the prison commission. Moss Side was placed at the disposal of the Ministry of Pensions and used as a colony for epileptic patients. In February, 1922, on the completion of extra accommodation, the women from Farmfield were transferred to Rampton, and Farmfield was closed. There was still found to be a shortage of accommodation for women at Rampton and on 25 July, 1923 Warwick Institution (formerly Warwick Prison) was reopened by the Board of Control to take the more hopeful cases. Thirty-one younger Rampton patients were transferred to be individually trained in a less restrictive environment 'to take their places as working members of the community'.

Two years later the chaplain's house was converted into a hostel and it was planned that suitable girls should live there while being employed on daily work, mainly domestic, outside the institution. Successful completion of this part of the training would be followed by living-in arrangements during release on licence.

Warwick Institution was anomalous in that it provided for female defectives of dangerous or violent propensities under section 36 of the Mental Deficiency Act 1913, yet there were fewer restrictions than at Rampton and an 'open-door' policy operated in the hostel. Nevertheless the superintendent stressed that the girls could not be suitably cared for elsewhere; in effect, it was claimed that the state institution had greater expertise and more appropriate management techniques for dealing with such cases. After five relatively successful years there was a change for the worse in the type of girl admitted from Rampton; many were so low-grade that they were permanently unfitted to move on to the hostel. The majority of such cases were transferred back to Rampton, as had been their predecessors who did not adapt to the progressive system, but some were transferred to institutions certified for defectives under the Mental Deficiency Act of 1913 and some to Poor Law institutions.

By the early thirties Rampton had reached the limit of expansion and the male wards were overcrowded. This was alleviated by Moss Side coming into the possession of the Board of Control for the third time and fifty men and fifty-one women[8] being transferred there in October, 1933. Warwick Institution was closed and the patients there transferred back to Rampton. Initially there was a hostel at Moss Side providing accommodation for six women for whom outside daily work was sought, but this venture seems to have been abandoned at the outbreak of war.

In 1930 Rampton opened a juvenile section for the care and treatment of children who could not be satisfactorily dealt with elsewhere. It consisted of two houses, one for the boys and one for the girls, each accommodating thirty-six children, and a school, all set some distance apart from the main institution. About 40 per cent of the children were victims of the encephalitis lethargica or 'sleepy sickness' epidemics, a viral disorder which in the words of Dr Rees Thomas, the medical superintendent, 'produces in a few weeks a mental condition and outlook that half a century of indulgence in the grossest vices cannot effectively imitate'. In its acute form delirium alternates with somnolence and the after-effects in children take the form of impulsive, overactive, and aggressive behaviour which nearly always necessitates institutional care. The average age of the children in Rampton at the end of 1930 was 12.8 years for the boys and 11.2 years for the girls. The juvenile section flourished until 1940, when a marked reduction in the number of admissions was noted but not explained. The maintenance of separate facilities for children in Rampton was discontinued in 1956 but the admission to the special hospitals of under-16-year-olds when necessary continues up to the present day, although no patient under the age of 13 has been admitted since 1980.

In 1948 the ownership of the two state institutions, Rampton and Moss Side, passed to the Minister of Health under section 49(4) of the National Health Service Act of 1946, but they continued to be managed by the Board of Control, which was responsible for the admission and discharge of patients. The following year Broadmoor was also vested in the Minister of Health in accordance with section 62 of the Criminal Justice Act 1948, and it too came under the management of the Board of Control, but the admission and discharge of patients remained the responsibility of the Home Secretary. At this time Broadmoor dropped the title of 'Criminal Lunatic Asylum' and was named

'Broadmoor Institution'; Rampton and Moss Side were called 'hospitals'.

The Mental Health Act 1959

In February, 1954 a Royal Commission was set up to review the law relating to mental illness and mental deficiency. The commission reported in May, 1957 and the climate of opinion and the will of Parliament were such that the subsequent Mental Health Bill passed through all stages in both Houses and received the Royal Assent in July, 1959.

The implementation of the new Mental Health Act brought revolutionary changes: it allowed for the majority of the mentally disturbed to be admitted informally and it abolished most of the statutory distinctions between mental illness and mental deficiency. With regard to secure provision, section 97 obliged the Minister of Health to provide institutions for persons who 'require treatment under conditions of special security on account of their dangerous, violent or criminal propensities',[9] and Broadmoor, Rampton, and Moss Side were deemed to be such institutions. From now on they would be known as 'special hospitals'. The Board of Control was dissolved and the three special hospitals became the direct responsibility of the Ministry of Health, now the Department of Health and Social Security.

Regional secure units

Anticipating that there would be changes in the number and type of patients admitted to Broadmoor, Rampton, and Moss Side, the then Minister of Health, Enoch Powell, appointed a working party 'to consider the role of the special hospitals and the classes of patients to be treated in them, having regard to the new mental health law and to the provision to be made by the hospital service generally'.

Reporting in 1961, the working party realized that developments in the NHS would directly affect the special hospitals and stated as a therapeutic principle that some secure provision should be provided. They recommended 'that the Regional Hosptial Boards should arrange their psychiatric services so as to ensure that there is a variety of types of hospital unit, including some secure units, and that transfer can be made between them as necessary'. This proposal for secure units was not new. The concept originated in 1957 in the report of the Royal Commission, which proposed that dangerous patients should be accommodated in a few hospitals having suitable facilities for their treatment and custody. The idea was then taken up by the Ministry of Health in a circular to the regional hospital boards, hospital management committees, and boards of governors in May, 1959, two months before the Mental Health Bill received the Royal Assent. The ministry, warning against indiscriminate application of the open-door principle, advised that there were 'some patients – not all of them may have been before the courts – for whom the maintenance of adequate security precautions must be regarded as an essential part of their hospital care, either in their own interest or that of the community'. Two methods of achieving this security were outlined; the first was for each hospital to maintain some special security precautions, and the second, as subsequently advised by the working party, was to establish regional units.

Having advocated provision for secure facilities in the NHS and recommended the establishment of secure diagnostic centres for difficult patients, the working party advised that 'a patient should be accepted for admission to a special hospital only after all the other possibilities have been carefully examined and considered unsuitable.' No positive criteria were proposed. This passive approach to special hospital admission was reflected in practice; for the years 1962–69 inclusive 77 per cent of all applications for admission were accepted.

The working party's recommendations were endorsed by the Minister of Health and were circulated to the regional hospitals boards and others. The boards were informed of the ministry's intentions to establish diagnostic and treatment centres. Ultimately only one such centre was ever built, the Northgate Clinic in the North-West Metropolitan Region, and this is now used as an adolescent unit and not as originally intended.

In 1963 a Hospitals Building Note (No. 30) giving advice on the planning of hospital accommodation for psychiatric patients was issued by the Ministry of Health. This commended special secure units as the most effective method of providing for patients who require a degree of security short of that offered by the special hospitals. Eight years later in 1971 the Department of Health and Social Security (as the Ministry of Health had now become) in the memorandum *Hospitals Services for the Mentally Ill* (DHSS, 1971a) reiterated departmental policy that the NHS should provide some security arrangements. In the same year a departmental working party was set up under the chairmanship of Dr J. E. Glancy to review the existing guidance on security to NHS psychiatric hospitals and to make recommendations on the present and future need for such security. Reporting in March, 1974 the working party found that most hospitals were expected to make their own arrangements for dealing with difficult patients, which usually consisted of one or two locked wards with the patients participating in varying degrees in the common occupational and recreational facilities of the rest of the hospital. A few regional units had been established for mentally handicapped patients but these did not meet the criteria for secure units. The working party reaffirmed that it was the responsibility of the regional health authorities to provide secure facilities and that these should take the form of special units to meet regional requirements. They recommended immediate planning for 1,000 places.

Four months later in July, 1974 the Committee on Mentally Abnormal Offenders (the Butler Committee) published an interim report stressing the urgency of providing regional secure units. There was a 'yawning gap' between NHS hospitals with no secure provision and the overcrowded special hospitals. The absence of any intermediate security, together with the development of treatment in open conditions in local hospitals, had adverse effects on the special hospitals, the criminal justice system, and the prisons. The special hospitals felt obliged to accept dangerous psychiatric patients from the open NHS hospitals but experienced difficulties in transferring to the NHS patients who were no longer dangerous. The courts found it increasingly difficult to obtain NHS beds for mentally disordered offenders and, even when a bed was available, the lack of security often rendered it unsuitable. For such offenders, unless they satisfied the criteria for admission to a special hospital, the courts often had no option but to impose a prison sentence. The Prison Medical Service had given evidence to the committee of the growing number of mentally disordered in the prisons. Not only were mentally abnormal offenders imprisoned for want of a hospital bed, but the prisons were unable to transfer to the NHS inmates who became mentally disordered whilst serving their sentences.

The Butler Committee doubled the estimate of the Glancy working party and recommended an initial target of 2,000 secure places to meet the needs of the NHS, the special hospitals, the courts, and the prisons. The DHSS responded immediately to the Butler Interim Report; in a circular issued in the same month they accepted an immediate need for 1,000 places in regional secure units which might be increased to 2,000 'as and when resources permit'. The Butler Committee considered that lack of finance was one of the main reasons why not a single secure unit had materialized since the report of the 1961 working party despite the repeated exhortations and advice from DHSS. To overcome this they recommended that the regional health authorities should receive a direct allocation of central government funds expressly for the provision of secure units. This was also accepted by the government in the July, 1974 circular but the final report of the Butler Committee in October, 1975 noted that little progress had been made: some regions seemed unwilling to formulate plans or to give the establishment of secure units the priority thought necessary by both the Butler Committee and the government. As a further inducement the committee recommended that the government meet the future running costs of the units as well as the capital costs. The acceptance of this was announced in the House of Commons on 26 January, 1976 but in the first year of central government financing, 1976–77, nearly a quarter of the £5.2 million allocated was used by the regional health authorities either as general revenue or to offset overspending, and two-thirds was carried over to the next financial year. Only £351,263, less than 7 per cent, was spent on secure facilities (Cohen 1977). By 1983 progress was discernible: all regions had some form of interim secure arrangements and the proportion of the revenue allocation spent on secure units had risen to 60 per cent and a further 30 per cent was spent on other psychiatric services. (As to the current progress in establishing regional secure units, see Chapter 5.)

The type of patient to be treated in the regional secure units was considered by the 1961 working party, who envisaged that they would cater for difficult patients from any of the four categories of mental disorder specified under the Mental Health Act 1959. Such patients would include potential absconders who would present a risk to the public at large, those who seriously disrupt the hospital regime, and the persistently or unpredictably violent. Dangerous or violent patients who were thought not to require treatment in a secure unit included emergency admissions whose violence proved transient, those liable to predictable and infrequent violent episodes, and the severely subnormal prone to occasional outbursts of impulsive violence.

This categorization was in general endorsed by the Glancy working party in 1974 who stated that 'secure accommodation in units may be required for patients who present severely disruptive behaviour, who may be mentally ill or mentally handicapped, or those who suffer from psychopathic or severe personality disorder, whether alone or in conjunction with mental illness or mental handicap.' Secure units were not thought to be suitable for the severely mentally handicapped because their main requirement was highly skilled nursing care and attention, and if properly supervised they were not likely to abscond. The secure units were not for long-term patients; if progress had not been made after eighteen months, 'consideration should be given to an alternative placement such as return to prison, admission to a special hospital or return to an ordinary psychiatric hospital.' The Butler Interim Report strongly supported this latter recommendation but, apart from excluding aggressive psychopaths and any other patients who would present an immediate danger to the public if at large, the committee did not specify criteria for admission.[10] (For a full discussion of regional secure units, see Chapters 5 and 6.)

A new special hospital

One reason underlying the Butler Committee's recommendations for the urgent establishment of regional secure units was to relieve the overcrowding in both the special hospitals and the prisons. Broadmoor in particular had been overcrowded for years, the greatest pressure for places being in 1958. In 1962 it had been planned to modernize the hospital, based on the expectation that the number of male patients would fall, but eventually it became clear that the number of patients would increase and that additional accommodation would be required. This led to the parallel decision to build a new special hospital for mentally ill male patients; in view of the comparative costs, it was decided to rebuild rather than just modernize Broadmoor (Ministry of Health 1968). The announcement of these plans was precipitated by the forthcoming inquiry into the special hospitals and the Scottish state hospital by the Parliamentary Estimates Committee. The Estimates Committee were appalled to see the extent of overcrowding in the century-old Broadmoor and were very critical of the length of the time taken to reach a decision to remedy the situation.

The site chosen for the new special hospital was adjacent to the existing special hospital, Moss Side. The two hospitals were to be completely separate within their own perimeter walls but were to share administrative service facilities. Delays in making decisions were followed by delays in execution. Planning for the new hospital was interrupted by a public inquiry in the autumn of 1969, the result of which was a recommendation not to build on the Moss Side site. This was overruled by the Secretary of State for the Environment in

August, 1970 and planning was resumed. The hospital, named Park Lane, was officially opened in September 1984.

In October, 1974 an advance unit of Park Lane was opened in buildings which were previously part of Moss Side hospital. For the second time in its history the overcrowding at Broadmoor was relieved by the transfer of patients to a similar institution in the North of England: seventy male patients from Broadmoor were admitted to the advance unit at Park Lane Hospital and, as when Rampton opened as a criminal lunatic asylum in 1912, preference was given to patients with North Country affiliations. Park Lane can currently accommodate 310 patients and nearly all those in residence have been transferred from Broadmoor. (See further Chapter 3.)

The rebuilding of Broadmoor, announced concurrently in 1967 with the proposal to build a new special hospital, has been subject to even greater delays; the first stage of a five-part rebuilding programme did not go out to tender until July, 1983 although preliminary work to the value of nearly £5 million has been completed.

The mentally disordered in the penal system

The overcrowding in the prisons noted by the Butler Committee began after the second world war when the prison population increased by over 300 per cent between 1945 and 1978, the situation in the later years being aggravated by the reported increase in the numbers of mentally disordered in the penal system. The principle that prisoners who fell within the existing lunacy or mental health legislation of the day may be transferred to an asylum or hospital was well established by 1840, although prior to 1913 this applied only to lunatics, idiots, and imbeciles unfit for penal discipline. The passing of the Mental Deficiency Act of 1913 permitted imprisoned defectives who came within its scope to be transferred to the new institutions established under its provisions. The Act only began to operate effectively after the 1914–18 war; it was found that only a third of the mental defectives sent to prison were 'subject to be dealt with' under its powers (Hobhouse and Brockway 1922) and that there were many mentally abnormal prisoners who were not certifiably defective or insane. The publication of the East–Hubert report *The Psychological Treatment of Crime* (1939) marked a policy change with regard to such prisoners. From this time it was accepted that they should be treated within the penal system and the opening of a psychiatric prison, Grendon Underwood, in 1962 was a direct albeit delayed response to the report's main recommendation.

A few years later the prison department was commenting on the increasing need for psychiatric treatment in the prison population (Home Office 1970) and repeatedly referring to the difficulties of obtaining beds in NHS psychiatric hospitals for prisoners who were mentally disordered within the terms of the Mental Health Act 1959 (Home Office, 1971, 1972, 1973, 1974, and 1975). The results of a survey among prison medical officers indicated that there were an estimated 500 prisoners who would be better placed in hospital outside the penal system (Home Office 1974). As described previously, the proposed regional secure units were intended to relieve the prisons of this group but the Butler Committee did express reservations concerning the appropriateness of hospital admission of psychopathic patients (Home Office and DHSS 1975).

Subsequent to the Butler Committee the mentally disordered in the prisons attracted the attention of a subcommittee of the Parliamentary Expenditure Committee which was considering ways of reducing the pressure on the penal system and which identified categories of prisoners, including the mentally disordered, which could be reduced in number. It was reported that in December, 1976 there were approximately 600–700 prisoners who in the opinion of the prison medical officers met the Mental Health Act criteria for transfer to hospital, but this estimate included unsentenced prisoners who formed a third of the total. In their recommendations the Expenditure Committee advocated 'that the provision of regional secure units be treated as a matter of great urgency' but recognized that the prisons would always contain difficult, dangerous, and abnormal offenders who were not actually mentally disordered in terms of the then Mental Health Act. To deal with this group the committee recommended increased psychiatric facilities in the penal system (House of Commons 1978).

Meanwhile the Home Office in 1977 had asked the prison medical service to make six-monthly returns of all inmates who were considered to meet the criteria laid down in the Mental Health Act for transfer to hospital, and in 1979 encouraged the prison medical officers to continue to make recommendations for transfer to hospital. Increased efforts were made by both the Home Office and the DHSS to secure places and as a result the number of transferred mentally disordered prisoners has risen annually to 110 in 1983 (Home Office 1984).

It would seem that the difficulties of obtaining hospital admission deter the prison medical officers from proposing inmates for transfer. Apart from the small number of men transferred each year, further empirical justification of the Home Office action in encouraging the admission to hospital of the mentally disordered in the penal system lies in the finding that, of the mentally ill apparently eligible, applications for transfers are only taken out in respect of a quarter (Cheadle and Ditchfield 1982) and in an even smaller proportion of cases are transfers actually effected (Robertson and Gibbens 1980; Cheadle and Ditchfield 1982).

The potential to respond to treatment has emerged as a consideration of major importance in the admission of offenders to hospital. Those less likely to be accepted by the National Health Service include mentally ill prisoners requiring long-term care (Cheadle and Ditchfield 1982) and among remanded men those with a diagnosis of psychopathic disorder, mental subnormality, alcoholism, or residual schizophrenia (Bowden 1978). The vast majority of people transferred have been classified as mentally ill and very few as subnormal or psychopathically disordered (Robertson and Gibbens 1980), a process of selection whereby 'treatability' is maximized. The outcome of this practice is that the prisons are relieved of the acutely mentally ill but are left with the mentally disordered whose main requirement is long-term care and/or training. A large proportion of this latter group have been psychiatric in-patients at some period in their lives (Robertson and Gibbens 1980) and they would appear to constitute part of the 'stage army' described by Walker and McCabe (1973) which continually features in both psychiatric and prison populations. Their presence in the penal system points to the paucity of suitable facilities elsewhere and, in particular, the absence of any secure provision for long-stay patients who do not require the level of security provided by the special hospitals. (For a full discussion of the problems of mentally disordered persons in the prison system, see Chapter 4.)

Secure provision for juveniles

Secure facilities specifically for disturbed children, apart from the former villas for juveniles at Rampton, are comparatively recent phenomena, appearing in the last decade. For young offenders some secure accommodation has always been considered necessary: imprisonment for juveniles was largely abandoned in 1908 under the Children Act but the reduction in closed places was to some extent compensated for by the development of Borstal training authorized under the Prevention of Crime Act in the same year. The Children and Young Persons Act in 1933 transformed the reformatory and industrial schools into a national system of open approved schools for children between 10 and 17 years of age. A sharp increase in absconding in the 1950s together with a series of disturbances at a senior boys' approved school focused attention on the need for some closed provision in the system which ultimately materialized during 1964–66 in the form of three secure units designed for persistent absconders and exceptionally unruly and uncooperative boys.

Prior to this, in 1960, a Home Office working party on closed and other special facilities in approved schools had considered 'what arrangements should be made for approved school boys who create problems through a combination of exacting medical or psychiatric requirements and difficult behaviour (e.g. some epileptics and psychopaths)'. Hospital treatment for appropriate cases was endorsed but the difficulty of finding beds, particularly for the 16–18 year olds, was commented upon. The situation was expected to improve particularly in respect of psychopaths with the implementation of the Mental Health Act 1959. The establishment of an approved school with special medical facilities was discussed but rejected on grounds of expense and the fear that the courts might make approved-school orders because of the available medical treatment in otherwise unsuitable cases. The working party eventually recommended that 'the boys in question should be provided for partly in the proposed closed units and partly by a greater degree of specialization at some existing schools. ... If these measures prove to be inadequate to deal with the problem, the provision of a school equipped with special medical facilities could be further considered.'

This policy was found to be unsatisfactory in practice and a series of difficult-to-place cases in the 1960s led to discussions between the Home Office and the Ministry of Health (Cawson and Martell 1979). Finally another working party was set up in March, 1967 with representatives from the Home Office, Ministry of Health, the approved-school service, the local authority child-care service, and the Maudsley Hospital. Their terms of reference were:

'To consider the extent and nature of the facilities required for the care and treatment of severely disturbed children and young persons who are now subject to an approved school order, with special reference to any who may require such care and treatment in secure conditions, and to make recommendations.'

Three types of severely disturbed children were identified – the mentally ill, the psychopathic, and a group presenting symptoms of an anti-social disorder. Mental illness was stated to be rare in adolescence; only 0.2 per cent of boys and 1 per cent of girls in approved schools were so diagnosed and it was reported that the schools were usually able to secure their admission to a psychiatric hospital. The anti-social children (5 per cent of the boys and 18 per cent of the girls) were unruly, disruptive, and persistent absconders but psychiatric symptoms were minimal. It was recognized that with their then current resources the ordinary approved schools could not successfully manage this group and the working party therefore recommended an increase in the number of places in the closed units.

It is not known to what extent the children described as psychopathic (0.8 per cent of the boys and 7 per cent of the girls) would meet the criteria of psychopathic disorder contained in the Mental Health Act of 1959. The definition used by the working party, 'a persistent disorder of the mind that can result in severely aggressive and anti-social behaviour', parallels that of the Mental Health Act 1959 but omits the phrase 'and requires or is susceptible to medical treatment' which appears in the latter. The psychopathic approved-school children were described as likely to be dangerous and disruptive, unmanageable both at home and in the approved-school system and with an uncertain prognosis. Improved prospects would result from continuous long-term care in an accepting environment. It was reported that some of this group were transferred to special hospitals and some to National Health Service psychiatric hospitals with special provision for such cases but the children's aggressive and disruptive behaviour together with their proclivity to abscond sometimes resulted in psychiatric hospitals asking the approved schools to readmit them. The hope of the 1960 working party that the implementation of the Mental Health Act 1959 would relieve the position had not been realized. The 1967 working party reported that the Ministry of Health accepted that the hospital psychiatric services should provide for young people suffering from a mental disorder which requires and is susceptible to medical treatment but it was not considered that such services should extend to young persons not susceptible to treatment or to those who although susceptible to treatment would not require admission as in-patients. This meant that whereas the mentally ill teenagers would continue to be admitted, the psychopaths would have to both require *and* be susceptible to treatment (note the substitution of 'and' for the word 'or' which appears in the Mental Health Act 1959) and require in-patient admission. This view of the psychiatric services was accepted by the working party as was the implication that the majority of psychopaths in approved schools would have to be catered for outside the National Health Service. Some of the psychopathic children would be 'the proper concern of the special hospitals once their condition has been diagnosed as requiring ... institutional care and treatment in conditions of special security for a period beyond the age range of the children's services'. A few who did not require maximum security would be provided for by the limited facilities available in the National Health Service. For the majority of the children, particularly those under 16, it was concluded that there was no existing appropriate provision and the working party recommended collaboration between the health and child care services to provide establishments 'which combine the treatment possibilities of both a hospital and an approved school'. It was considered that a medical setting would reduce the anti-authority attitudes exhibited by the children and therefore a medical director was proposed. There should be some secure provision both for the protection of the public and to ensure continuity of treatment for absconders but the children should progress from secure to open conditions.

The new establishments materialized as youth treatment centres provided for initially under section 64 of the Children and Young Persons Act 1969 and currently under section 80 of the Child Care Act 1980; St Charles at Brentwood, Essex opened in July, 1971 and Glenthorne, near Birmingham, opened in February, 1978. The centres were conceived as a national resource to be managed centrally by the Department of Health and Social Security, which resumed responsibility for all child-care services in January, 1971.

The orginal intention to provide combined hospital and approved schools has not been realized. The only medical director to be appointed was initially at St Charles, a consultant psychiatrist who resigned after twelve months. Subsequently policy evolved so that directors of youth treatment centres are now required to have occupational experience of residential child-care services. St Charles has developed as a psycho-therapeutic community with psychiatric input from a visiting consultant who provides support for the staff and on occasions undertakes individual psycho-therapy with the young people. The treatment approach at Glenthorne is that of behaviour-modification organized by a psychologist. Up to the present there has been no psychiatric intervention but there are now plans to employ a visiting psychiatrist on a similar basis to St Charles. The staff at the centres are drawn variously from the teaching, nursing, or residential child-care services.

The youth treatment centres were mainly intended for severely disturbed children who were in local authority care as a result of court orders but it was accepted from the start that at the request of the Home Office some juveniles would be admitted who had been convicted of grave crimes under section 53 of the Children and Young Persons Act 1933. The section 53 children currently constitute just over 50 per cent of St Charles's population and over 40 per cent of the population at Glenthorne. The presence of the two groups of young persons has resulted in conflicting objectives in that for the care-order children the aim is to rehabilitate them back into the community whereas the section 53 children will usually be returned to custody in the penal system. The difficulties of providing a therapeutic milieu for both groups in the same institution has been described by the St Charles Youth Treatment Evaluation Team (DHSS 1979) and by Millham, Bullock, and Hosie (1978).

The implications of the Mental Health Act 1983

The Mental Health Act 1983 mainly came into force on 30 September, 1983. (For an explanation and analysis of its provisions relating to mentally disordered offenders, see Chapter 7.) The objectives represent two competing philosophies, legalism and treatment. While still embodying the treatment philosophy of the 1959 Act the Mental Health Act 1983 incorporates a resurgence of legalism in its provision of greater safeguards for detained patients. The implications for secure provision may be divided into those parts of the Act which might raise and those which might reduce the numbers and types of patients detained in security.

The sections of the Act which may increase the numbers in secure provision are the new powers given to the courts to remand defendants to hospital for a medical report, and a new sentence of an *interim* hospital order.[11] As yet it is not known what use the courts will make of these provisions, but of the patients dealt with under the new sections it may be expected that a proportion will require secure placements.

The power to remand to hospital for a medical report in addition to increasing the total number of such reports has the potential to shift a substantial area of work from the Prison Medical Service to the National Health Service (8,003 individuals were remanded in custody for psychiatric reports in 1981), provided that the Health Service has the necessary resources. It is the provision of such facilities which underlies the delay in implementation. For remand patients requiring an element of security the regional secure units would seem ideally placed, not only on account of their security but also because of the central position they will occupy within the regions' forensic psychiatric services. The special hospitals are also planning to provide an assessment service for such patients for whom greater security is considered necessary.

An interim hospital order is intended to assist the courts and hospitals in determining whether a hospital order would be an appropriate disposal.[12] It is difficult to predict the effects of this provision as some defendants who would not previously have been given a hospital order will now after a trial run on an interim order prove responsive to hospital treatment, and vice versa. Any offender who suffers from one of the four types of mental disorder specified in the Act is eligible for an interim order but it will be of special relevance to psychopaths whose response to treatment is particularly difficult to determine in advance in that it will afford a period of medical care which will provide an empirical basis for the eventual disposal, be it a full hospital order or not.

The courts are empowered when considering making a hospital order to request the regional health authorities to supply information as to the availability of suitable beds (s. 39). In their explanatory memorandum to the new Act the Department of Health and Social Security (1983a) widely interpret this provision as implying 'the need to ensure that the facilities of the Region offer in total a comprehensive service for the Region's patients, both offenders and non-offenders' – an interpretation consonant with their exhortations to regions since 1959 to retain some secure units. The conditions under the 1983 Act for making hospital orders in cases of psychopathic disorder or mental impairment include a new treatability criterion – i.e. that medical treatment is likely to alleviate or prevent a deterioration of the offender's condition. The new treatability requirement is designed to ensure that psychopathic and mentally impaired offenders will only be admitted to hospital on a hospital order when there is some real prospect of benefit to the patient. The effect of this change is uncertain. The number of hospital orders for subnormal patients has fallen steeply and the number of orders for cases of psychopathic disorder has always been relatively small

(Robertson 1982), which may indicate that the offenders given hospital orders under the 1959 Act are those amenable to therapeutic intervention and therefore might also satisfy the criteria of the 1983 Act. If so, the treatability provision of the 1983 Act would not be expected to alter significantly the number of hospital orders for the psychopathic or mentally impaired offenders.

The provisions of the Act which may reduce the numbers of patients in secure provision are mainly concerned with the increased opportunities for patients detained under both civil and criminal powers to apply to the Mental Health Review Tribunals for discharge and the compulsory referral to the tribunals of patients who fail to exercise their rights within a specified period. In addition, with regard to restricted patients the previously sole power of the Home Secretary to discharge has now been extended to the tribunals, who have now the power to discharge providing specified criteria are met. In certain circumstances the tribunals have a statutory obligation to consider 'response to treatment' but only with regard to *non-restricted* patients. This is in accordance with the well-established tradition in English mental health legislation of allowing indefinite detention of persons in psychiatric hospitals for mainly custodial reasons (Parker 1980). By not requiring tribunals to consider response to treatment with regard to restricted patients the Act has provided the means to detain persons deemed to be dangerous even though their stay in hospital is fulfilling a custodial and not a medical purpose.

Security

The actual containment of patients in secure provision is achieved by a complex interplay of factors of which four can be readily identified: physical security; quality of nursing care; the control of patients, particularly by medication; and patient motivation.

PHYSICAL SECURITY

The physical security of the special hospitals has always been influenced by that obtaining in the penal system. Sir Joshua Jebb, the director of convict prisons and penal architect, was responsible for the planning and design of Broadmoor. The expertise of the Home Office in security matters acquired as a result of their responsibility for the penal system was drawn upon in the building of the new special hospital, Park Lane, and presumably also applied to Rampton, which was originally built by the Home Office as a criminal lunatic asylum under the provisions of the Criminal Lunatics Act of 1800. Moss Side Hospital, acquired by the Board of Control in 1914, was not purpose-built for the dangerous and violent defectives it housed and even as late as 1967 was considered to be the least secure of the special hospitals.

In 1877 a committee appointed to investigate the high maintenance costs incurred by Broadmoor considered that it satisfactorily fulfilled its custodial function. It was shown that since the asylum had opened, only 0.08 per cent of patients had escaped, whereas previously for the period 1856–62 inclusive the percentage for escaped and not recaptured criminal lunatics had been 0.62; from this spurious comparison it was concluded that the safe custody of such patients was eight times greater in Broadmoor compared with other asylums. The committee reported that work was in progress to raise the height of the boundary walls, a proposal first made by the council of supervision in 1862, and recommended that an alarm bell and an internal communications system be installed and that all the locks be changed because the ones *in situ* were thought to be easily pickable.

Sixty-five years later, in 1952, the adequacy of the security arrangements at Broadmoor was the subject of another inquiry, following the escape of John Straffen, who had been committed to Broadmoor after having been found unfit to plead to a charge of strangling two young girls and who, within hours of his escape, strangled a child. The inquiry committee confirmed the traditional view of the primacy of security but recognized that treatment was becoming an increasingly important function of the institution. Once again it was recommended that the locks be changed, this time as a matter of urgency, as it was found that two previous escapes had been effected by means of keys made by patients. Other recommendations included a siren to be coupled to an alarm at Wokingham police station to warn the neighbouring vicinity when an escape occurred and which would also be a signal for outside working parties to return and for off-duty staff to report for duty.

A more qualified definition of the objectives of security in the special hospitals was put forward by a Ministry of Health working party on special hospital security, set up as a consequence of several notorious escapes from the prisons, and the resulting Mountbatten inquiry: in evidence to the House of Commons Estimates Committee in 1967 the working party stated: 'the public must be provided with strong protection against the more serious risks and with adequate protection against lesser risks.' For seriously dangerous patients this protection was defined as not being 'less than that required for the most dangerous prisoners'. The Mountbatten Report identified the most dangerous prisoners as those 'whose escapes would be highly dangerous to the public or the police or to the security of the State' and recommended that they be allocated to category A of a four-level security classification. Following the advice of the Advisory Council on the Penal System and against the advice of the Mountbatten Inquiry the Home Office decided to disperse the category-A prisoners among the more serious of the category-B prisoners in seven high-security dispersal prisons. The Department of Health and Social Security now claims that all special-hospital patients are subject to the degree of security provided for category-A prisoners.

It is difficult to assess how far the security provided by the special hospitals does equate to that of the dispersal prisons as it is clear from both the evidence of the Ministry of Health to the Estimates Committee and the evidence given by the Home Office (Home Office 1979b) to the Inquiry into the United Kingdom Prison Services under the chairmanship of Mr Justice May that there are varying degrees of security in both types of institution which are largely determined by the age, structure, and previous usage of the buildings into which the secure measures are installed. Nevertheless a new purpose-built special hospital does not duplicate all the features of perimeter security such as double fences, high-mast floodlighting, dog patrols, geophonic alarms, television cameras, and rocket-proof walls which characterize a new dispersal prison. Some of these precautions are obviously designed to repulse organized outside assistance in an escape attempt, a possibility considered to be most unlikely with regard to special-hospital patients by the Ministry of Health working party in 1967 but to which, in the light of the increased security-consciousness in the prisons originating in the occurrences which culminated in the Mountbatten Report and stimulated by events in Northern Ireland, the Department of Health and Social Security is now giving closer consideration.

In its evidence to the Estimates Committee the Ministry of Health gave a description of the security measures in operation at the then three special hospitals, which included an account of the gradations of security implied in their statement of the objectives of special hospitals security quoted earlier. Since 1967 the only published account of security in a special hospital is to be found in the Report of the Review of Rampton Hospital, an inquiry carried out in 1980 under the chairmanship of Sir John Boynton following allegations by Yorkshire Television of ill treatment of patients by staff. On the whole the Boynton Committee found the security arrangements at Rampton to be satisfactory but found little or no evidence of gradations. The committee considered it to be wrong in principle for a patient to be subject to a higher degree of security than necessary and recommended the introduction of less rigorous regimes in certain areas of the hospital, particularly with regard to those patients who had been approved for discharge or transfer to a National Health Service hospital.

The changing balance between security and treatment and the ascendency of the latter were confirmed by the Estimates Committee, which endorsed the conclusion of the Ministry of Health working party that security should not interfere with therapeutic requirements. The Boynton Committee considered and rejected the idea of a separate security staff for economic reasons and the fear that other staff would become less security-conscious resulting in a serious reduction in standards of security. On the other hand the committee reported that

'to give security absolute priority is nevertheless an attitude we cannot endorse. Anything approaching total security would only be achieved at the expense of most if not all therapeutic activity and this would be unacceptable. ... It should be accepted by all concerned that a certain amount of security risk may have to be tolerated for the sake of the treatment or other benefits which can be gained in return.'

This statement, which insofar as the Department of Health and Social Security accepted the Boynton Report, indicates a fundamental difference between the DHSS in respect of security in the special hospitals and the Home Office in respect of security in the dispersal prisons and calls into question the extent to which special-hospital patients are in fact subject to a level of security commensurate with that of category-A prisoners.[13]

From the start it was recognized that the level of physical security in the regional secure units should be less than in the special hospitals (Ministry of Health 1961) but a definition of what would constitute appropriate security measures has not been achieved. The Glancy Committee recommended that physical security should be as unobtrusive as possible and advised that there should be gradations of security within a unit, which at a maximum would 'contain all but the most determined escapers'. Subsequent to this the design of regional secure units was the subject of some guidelines issued by the Department of Health and Social Security (DHSS 1975) and of a seminar held by the Institute of Hospital Engineering, both of which attempted to operationalize the recommendations of the Glancy Report. The Confederation of Health Service Employees, COHSE, also issued a policy statement on National Health Service secure treatment units (COHSE 1979). The restrained approach to physical security is epitomized by the attitudes to a secure perimeter. In keeping with the recommendation that the units provide differing levels of security the Glancy Committee considered total boundary security to be unnecessary. At least one regional health authority has disagreed with this view but nevertheless conceived perimeter security only as 'a delaying mechanism which would enable staff to observe that an attempt to abscond was being made' (Williams 1976). In their policy statement COHSE stated that 'the primary purpose of a perimeter fence is to reassure the community living close to the unit.'

Gradations of security were also envisaged for youth treatment centres ranging from a secure zone through medium-secure accommodation to open conditions (DHSS 1971b) and such a three-level system is in operation at both St Charles and Glenthorne.

The recommendations of the Boynton Committee regarding greater flexibility with regard to security at Rampton have still to be implemented. It has yet to be seen whether the regional secure units will be able to operate a continuum of security but the experience of the special hospitals and the youth treatment centres is not promising; external influences and organizational pressures are towards uniformity, which in secure provision means that the maximum security available in any one institution tends to be applied to all patients – a phenomenon noted at ward level in the Boynton Report (para. 18.2.1).

QUALITY OF NURSING CARE

From the beginning of the nineteenth century it has been recognized that the quality of nursing care is directly associated with security and that physical security as such tends to militate against the exercise of proper nursing practice. In 1813 Samuel Tuke, grandson of William Tuke who founded the Retreat at York, wrote:

'In the construction of [asylums], cure and comfort ought to be as much considered as security, and I have no hesitation in declaring that a system which, by limiting the power of the attendant, obliges him not to neglect his duty, and makes it his interest to obtain the good opinion of those under his care, provides more effectually for the safety of the keeper, as well as of the patient, than all the apparatus of chains, darkness and anodynes.'

(Tuke 1813)

In the special hospitals, security and nursing care are both vested in the nursing staff, and evidence was given to the Estimates Committee of the difficulties experienced by the staff in combining both functions. The custodial role is affirmed by the nurses belonging to the Prison Officers' Association and, in all but one of the special hospitals, wearing uniform identical to that of prison officers. The dual nursing/security commitment was accepted by the Boynton Committee, which nevertheless recommended that a uniform more appropriate to a therapeutic environment be introduced at Rampton Hospital.

Unencumbered by the traditionally custodial role of the special hospitals and adopting a limited approach to physical measures of security, the regional secure units are, at least in theory, in a position to develop the concept of security as a product of the quality of the nursing care. The Glancy Committee considered that security could take the form of physical measures or 'high staffing ratios coupled with the development of specialised therapeutic techniques', and recommended a combination of both in the proposed units. The DHSS repeated this in their guidelines: 'the overall aim should be to provide the majority of the security required by personnel involvement' (DHSS 1975) and comparable sentiments were expressed by the speakers at the seminar held by the Institute of Hospital Engineering. COHSE considered that 'the chief source of security in the unit is the high staff ratio' (COHSE 1979: para. 3.9). How far the regional secure units will succeed in providing the greater part of their security by means of therapeutically orientated staff/patient relationships remains to be seen.

Security in the youth treatment centres has been discussed only in physical terms; although it is recognized that 'management by the staff collectively is perhaps the most important single factor in treatment', security as such is not seen as evolving from interpersonal relationships (DHSS 1971b).

CONTROL OF PATIENTS

The physical confinement of patients, however effected, is for the protection of the public, but secure institutions also have a responsibility to protect both staff and patients within the establishments and such 'internal' aspects of security coincide with and are indistinguishable from the wider organizational requirements for control. Aspects of internal security may include, as in the special hospitals, the frequent counting and searching of patients, the monitoring of the movement of patients around the hospital by centralized radio contact, and the use of drugs as a means of controlling violent and disruptive patients. The association between drugs and security was explicitly expounded in a policy statement issued by the Royal College of Psychiatrists in 1980: 'The prompt but appropriate judicious use of medication where it is properly indicated is another measure related to security.'

Concern has been expressed about the 'medication of control' in both the penal and child-care systems (Fitzgerald and Sim 1979; Taylor, Lacey, and Bracken 1979). Prisoners, as with patients generally, may not be treated against their wishes. Previously the only exception to this was in extreme situations where the life of the prisoner might be at risk (Home Office and DHSS 1975) but it is said that the Home Office now follows the recommendations of the Butler Committee that a mentally disturbed offender may be compulsorily treated if it is necessary to prevent deterioration in his condition, to save his life, or 'to prevent the patient behaving violently or being a danger to himself or others' (Council for Science and Society 1981). This last clause explicitly legitimizes control by medication as it is not necessary for the violent behaviour to derive from the mental disorder.

PATIENT MOTIVATION

The final aspect of security to be considered is that of the patients' motivation, a factor which may reduce the expected close association between the degree of assessed dangerousness and the level of security required. Not all patients would abscond from secure establishments if 'open' conditions suddenly prevailed and not all patients who are deemed to be dangerous necessarily need treatment in secure conditions. The importance of patient motivation was recognized in the Guidelines on the care and treatment of Mentally Disturbed Offenders jointly drawn up by the Royal College of Psychiatrists and the Department of Health and Social Security in 1977.

'A patient who might be very dangerous when at large in the community may well prove co-operative in a therapeutic situation and make no attempt to abscond. Conversely, a patient who is less dangerous when at large in the community but who is a persistent absconder might need to be detained under conditions of special security because of his persistent efforts to abscond.'

The effects of the institution itself in modifying patient motivation were noted by the Hospital Advisory Service in its report on Broadmoor. Long-stay patients were vulnerable to institutionalization and it was observed that after a decade few patients wished to return to the demanding and unsupported life outside. Positive patient motivation deriving from a co-operative approach to treatment, or absence of motivation due to prolonged in-patient care, act to reduce the level of security which would otherwise be considered necessary.

Diminishing provision and falling demand

The account so far of the development of secure psychiatric facilities and the contemporary building programme of a new special hospital and regional secure units has probably led to the reasonable conclusion that increasing numbers of patients are being detained in conditions of physical security. The truth is in fact quite the reverse: the special hospital population has fallen by over 25 per cent from a peak of 2,554 patients in 1973 to 1,746 patients at the end of 1982. This parallels a fall by over a third in the number of secure beds in mental illness hospitals: from 2,341 in 1974 to 1,496 in 1981. The number of secure beds in mental handicap hospitals has remained steady, usually between 700 and 800 per annum. The number of beds in regional secure units at the end of 1981 was about 500, which only compensates for about 60 per cent of the reduction in secure beds in the mental illness hospitals.

The smaller special-hospital population came about as efforts were made to reduce the overcrowding by means of a more stringent application of the criteria for admission. The DHSS had to be satisfied that a patient required the level of security obtaining in the hospitals, which was defined as being designed to deter the scheming, determined absconder or to prevent the escape of a patient who would, if at large, present a grave, immediate danger to the public. Patients were no longer admitted because of the absence of suitable facilities elsewhere. Additionally, patients deemed to be suffering from psychopathic disorder were, in the words of the

Mental Health Act 1959, required to be 'susceptible to treatment'. This policy not only served the main objective of reducing overcrowding but also resulted in a practical demonstration to the regional health authorities of the need to provide the secure units which the government had been pressing them to do for some years.

The reduction in the number of secure National Health Service beds is a consequence of the operation of the open-door policy and changing attitudes following the implementation of the Mental Health Act 1959, by which the majority of patients are admitted on a voluntary basis. A greater emphasis on treatment, facilitated by the development of psychotropic drugs, rather than simply providing containment, eventually resulted in difficult chronic patients being unwanted by the National Health Service, and reinforced the traditional reluctance to admit mentally abnormal offenders.[14] Other factors aggravating the situation are a lack of resources including staff, negative staff attitudes, lack of appropriate training, and the development of district general hospital units (Royal College of Psychiatrists 1980). Not all mentally abnormal offenders or difficult patients require secure provision but it is from within these groups that the majority of those identified as requiring security will be drawn, and it is precisely this type of patient which the National Health Service has been so successful in rejecting (Gunn 1982).

The unwelcoming attitude of the National Health Service underlies the decline in the number of hospital orders given by the courts under Part V of the Mental Health Act 1959 (Parker and Tennent 1979). The total number of hospital orders almost halved, from a peak of 1,448 in 1966 to 762 in 1979, the number rising in 1981. A court may only make a hospital order if a hospital makes a bed available and the judiciary have complained of having, in the absence of a bed, to send mentally disordered offenders to prison rather than hospital. As described earlier, this led to the prison authorities protesting about the increasing numbers of mentally abnormal prisoners and the difficulties they also experienced in effecting admission to hospital.

The advent in 1976 of interim secure units, the precursors of regional secure units, alleviated the situation by providing some secure accommodation. The overall extent of the relief to the different services in terms of numbers admitted from the psychiatric and special hospitals, prisons, and courts is not known but figures from four interim units show that of 193 first admissions nearly half, 47 per cent, came from the courts or prisons, a further quarter, 24 per cent, were admitted from the National Health Service, and a fifth from the special hospitals, which indicates that these four units are providing a significant service to the three main referral sources (Treasaden and Shepherd 1983).

It is curious that with fewer secure places than at any time since 1974 there is not a greater expressed demand. The referral rate to the special hospitals between 1979 and 1982 inclusive has remained steady within the range of 316 to 381 patients a year, as has their acceptance rate of about 57 per cent. The prison department last complained of difficulties in gaining the admission of offenders to psychiatric hospitals in 1979 (Home Office 1980) and, although the courts may still experience difficulties in placing a mentally disordered defendant, this seems to be a rare occurrence. And of course, only a proportion of the places sought by the courts and the penal system will be in a secure provision.

One process which offers an explanation of the reduced demand for secure provision is the evolution of forensic psychiatry as a discipline, which has helped to foster changing attitudes in both the penal service and the National Health Service. The development of the regional secure units has been the main stimulus underlying the growth of this subspeciality. This development of forensic psychiatric expertise seems to have generated a reformulation and reassessment of the function of security and of the needs of patients within secure provision. In turn, this has led within the NHS to the development of methods of caring for difficult and disruptive patients which do not involve physical security; for example, the special care units in some hospitals and the recognition that some patients in security could be successfully treated in an open environment. Nevertheless, the promise of these innovations is somewhat offset by the fact that they have been facilitated by the hospitals having successfully banished the least desirable patients, a significant number of whom do require treatment in some degree of physical security and for whom the new developments would not be suitable (Gunn 1982).

Evidence of a changing attitude in the penal system is hard to come by but there are two straws in the wind. Firstly there has been a change of emphasis in the reports on the work of the prison department: complaints about the difficulties in obtaining admission to the National Health Service were last voiced in 1979, the year subsequent to that in which the number of prisoners annually transferred to hospital began to rise.

Secondly, an investigation of persons convicted of manslaughter due to diminished responsibility (Homicide Act 1957, s. 2) found that, in cases where admission to a special hospital was not obtained, the prison medical officers, rather than seek admission to the National Health Service, drew the courts' attention to the facilities and resources available within the penal system for treating mental disorder and to the possibilities of transfer to a psychiatric hospital should this eventually prove necessary (Dell and Smith 1983). There are of course unique circumstances attending to this offence group but if the prison medical officers are willing to treat them within the penal system then might they not also be prepared to treat other abnormal offenders and indicate as much to the courts? The finding of this study together with the more positive and constructive tone of the reports of the work of the prison department seem to denote a changing attitude to mentally abnormal offenders within the penal system which parallels that taking place in the National Health Service.

Present problems and future developments

The range of secure psychiatric provision extends from, at one end of the continuum, that provided in the predominantly open NHS psychiatric hospitals through the regional secure units to the maximum security of the special hospitals. Ideally patients move through the system in both directions so that the level of security to which they are subject never exceeds the minimum required or considered to be necessary. In practice the system is neither comprehensive nor efficient. There is little or no provision for certain types of patient who require some degree of secure facility, and a non-psychiatric agency, the prisons, caters for many mentally disordered offenders. The movement of patients through the system particularly towards a lower level of security is hampered because of difficulties in transferring patients to another hospital or because of the shortage of suitable accommodation for those ready to be discharged into the community.

Approximately two-thirds of patients leaving the special hospitals are transferred to the NHS and are admitted either to a regional secure unit or to a psychiatric hospital. The regional secure units are still in the early stages of development and are not yet fully operational, and the psychiatric hospitals, as has been described, are reluctant to accept such patients. At any time there are about 200 special-hospital patients awaiting transfer, of whom about one-third have been waiting over a year.

In 1974 the opening of the Eastdale Unit in a NHS hospital represented a specific attempt to deal with this problem. The unit admits only male ex-special-hospital patients, predominantly from

Rampton Hospital, for a maximum period of six months, the original intention being that it would operate as a half-way house between the special hospitals and full transfer to an NHS hospital, cleansing patients of their special-hospital stigma and making them more acceptable to the hospitals by showing that they could be cared for outside a high-security institution. This original objective was never entirely fulfilled in that as the unit developed it became more autonomous, and its function now is to prepare patients for direct discharge into the community. The Boynton Report on Rampton Hospital commended the Eastdale Unit and advised that the possibility of providing a similar unit for female patients should be explored.

It is expected that under the Mental Health Act 1983 the number of patients to be transferred to the NHS or discharged into the community will rise due to the powers of discharge of the mental health review tribunals being extended to restricted patients and the compulsory referral of patients who have not previously applied within a specified period of time. The presence of patients in the special hospitals who do not require maximum security has already attracted criticism (Dell 1980; DHSS 1980) and further concern is likely to be expressed by the Mental Health Act Commission, a body set up under the new Act to protect the rights of detained patients. At a time of economic stringency and diminished spending on the NHS the most promising approach to reducing the number of patients waiting to leave the special hospitals is to make better use of existing resources. For special-hospital patients awaiting transfer to the NHS such resources are the Eastdale Unit, the regional secure units, and the mental illness and mental handicap hospitals. It is a notable feature of both the Eastdale Unit and those interim secure units for which information is available that they do not operate to their full capacity. Eastdale is a thirty-bed unit but never has more than twelve patients at a time. From the figures supplied by Treasaden and Shepherd for four interim secure units it is possible to calculate that one operates at about 86 per cent capacity, two at about 76 per cent capacity, and the fourth, which has been open for over four years, at only 46 per cent capacity. If these figures are representative of interim secure units generally then the operational efficiency of a quarter of them could be reasonably increased by 40 per cent and of an additional half by 10 per cent with a commensurate advantage to the special hospitals as well as to the NHS hospitals and the penal system. Whatever the reasons underlying this under-usage they are not financial, as the DHSS meets the revenue costs, and not all of the allocated money is spent by the regions on secure facilities. On the other hand, the Eastdale Unit did suffer from lack of resources, but this has now been rectified; full use of Eastdale could result in approximately a further thirty-two special-hospital patients a year being transferred. The Boynton recommendation that a similar unit be established for female patients is most likely to be realized by the future enlarged intake into Eastdale including women as well as men.

Increasing the number of patients transferred to mental illness and mental handicap hospitals is primarily dependent on overcoming their resistance to such patients, a task which is made more difficult by the run-down of the old mental hospitals. Severely mentally handicapped patients are particularly difficult to place: at the end of 1982 nearly 40 per cent of special-hospital patients awaiting transfer for over two years were so classified and it has been suggested that the problem of effecting transfers for this group is largely a reflection of the inadequate services for the mentally handicapped generally (Dell 1980). Following the publication of the Boynton Report in 1980 the Secretary of State for Social Services wrote to the chairmen of the regional health authorities expressing deep concern and requesting their personal help in placing named patients. This did result in an increase of patients transferred in 1981 but the effects of industrial action in the NHS caused the numbers to fall in 1982. The change of attitude detected in the NHS consequent upon the development of forensic psychiatry generally combined with constant pressure from the special hospitals and possible future intervention by the Mental Health Act commissioners may eventually succeed in clearing the backlog of patients waiting to be transferred.

In comparison with patients selected for transfer, the problems of patients discharged directly into the community are very much less severe. The majority, not being self-sufficient, become the responsibility of the local authorities and enter hostels run by such authorities or by voluntary agencies. At any one time there are normally about thirty-five special-hospital patients whose conditional discharge is pending arrangements being made for hostel accommodation, but this figure does not include any patients whose absolute discharge by the consultant is dependent on suitable accommodation being found in the community.

Hostels for former mental patients are under increasing pressure generally because of the shrinking number of in-patient beds; in future special-hospital patients will be in more direct competition with other psychiatric patients for hostel accommodation. A recent inquiry has pointed to the inadequacy of community services for ex-patients and called for legislation to place a mandatory duty on local authorities to provide proper facilities (Richmond Fellowship 1983). The history of the special hospitals suggests one way in which this potential problem might be broached: both Rampton and Moss Side hospitals have at different periods operated pre-discharge hostels for patients who did not require full special-hospital treatment but for whom it was not possible to find placements elsewhere. Currently plans are again underway at Rampton in collaboration with the Mental After Care Association to open a pre-discharge hostel for female patients which could act as a staging post from which patients could more fully enter the community or be transferred to an NHS hospital. Despite the enterprise shown by Rampton it is doubtful whether these plans will ever come to fruition due to anticipated objections by the local community to a hostel specifically catering for special-hospital patients.

Whereas the patients in a pre-discharge hostel are still the responsibility of the parent hospital, discharged patients are usually the responsibility of the local authority and there are objections in principle to the DHSS financing hostel accommodation for ex-special-hospital patients. It is argued that the needs of these patients should be met by the local authorities and that the funding of such patients in the community would act as a disincentive to the local authorities to meet their obligations. A general realization that rigid categorization of financial responsibility was not in the best interests of patients led to the regional health authorities being empowered to make grants from a central monetary allocation towards expenditure on services of common interest to both themselves and the local authorities (Health Services Act 1980, which inserted section 28A into the National Health Service Act 1977).[15] More recently these joint finance arrangements were extended so that the movement from hospital into community of National Health Service patients requiring long-term care could be accompanied by a permanent transfer of necessary financial resources (DHSS 1983b). These provisions relate only to the health service and local authorities and will not benefit special-hospital patients, who are the direct responsibility of the Department of Health and Social Security. Nevertheless, if such innovatory concepts were applied to the special hospitals in respect of their links with both the National Health Service and the local authorities, there is no doubt that it would facilitate the transfer and discharge of patients and rapidly reduce the numbers of patients awaiting departure.

It would be expected that the difficulties the special hospitals experience in effecting the transfer or the discharge of patients might also be shared to a certain extent by the regional secure units. That this is so is demonstrated by one interim secure unit which, in order to facilitate discharge, has bought a local house which is used as a four-bed hostel, and in the plans approved for a permanent unit has included a three-bed flat. Regional secure units which find it difficult to place patients when they are ready to leave are eligible as a National Health Service facility to benefit from the joint funding arrangements described above.

The closely defined criteria for admission to special hospitals and the regional secure units exclude two groups of patients who require some degree of security but less than that provided by a special hospital: those mentally ill patients requiring long-term care and a modicum of security and severely mentally impaired patients requiring secure provision. This latter group do not officially exist; the Glancy Committee considered that the proper management of severely subnormal patients lay in skilled nursing care and an appropriate environment. However, the admission each year of a few such patients to the maximum security of the special hospitals suggests the presence of a somewhat larger group who could suitably be placed in a medium-secure provision. This need has been recognized by several regional health authorities who are currently considering special care facilities for the mentally handicapped. The long-term mentally ill who need a degree of security short of that provided in the special hospitals have not yet been identified as a group requiring specialist provision but their requirements will become more apparent as the old asylum-type hospitals are phased out.

The future development of secure provision in NHS hospitals appears to lie in the development of special care facilities (which do not necessarily include physical security) for those patients for whom an open ward is unsuitable; the regional secure units and the special hospitals will cater for patients who need greater levels of security. That the special hospitals will continue to be needed has been confirmed by the Royal College of Psychiatrists (1983), but the short-stay policy of the secure units together with the developing forensic presence in the regions creates the possibility that the regional secure units will deal with patients treatable within the short term and the special hospitals will be left with the long-stay and untreatable patients.

An even greater concentration of unrewarding patients who are unacceptable elsewhere would increase the distance between the special hospitals and the other mental health services. The isolation of the special hospitals generally was noted by the Estimates Committee in 1969, and the Boynton Committee in 1980 considered that Rampton Hospital suffered seriously from geographical, organizational, professional, and social isolation, which had produced an inbred and inward-looking community. The management structure of the special hospitals is a major factor influencing their links with other psychiatric services. Since 1959 they have been managed centrally by the DHSS outside the NHS but this arrangement has been subject to criticism mainly on grounds of remoteness and the lack of local involvement (House of Commons 1968; DHSS 1980; Royal College of Psychiatrists 1983). Following a recommendation of the Boynton Committee a review board has been established to manage Rampton Hospital on behalf of the Secretary of State, the members having regional connections. A proposal that the other special hospitals should have the option of adopting a local management committee if they so wish has been put forward by the Royal College of Psychiatrists (1983). Other modes of management are by an independent central board or by the appropriate regional health authority. This latter possibility has the obvious advantages of drawing the medical and nursing staff in the special hospitals closer to their colleagues in the NHS and of introducing appropriate professional expertise into the special hospitals' administration. However, some responsibilities such as decisions concerning patient admissions would have to be retained centrally in order to ensure uniformity of practice. In the current economic climate it is unlikely, should such a proposal be made, that it would find favour with the health authorities. The so far protected expenditure on the high-cost special hospitals would prove an embarrassment to authorities struggling with successive cuts in NHS financing, and the diversion of monies provided for the regional secure units is a cautionary tale.

The present form of secure psychiatric facilities seems to be well established and it remains to be seen how the developing forensic services affect the number of persons deemed to require security and their allocation between the NHS, regional secure units, special hospitals, and the penal system. Secure psychiatric facilities evolve in response to the rejection by existing services of difficult and disruptive patients, but once developed the new provision tends to become selective. At present this selectivity is operated throughout the psychiatric services via the concept of treatability: as has been described, persons diagnosed as suffering from certain forms of legally recognized mental disorder are only permitted access to psychiatric care if the condition is considered to be amenable to therapeutic intervention, preferably in the short term. The asylum aspect of psychiatric care is currently in abeyance. However, the notion of treatability itself derives from real advances in the understanding and treatment of mental disorder and it is further therapeutic advancement which is the factor of the greatest significance in the future role of secure facilities and psychiatric provision generally.

Notes

1 The opinions expressed in this paper are those of the author and are not to be construed as necessarily reflecting the views of the Department of Health and Social Security.

2 The Lunatics Act 1845 repealed sections 20 and 21 of the Vagrancy Act 1744 relating to possibly mad and dangerous lunatics and made it lawful for persons wandering about and deemed to be insane and dangerous by the justices to be detained in asylums on the same orders and certificates as pauper lunatics. Again, nothing was to prevent such patients being taken into the care of relatives or friends.

3 This section was repealed in 1838 (1 and 2 Vict., c. 14) and the new Act empowered magistrates to detain insane or dangerous idiots in asylums on the same orders and certificates as pauper lunatics. Nothing was to prevent such patients being taken into the care of relatives.

4 This number was considered to be a gross underestimate as some counties denied having any criminal lunatics.

5 A full description of the conditions covered by the terms lunatic, person of unsound mind, idiot, imbecile, and mental defective may be found in the Report of the Royal Commission on the Law Relating to Mental Illness and Mental Deficiency 1954–57, paras 146–58. Generally 'lunatics' and 'persons of unsound mind' would now be termed 'mentally ill'. 'Mental defective' was applied to any degree of handicap. 'Idiot' would now equate to the severely mentally handicapped and the terms 'imbecile' and 'feeble-minded' were used to denote less severe forms of mental handicap. (For the current statutory terms, see Chapter 7.)

6 With the exception of eighteen found in prison to be insane, all the patients were HMP cases. The new patients occupied the two completed blocks; ultimately Rampton would provide accommodation for 800 patients, 590 men and 210 women.

7 From 1 January, 1914 to 1 January, 1918 the population of the county, district, and borough asylums fell from 105,504 to 95,811 patients, a reduction of 9.2 per cent. The figures for Broadmoor showed a fall of 16.3 per cent, from 767 to 642 patients.

8 The women were transferred not because of overcrowding at Rampton but to provide workers for the kitchen, laundry, and sewing-room at Moss Side. The use of patients as a cheap and available source of labour has stopped in the special hospitals, mainly because the occupations now form part of the therapeutic process, but also because any industrial action by the nursing staff which includes non-movement of patients results in a breakdown of domestic services.

9 This duty was subsequently re-enacted in the National Health Service Reorganisation Act 1973, section 40, and is currently to be found in the National Health Service Act 1977, section 4.

10 The type of patients actually admitted to regional secure units and their length of stay is currently the subject of a research project being undertaken by Professor H. Gwynne Jones at Birmingham University.

11 These particular powers came into force, not on 30 September, 1983, but on 1 October, 1984.

12 An interim order may be made in the first instance for a period not exceeding twelve weeks and may be renewed for further periods of twenty-eight days up to a maximum total of six months.

13 A statement covering the overriding importance of security in penal establishments was given by the Home Office in evidence to the May Committee in Paper IIA(2), entitled 'The Concept of Imprisonment and the Priorities of Policy', paras 2 and 21 (Home Office, 1979a). This was endorsed in the May Report, p. 61, para. 4.2.

14 In a written answer to a Parliamentary Question the Secretary of State for the Home Department stated that there were 286 persons in prison department establishments on 30 September, 1982 who were considered by the prison medical officer to be mentally disordered within the meaning of the Mental Health Act 1959 (*Hansard* December 1982). Additionally, at any one time there are approximately 200 special-hospital patients awaiting a National Health Service bed, of which about one-third have been waiting for more than a year.

15 As a financial inducement to promote a desired change of practice in mental health administration the joint financial arrangements are in direct descent from the grant-in-aid of pauper lunatics in 1874. As an effort to move pauper lunatics from the workhouses to the county asylums the boards of guardians were paid four shillings from the consolidated fund for each patient so transferred (Jones 1960).

References

Allderidge, P. (1979) Hospitals, Madhouses and Asylums: Cycles in the Care of the Insane. *British Journal of Psychiatry* 34: 321–34.

Ayers, G. M. (1971) *England's First State Hospitals and the Metropolitan Asylums Board 1867–1930*. London: Wellcome Institute of the History of Medicine.

Bowden, P. (1978) Men Remanded into Custody for Medical Reports: The Selection for Treatment. *British Journal of Psychiatry* 132: 320–31.

Cawson, P. and Martell, M. (1979) *Children Referred to Closed Units*. DHSS, Statistics and Research Division. Research Report No. 5. London: HMSO.

Cheadle, J. and Ditchfield, J. (1982) Sentenced Mentally Ill Offenders. Unpublished work jointly sponsored by the Home Office and the DHSS.

Cohen, R. (1977) Where Did the Money Go? *Health and Social Service Journal* 30 September.

COHSE (1979) *NHS Secure Treatment Units*. Surrey: COHSE.

Council for Science and Society (1981) *Treating the Troublesome*. London: Council for Science and Society.

Dell, S. (1980) The Transfer of Special Hospital Patients to National Health Service Hospitals. Special Hospitals Research Report No. 16.

Dell, S. and Smith, A. (1983) Changes in the Sentencing of Diminished Responsibility Homicides. *British Journal of Psychiatry* 142: 20–34.

DHSS (1971a) *Hospital Services for the Mentally Ill*. DHSS memorandum. December.

—— (1971b) *Youth Treatment Centres*. London: HMSO.

—— (1975) *Regional Secure Units: Design Guidelines*. London: DHSS.

—— (1979) Report of St Charles Youth Treatment Centre Evaluation Team. London: HMSO.

—— (1983a) *Mental Health Act 1983*. Memorandum on Parts I to VI, VIII and X. London: HMSO.

—— (1983b) Circular HC(83)6; LAC(83)5.

East, W. Norwood and Hubert, W. H. de B. (1939) *Psychological Treatment of Crime*. London: HMSO.

Fitzgerald, M. and Sim, J. (1979) *British Prisons*. Oxford: Blackwell.

Gunn, J. (1982) Forensic Psychiatry as a Subspeciality. *International Journal of Law and Psychiatry* 5: 65–79.

Hansard (1982) House of Commons, vol. 33.

Hobhouse, S. and Brockway, A. F. (1922) *English Prisons Today*. London: Longmans, Green.

Home Office (1979a) The Concept of Imprisonment and the Priorities of Policy. Paper II A(2). In *Inquiry into the United Kingdom Prison Services*. Vol. 1. Evidence by the Home Office, the Scottish Home and Health Department, and the Northern Ireland Office: Introduction and descriptive papers. London: HMSO.

—— (1979b) The Dispersal System: England and Wales. Discussion paper 9. In *Inquiry into the United Kingdom Prison Services*. Vol. 2. Evidence by the Home Office, Scottish Home and Health Department, and Northern Ireland Office: Descriptive and discussion papers. London: HMSO.

Jones, K. (1955) *Lunacy Law and Conscience 1744–1845*. London: Routledge & Kegan Paul.

—— (1960) *Mental Health and Social Policy 1845–1959*. London: Routledge & Kegan Paul.

Millham, S., Bullock, R. and Hosie, K. (1978) *Locking up Children*. Farnborough: Saxon House.

Ministry of Health (1959) Circular. 4 May. HM(59)46, paras 8–9.

—— (1961) Circular. 13 July. HM(61)69.

—— (1963) *Accommodation for Psychiatric Patients*. Hospital Buildings Note No. 30. London: HMSO.

O'Donoghue, E. G. (1914) *The Story of Bethlem Hospital*. London: T. Fisher Unwin.

Parker, E. (1980) Mentally Disordered Offenders and Their Protection from Punitive Sanctions. *International Journal of Law and Psychiatry* 3: 461–69.

Parker, E. and Tennent, G. (1979) The 1959 Mental Health Act and Mentally Abnormal Offenders: A Comparative Study. *Medicine, Science and the Law* 19: 29–38.

Richmond Fellowship (1983) *Mental Health and the Community*. London: Richmond Fellowship Press.

Robertson, G. (1982) The 1959 Mental Health Act of England and Wales: Changes in the Use of Its Criminal Provisions. In J. Gunn, and D. P. Farrington (eds) *Abnormal Offenders, Delinquency and the Criminal Justice System*. London: Wiley.

Robertson, G. and Gibbens, T. C. N. (1980) Transfers from Prisons to Local Psychiatric Hospitals under Section 72 of the 1959 Mental Health Act. *British Medical Journal* 1: 1263–66.

Royal College of Psychiatrists (1980) *Secure Facilities for Psychiatric Patients: A Comprehensive Policy*. London: Royal College of Psychiatrists.

—— (1983) Report on the Future of the Special Hospitals. London: Royal College of Psychiatrists.

Royal College of Psychiatrists and DHSS (1977) Guidelines on te Care and Treatment of Mentally Disturbed Offenders. News and Notes, Supplement to the *British Journal of Psychiatry* April: 7–12.

Taylor, L., Lacey, R., and Bracken, D. (1979) *In Whose Best Interests?* London: The Cobden Trust and Mind.

Treasaden, I. H. and Shepherd, D. M. (1983) Evaluation of the Lyndhurst Interim Secure Unit. Unpublished paper.

Tuke, S. (1813) *Description of the Retreat*. York: W. Alexander.

Walker, N. and McCabe, S. (1973) *Crime and Insanity in England*. Vol. 2. Edinburgh: Edinburgh University Press.

Williams, A. (1976) The Design of Security Units: Engineering Considerations. In *Hospital Engineering* 30: 6.

REPORTS OF OFFICIAL COMMITTEES

1835   *Report of the Select Committee of the House of Lords on the Present State of the General Gaols and Houses of Correction in England and Wales*. Ordered to be printed 28 July, 1835.

1844   *Report of the Metropolitan Commissions in Lunacy to the Lord Chancellor*.

1846   *Annual Reports of the Commissioners in Lunacy to the Lord Chancellor*. 1846–1914. 69 volumes.

1860   *Annual Reports of the Directors of Convict Prisons*. 1860–93. London: HMSO.

1877   *Report from a Committee Appointed to Inquire into Certain Matters relating to the Broadmoor Criminal Lunatic Asylum.* C. 1674. London: HMSO.

1914   *Annual Reports of the Board of Control. 1914–38, 1945–59.* 40 volumes. London: HMSO.

1952   Ministry of Health. *Report of the Broadmoor Inquiry Committee.* Cmd 8594. London: HMSO.

1957   *Report of the Royal Commission on the Law Relating to Mental Illness and Mental Deficiency 1954–57.* Cmnd 169. London: HMSO.

1960   Home Office. Report of the Approved Schools Central Advisory Committee on closed and other special facilities. Unpublished.

1961   Ministry of Health. *Special Hospitals. Report of Working Party.* London: HMSO.

1966   Home Office. *Report of the Inquiry into Prison Escapes and Security, etc.* Cmnd 3175 (Mountbatten Report). London: HMSO.

1968   Home Office. *Report of the Advisory Council on the Penal System. The Regime for Long-Term Prisoners in Conditions of Maximum Security.* London: HMSO.

1968   Home Office. Report of a Working Party on generally disturbed children and young persons in approved schools. Unpublished.

1968   House of Commons. *Second Report from the Estimates Committee. The Special Hospitals and the State Hospital. Session 1967–68.* London: HMSO.

1968   Ministry of Health. *Annual Report for 1967.* London: HMSO.

1970   Home Office. *Report on the Work of the Prison Department 1969.* Cmnd 4486. London: HMSO.

1971   Home Office. *Report on the Work of the Prison Department 1970.* Cmnd 4724. London: HMSO.

1972   Home Office. *Report on the Work of the Prison Department 1971.* Cmnd 5037. London: HMSO.

1973   Home Office. *Report on the Work of the Prison Department 1972.* Cmnd 5375. London: HMSO.

1974   DHSS. *Revised Report of the Working Party on Security in NHS Hospitals* (Glancy Report). Unpublished.

1974   Home Office. *Report on the Work of the Prison Department 1973.* Cmnd 5767. London: HMSO.

1974   Home Office and DHSS. *Interim Report of the Committee on Mentally Abnormal Offenders.* Cmnd 5698 London: HMSO.

1975   Home Office. *Report on the Work of the Prison Department 1974.* Cmnd 6148. London: HMSO.

1975   Home Office and DHSS. *Report of the Committee on Mentally Abnormal Offenders* (Butler Report). Cmnd 6244. London: HMSO.

1978   House of Commons. *Fifteenth Report from the Expenditure Committee. Session 1977–78. The Reduction of Pressure on the Penal System.* Volume 1 Report. London: HMSO.

1979   Home Office, Scottish Home and Health Department, and Northern

Ireland Office. *Committee of Inquiry into the United Kingdom Prison Services Report* (May Report). Cmnd 7673. London: HMSO.

1980 DHSS. *Report of the Review of Rampton Hospital* (Boynton Report). Cmnd 8073. London: HMSO.

1980 Home Office. *Report on the Work of the Prison Department 1979.* Cmnd 7965. London: HMSO.

1982 Home Office. *Report on the Work of the Prison Department 1981.* Cmnd 8543. London: HMSO.

1984 Home Office. *Report on the Work of the Prison Department 1983.* Cmnd 9306. London: HMSO.

Part II The Services

2 Secure facilities in local psychiatric hospitals

Malcolm Faulk

Introduction: towards an understanding of security

The term 'security' is used to imply a degree of control by the managing agents of the patient, total security giving total control of the patient's movements and behaviour. No security means no control over the patient, except that control exerted by the patient. Near total control (obtained through close staff surveillance and physical barriers) is required for very dangerous patients. Similarly it is possible for psychiatric hospitals to look after the majority of patients with minimal control, and certainly without the need for physical barriers. No hospital is, in practice, without some controls when needed. The control may be exerted through the calming effects of a nurse purposefully talking to, or counselling, an aroused patient, or, more strongly, it may be exerted through medication deliberately administered to treat and calm a severely distressed patient. It may be exerted through 'nicer' forms of control: physical barriers, such as doors with two handles in psychogeriatric wards, which are sufficiently complicated to prevent demented patients operating the door. 'We have no locked wards,' says the hospital, but certainly these doors are effectively locked, possibly necessarily, to the patients they must contain. The 'open' hospital has devices which it employs (psychological, physical, medical) as required to control its patients, although every good hospital will temper this control by the attention and care which it gives to the patient. The degree of control which an 'open' hospital can exert in the very short term (hours or days) can be considerable, particularly if it has sufficient staff to give the extra time to the patient that is required, and there is a willingness among the staff to do so. However, the fewer the staff the more mechanical and authoritarian they are obliged to be; fewer staff also creates more anxiety concerning potentially difficult or dangerous patients. Attempts to prevent a patient from absconding from the hospital can be made by 'specialing' and by placing the patient in night-clothes, as well as by giving better attention. However, in busy, acute admission wards with no physical barriers and low staffing, sooner or later the patient, if determined, will abscond. Hospitals, therefore, either have had to exercise more control or have simply had to turn certain patients away as not being manageable. The less the control the hospital is willing, or able, to bring to bear, the greater the chance that difficult patients will be refused admission.

A ward which can be locked to prevent a patient leaving at will represents conventionally the next line of control. It is the line which produces most emotion in debates on the subject (Royal College of Psychiatrists 1980). Nevertheless there are reports to be discussed later of such wards being run successfully with reasonable claims to making a useful contribution to the patients' care and without any obvious detrimental effects. This chapter will discuss the development of the 'open door' policy and its benefits; the scientific evidence relating to the effects of locking a ward within an ordinary mental hospital; and the need for a secure ward within an ordinary mental hospital. This will be followed by discussion of possible solutions to the problems that have developed from the 'open door' policy.

Development of the 'open door' policy

By the end of 1954 the in-patient population of psychiatric hospitals reached a peak at 150,000 (Wing 1981). A revolution in psychiatric hospitals was starting to occur; hospitals were beginning to lessen the control they exercised over patients. This led in many cases to removing entirely any physical restraints over patients in hospital. The beneficial effect of unlocking large, overcrowded hospitals was demonstrated in a number of studies (Rees and Glatt 1955; Bell 1955; Stern 1957; Mandelbrote 1958). For unlocking to be a success certain features were required (Sterne 1957): patients must be happily occupied on the wards; occupation and high-class recreation should be offered outside the wards; the patient must be respected as a person and treated with patience and gentleness; the constant aim of the programme should be resocialization. There were several material benefits accompanying these principles: clothing was improved, holiday visits were encouraged, and staff were continually stimulated and supported. A similar experience was reported from Coney Hill and Horton Road Hospitals, Gloucestershire (Mandelbrote 1958). In those hospitals the wards were broken into small group units under particular nursing staff, each with a planned programme depending on the level of integration of the patient, including group psychotherapy, practical occupation, habit training, and play therapy. Great emphasis was placed on good communications between staff, patients, and the doctors in order to foster personal contacts. Repeated absconders, who failed to respond to persuasion, and those likely to harm the public were placed in small closed groups of up to six patients under the constant supervision of a nurse responsible for their day. There were very low numbers of absconders, the majority of whom simply went to their homes to be brought back by their relatives. The majority were wanderers in the older age group and deluded patients responding to their hallucinations. Patients came to realize that the unlocked hospital environment was in fact a safer and more secure one for them. Previous violence and hostility virtually disappeared, wards catering especially for disturbed patients became popular with staff and the use of seclusion fell markedly. The conclusion was reached that the restrictions produced by locking doors had a marked adverse effect on the relationships between patients and staff, and the consciousness of captivity had caused a variety of additional symptoms and preoccupations.

These studies and other similar ones, combined with clinical experience over the years, have resulted in the widely held belief that physical security within a local hospital must necessarily have an adverse effect upon patient care and staff morale. It has been assumed that all patients can be contained and treated without physical security except for those who should be placed in a special hospital. As a result, there has been a pronounced development away from the use of locked wards in local NHS hospitals. The next section of this chapter will seek to demonstrate that a locked ward can be a positive advantage to a hospital service and that an entirely open hospital is less likely to provide care for all the patients who require it.

The effect of locking a ward

There are very few scientific studies dealing with the effects on patients and staff of locking a ward in a psychiatric hospital. Folkard (1960) studied one ward before and after unlocking. The opening was preceded by a period of therapeutic activity which was to continue and increase after the opening of the doors. Aggressive incidents dropped markedly before the door was open, simply due to the effect of the extra therapeutic input. The improvement continued after the door was opened. However, five weeks after the door was opened the nursing staff in charge of the ward were changed, at which point, even though there was no change in policy and though the doors remained open, the number of aggressive incidents increased rapidly. It appears, therefore, that aggression arises from various forms of social interaction between patients and staff and not simply from locking the ward. These sources of aggression are not likely to be eliminated by the simple opening of doors. The other sources of frustration for the patients, apart from the locked ward, include such things as strict discipline, withholding of parole, and withdrawal of privileges. While applauding the achievements of the open-door policy for most patients, Folkard recognizes that despite earlier claims there may well be patients who do not respond to an open-door approach, and require additional conditions of security.

A study by Cobb and Gossop (1976) showed that when staff had to accept more disturbed patients, their attitudes and management decisions changed in favour of locked wards. A locked ward had to be repaired and the patients had to be distributed among two unlocked wards. The highly staffed, very therapeutic ward which received the more disturbed patients became locked for increasing lengths of time, despite the fact that the nurses in it initially believed that locking a ward would increase tension. Violent incidents did not increase on that ward with the length of time it was locked. Patients were admitted exhibiting aggressive, destructive behaviour which rapidly calmed even with the ward locked, allowing them to be moved to open wards after relatively brief stays. Nursing attitudes moved, therefore, strongly in favour of a locked ward for this group of patients as a result of their experience.

In summary, therefore, the two studies suggest that locking in itself is not necessarily deleterious provided that the right therapeutic activity is supplied by staff. Indeed, locking a ward, given the right therapeutic milieu, may be a very positive way of contributing to the care and management of patients who are aggressive or destructive. The results of these two studies concur with the experience of the interim secure units and special locked wards which are described later.

The need for a locked ward

Most studies have concerned themselves with 'forensic' patients, i.e. that group of patients who have come before a court charged with a criminal offence and who have been sentenced to receive psychiatric treatment. The studies on forensic patients demonstrate an unmet need although the absolute numbers involved are very small compared with the numbers of patients resident in hospitals. Only one study (Wykes, Creer, and Sturt 1982) has attempted to assess the need in the general psychiatric population for treatment in a secure setting. Even this study makes only a partial estimate of the total need for security. This section of the chapter will review the studies which have sought to demonstrate and to estimate the need for secure psychiatric accommodation for forensic and other patients in ordinary psychiatric hospitals.

In 1961 an official report on special hospitals warned of the dangers of dispensing with all security precautions for patients in ordinary psychiatric hospitals (Ministry of Health 1961) (see further Chapter 1). It was noted that hospitals which did not have any security precautions made applications for transfer to special hospitals much more than those that had. It was recommended that certain hospitals in the region should take on the task of looking after more difficult patients by providing security arrangements short of those provided by special hospitals. They also went on to recommend that there should also be regional secure units, for diagnosis and treatment of special cases. Shortly after the 1959 Mental Health Act came into being it was observed that the open-door policy was resulting in a cycle among some disturbed patients of absconding, followed by reoffending, followed by readmission and further absconding (Rollin 1963). A sudden upsurge in admissions of patients suffering from chronic schizophrenia who had committed minor offences and who had been discharged from mental hospital in the preceding two years, due to the open-door policy, was observed. There was also a high absconding rate from locked wards within an ordinary psychiatric hospital. This rate compared very unfavourably with the very low absconding rate which occurred when the hospital as a whole was physically secure (Rollin 1966). It seems possible that the ineffectiveness of a simple locked ward to contain patients is due to the lower staffing and less active therapeutic atmosphere than exists in interim secure units and intensive care wards, which will be described later.

By the 1970s there was a considerable number of anecdotal accounts from courts, the Prison Medical Service, and special hospitals that patients who had previously been treated in psychiatric hospitals were no longer being offered hospital places; the hospitals apparently felt unable to contain or manage these patients (*BMJ* 1977; Gostin 1977). Government reports (Butler Committee 1974; Glancy Committee 1974) concluded that there had been an increasing difficulty in transferring patients from special hospitals and prisons to local psychiatric hospitals due, in part, to the absence of appropriate secure hospital accommodation. A study of one region demonstrated the connection between the presence of a locked ward and its effectiveness at looking after mentally disordered offenders (Bowden 1975). In a region of three and a half million people, there were eighty-seven mentally disordered offenders residing in hospital. The likelihood of a hospital taking such a patient was much greater if the hospital was larger, and particularly if it had a locked ward. While the number of closed beds fell by 40 per cent in a five-year period there still remained several levels of security: constantly locked wards, wards locked as required, and lockable single rooms. The use of locked wards was the commonest form of restraint. However, the wards seemed to be temporarily locked more because of staff shortages than to provide a secure therapeutic environment. Locked wards for disturbed patients were very labour-intensive if staffed properly and, therefore, administratively unpopular. Restriction orders (see Chapter 7) were also unpopular as they seemed to demand a higher degree of supervision, which could not be provided because of the understaffing within the hospital; restriction orders were also thought to provide much more administrative work. Bowden refers to the evidence in prison, special hospitals, and studies of common lodging houses to demonstrate that there has been an increase in the number of patients requiring local psychiatric hospital care who are not able to get it.

A study was carried out in the Oxford region (Department of Psychiatry, University of Oxford, 1976) in order to determine how many people from the region might require psychiatric treatment under conditions of security short of those provided by the special hospitals. Cases were identified by contacting hospitals, social services, probation, prison, and special hospitals, asking for details of patients requiring medium security (interpreted in the widest sense). The need for seven different categories of treatment facilities was identified. Thirty-seven mentally ill and sixty-three mentally handicapped patients required some degree of security within a hospital. A substantial number looked as if they might require long-term care. The large number of mentally handicapped patients was an unexpected finding at the time. These patients fell broadly into those with mild mental handicap with behaviour disorder, and those with severe mental handicap, also with behaviour disorder. The mentally ill fell into a group requiring some degree of security, as might be provided in a regional secure unit, and some who could be managed in an open psychiatric hospital provided a secure unit were immediately available. In this study there was no discussion about locked wards or secure facilities in ordinary psychiatric hospitals. However, the investigation did demonstrate that the hospitals within the Oxford region were unable to cope with all the patients in the region who did not require special hospitals.

The Prison Medical Service tried to collect statistics to demonstrate the failure of the National Health Service to provide treatment for mentally abnormal offenders in prison (Orr 1978) (see further Chapter 4). It was asserted that the number of sentenced men recognized as suffering from mental illness is increasing in absolute numbers in the prisons, in part because hospital places are not forthcoming for the mentally ill. In 1931, 105 sentenced prisoners were recognized as suffering from mental illness and transferred to mental hospital. In 1976 the number was 210 in prison; however the number transferred to hospital was less than half. It was believed that the reason for this low rate of transfer from prison to hospital is that local hospitals cannot provide the intensive nursing which the offenders require.

Further support for the proposition that local hospitals have not been able to adapt their policies to be able to admit mentally disordered offenders is provided by a study of the relationship between special and local hospitals (Dell 1980). This study shows the increasing difficulties of transferring patients from special to local hospitals, particularly mentally handicapped patients. This appears to be due to hospitals not wanting to accept patients who might turn out to be difficult or dangerous (see Introduction). Unfortunately this study does not throw light on what changes in the local hospitals would be required to facilitate transfers.

In contrast to studies of the needs for secure provision among forensic patients, a study in Camberwell examined the needs of another group of patients (Wykes, Creer, and Sturt 1982). Using the Camberwell Psychiatric Register the needs of all long-term mentally ill patients based in the community and in contact with mental illness services were investigated to see what services the patients required and whether they were being provided. One of the findings on the census day was that of the 158 patients studied, 18 needed and were receiving special supervision or security because they were a danger to themselves or constituted a serious nuisance or a danger to others. (There are some 130,000 residents of Camberwell living in the community.) At the same time there would be a need for security for some of those patients from Camberwell who were not based in the community but were long-term in-patients in a psychiatric hospital. The number in this group requiring security on the census day is not known, nor is the number of newly presented patients (as opposed to long-term) who would require security. Therefore the total number of patients from Camberwell requiring security on any particular day would include those drawn from long-term community-based patients (eighteen), long-term hospital-based patients (number unknown), and newly presented patients (number unknown). Even at the base level of 18 per 130,000 this study suggests a need for security for 13 per 100,000 population or some 6,500 per 50 million population. It remains to be seen whether further studies will replicate these findings. What makes this study particularly important is that it is the only one which examines patients' needs for psychiatric care in a secure setting by studying a large population of patients rather than relying on the impression of professional staff whose bias may be against recognizing this group.

The evidence, therefore, from these various studies does not support the assertion that open psychiatric hospitals are coping with all patients outside special hospitals. The evidence suggests that patients requiring a degree of security for their care can certainly be found among forensic patients (a relatively small number) and long-term community based patients (a larger number). Almost certainly, it is possible to add to this number some of the patients who present for the first time (number unknown) and some long-term in-patients who from time to time may deteriorate and require secure care (number unknown). Some of the studies indicate that some patients will need secure care for a longer rather than a shorter time. In Edinburgh it was found that there was a need for two long-term disturbed wards besides a short-term secure ward (Woodside et al. 1976). There is a great need for further studies to clarify in numerical terms this area of long-term care.

Administrative solutions

There have been a number of proposals put forward to provide secure accommodation for mentally disordered people who may be difficult or dangerous. One obvious solution that has been put forward is the building of more secure hospitals (*BMJ* 1967) and, if necessary, more special hospitals (*BMJ* 1973). Later it was proposed to try different schemes (*BMJ* 1979) though most recently (*BMJ* 1980) the recommendation has been for the widespread establishment of small specialist units resembling interim secure units of the types described below. These can be developed by adapting existing wards and avoiding the need for expensive building programmes, and they have been shown to be effective.

The official DHSS solution depends (as does the solution proposed in the Butler Report) on the setting up of regional (medium-) secure units, which it is assumed will cope with those mentally ill who fall into the gap between the services offered by the special hospitals and local mental illness hospitals (Glancy Committee 1974) (see Chapters 5 and 6). The Glancy Committee claimed, on the basis of their enquiries to regional health authorities, that there was an excessive (13,000) number of secure beds in ordinary hospitals, which included large numbers of patients who should not be there (e.g. elderly wanderers, severely subnormal) but that much of their 'security' was due to the shortage of staff or old-fashioned attitudes rather than to the dangerousness or difficulty of the patients. It is a measure of the uncertainty of the situation that the Butler Committee believed that 2,000 regional secure beds were required, whereas the Glancy Committee thought that only 1,000 would be required, as they argued that the number needing security was actually a very small number.

Some saw dangers in the proposals, seeing them as far too simplistic. Security is immensely expensive materially and in staff, it requires highly experienced, skilled nurses, who are very difficult to find, and there have been unmistakable signs that the units will select out a nicer band from the psychiatric spectrum of patients. It has been argued that the units will do nothing to relieve overcrowding in special hospitals, nothing for the mentally abnormal long-term dangerous convicts and nothing to encourage therapeutic developments in prisons; indeed they are likely to retard any such efforts (Scott 1974). It seems a strange notion that only 1,000 beds would be able to cope with the 13,000 already in locked wards (unless, presumably, the majority were there unnecessarily, as suggested by Glancy). The fear has been expressed that the units would end up merely taking the difficult patients from ordinary psychiatric hospitals and not assist special hospitals or prisons, or alternatively the units would become blocked with long-term patients who could not return to the community or to ordinary hospitals (Gostin 1977).

It was argued that there were bound to be grey areas in which patients would fall between the two stools of open hospitals and regional secure units, and little attention had been paid to non-offending difficult or disturbed patients and the way they were coped with in ordinary psychiatric hospitals. Regional secure units were only likely to cope with a small proportion of those difficult patients unsuitable for special hospitals (Bluglass 1978); the remainder would have to be accommodated and cared for in National Health Service psychiatric hospitals. If the NHS hospitals fail to accept this responsibility any plan to develop regional secure units will fail, which implies that there is a need for a revival of a part of the mental hospital to provide an area which is at once therapeutic and controlling.

Clinical solution

The discussion above has shown that there is a body of patients who cannot be cared for at all within the present open-door hospital. The question must then be posed what facilities might be made available in ordinary mental hospitals so that these patients can be provided with optimum care. The nursing trade union, COHSE, recommended that each large psychiatric hospital should consider the feasibility of setting up an adequately staffed 'special care' unit (COHSE 1977) with one consultant responsible for its policy to facilitate the care of the more difficult patient. This unit, well staffed and therapeutically orientated, would be able to assist the hospital in caring for violent patients and thus reduce the number who would have to be sent to regional secure units. Such a unit could also absorb acutely disturbed patients from admission wards, or deal with flare-ups among more chronically ill patients from the long-term wards, so that they could rapidly be treated in the best possible conditions, to enable them to return to open wards. There are at least two descriptions available of what might be called 'special units'. One is a high-staffed locked ward in the Royal Edinburgh Hospital (Woodside et al. 1976) set aside to deal on a short-term basis with all types of disturbed behaviour arising in psychiatric patients. Their experience showed them that the ward could cope with up to fifteen patients. All diagnoses are received and the patients come from within the hospital, community, prison, courts, and special hospitals. Only half are treated compulsorily. The ward is supported by two long-stay disturbed wards but many patients return to ordinary wards or to the community. This locked ward has been arranged to provide a degree of physical security with unbreakable and reinforced glass used in various parts of it. The ward's success seems to depend on sufficient nursing staff (five per day-shift) and good medical cover, to provide a warm, therapeutic atmosphere based on a multi-disciplinary approach. There were initial fears that the ward would be retrogressive, an unwelcome return to keys and custodial care. In fact it came to receive the wholehearted recommendation of the hospital. In their discussion of the results, the authors point out that there is a grave risk that regional secure units will become autonomous units, selective about their intake. Disputes are likely to arise about placement, particularly of non-forensic patients. As the main traffic of regional secure units is likely to be forensic patients, non-offenders could reasonably object to a transfer to an establishment with such a stigma. There is strength in their conclusion that the demand for accommodation for disturbed patients outside regional secure units is, therefore, likely to continue and the provision of special care units of the Edinburgh type will be needed.

A similar unit in Shenley Psychiatric Hospital (Carney and Nolan 1978) serves that hospital and two general hospitals with psychiatric departments. The unit has developed two twenty-four-bedded locked wards which aim to help the area hospitals with the management of disturbed behaviour in the mentally ill. The two wards in Shenley provide different degrees of security reflecting the disturbance of the patient. In practice most patients were psychotic and came from the main hospitals. Acting out and manipulative patients did not seem to do well in this particular unit. There was support for the Edinburgh findings that success depends on a high staff ratio and developing an active therapeutic regime. With time the work of the unit increased considerably, demonstrating the need for this kind of short-term secure unit. The unit is seen by the authors not as replacing a regional secure unit but as fostering links with such a unit. Its function was described as a crisis centre for the disturbed mentally ill and, in that respect, it was believed to have met with some success.

The description of these two units bears great resemblance to the description of two of the first interim regional secure units. The Lyndhurst Unit at Knowle Hospital (Faulk 1979) was a converted ward set up by the Wessex Region as an interim regional secure unit consisting of fourteen beds, a very high nurse/patient ratio, and considerable medical input. The unit received those patients who needed treatment and rehabilitation from special hospitals, courts, prisons, and other hospitals, and who were considered too dangerous to be managed on ordinary wards. The unit successfully contained and improved the behaviour of most of the patients referred to it. Rainford Ward, at Rainhill Hospital, Merseyside (Higgins 1979, 1981), is an interim regional secure unit set up by the Mersey Regional Health Authority. This unit, though physically more secure than the Lyndhurst Unit, provided for a similar number and kind of patients. It had similar high ratios of nursing and medical staff and was also able to demonstrate that it could accept and successfully contain difficult patients referred from many sources for treatment, so that they could eventually return to the community or source of referral.

A comparison of the interim regional units with the intensive care units in Edinburgh and Shenley indicates that there is only a matter of degree between them; the similarities are greater than the differences. All these units provide models for further special care units. The interim regional secure units tended to have more patients with forensic histories and with histories of committing grave crimes. The stay in the interim regional units was longer than in the other two units (average six months as opposed to one or two months) but the overall flavour of the units seemed to be similar. In all of them the emphasis is on the individual therapeutic approach to the patient, aimed at rehabilitating the patient to the community. A number of regions have adopted as policy the idea of developing intensive care units, or local small units like this, as well as having a regional secure unit. Wessex Region adopted the policy of having a central regional secure unit and each major local psychiatric hospital having a special-care ward, although there have been problems which have prevented this policy being put into practice, principally those due to a shortage of nursing staff. South-East Thames Regional Health Authority (1976) is planning a central medium-secure unit with four smaller medium-secure in-patient clinics placed around the region. These four in-patient clinics have many of the characteristics of the special care units.

The regional secure units and the special care wards described here have been able to contain patients and prevent absconding, in contradiction to the reports of the failure of locked wards to prevent absconding (Rollin 1963). It seems probable that the difference is due to much higher staffing levels and the more intensive therapeutic atmosphere which exists in special care wards and interim secure units.

The formula for a successful secure unit includes a combination of the following: (1) sufficient physical security appropriate to the patient; (2) high staff ratios; and (3) a therapeutic policy which encompasses individual programmes (including parole if appropriate) aimed at providing a decent life-style with return to the community as soon as is safe. ,

Conclusions

We do not know at this stage to what extent special care units will be required once regional medium-secure units are set up. If the finding from Camberwell (Wykes, Creer, and Sturt 1982) is replicated in further studies, then the 1,000 beds planned for the regional medium-secure units will not meet the need. The arguments above make a strong case for the coexistence of special care units in ordinary psychiatric hospitals plus especially good wards for chronically disturbed patients, and regional secure units. There are obvious advantages in such an arrangement. The number of patients transferred to the regional secure unit would be kept to a minimum, and patients would, therefore, be likely to be treated in their own locality. Regional secure units could remain small and movement from the units to the local hospitals would be likely to be easier. The whole system could do a lot to remove the anxiety associated with treating dangerous and difficult patients within a local hospital. What does seem to be demonstrated by the experience of the units already discussed is that patients who present as dangerous and very disturbing in ordinary psychiatric wards can, given the right quantity and quality of care, coupled with a degree of security, be considerably helped. It seems likely that the total open-door policy was too optimistic, but the gap can be filled positively.

References

Bell, G. M. (1955) A Mental Hospital with Open Doors. *International Journal of Social Psychiatry* 1: 42–8.
Bennett, D. H. (1973) Community Psychiatry. *Community Health* 5: 58–64.
Bluglasss, R. (1978) Regional Secure Units and Interim Security for Psychiatric Patients. *British Medical Journal* 1: 489–93.
Bowden, P. (1975) Liberty and Psychiatry. *British Medical Journal* 4: 94–6.
BMA Psychological Medicine Group (1962) Security Provisions in the Mental Health Service. *British Medical Journal* 1: 462–65.
BMJ (1967) Dangerous Patients. *British Medical Journal* 1: 317–18.
—— (1973) Dangerous Patients. *British Medical Journal* 1: 247–48.
—— (1977) Inhumanity to Man. *British Medical Journal* 4: 591–92.
—— (1979) Mentally Disordered Offenders. *British Medical Journal* 1: 1–2.
—— (1980) Secure Units. *British Medical Journal* 2: 81.

Butler Committee (1974) *Interim Report of the Committee on Mentally Abnormal Offenders.* Cmnd 5698. London: HMSO.
—— (1975) *Report of the Committee on Mentally Abnormal Offenders.* Cmnd 6244. London: HMSO.
Carney, M. W. P. and Nolan, P. A. (1978) Area Security Unit in a Psychiatric Hospital. *British Medical Journal* 1: 27–8.
Cobb, J. P. and Gossop, M. R. (1976) Locked Doors in the Management of Disturbed Psychiatric Patients. *Journal of Advanced Nursing* 1: 469–80.
COHSE (1977) *The Management of Violent or Potentially Violent Patients.* Banstead: Confederation of Health Service Employees.
—— (1979) *NHS Secure Treatment Units – A Policy Statement.* Banstead: Confederation of Health Service Employees.
Dell, S. (1980) *The Transfer of Special Hospital Patients to National Health Service Hospitals.* Special Hospitals Research Unit. Report No. 16. London.
Department of Psychiatry, University of Oxford (1976) *A Survey of the Need for Secure Psychiatric Facilities in the Oxford Region.* Oxford: Oxford Regional Health Authority.
Faulk, M. (1979) The Lyndhurst Unit at Knowle Hospital. *Bulletin of the Royal College of Psychiatrists* March: 44.
Folkard, S. (1960) Aggressive Behaviour in Relation to Open Wards in a Mental Hospital. *Mental Hygiene* 44: 155–61.
Glancy Committee (1974) *Revised Report of the Working Party on Security in the N.H.S. Psychiatric Hospitals.* London: DHSS.
Gostin, L. (1977) *A Human Condition.* Vol. 2. London: National Association for Mental Health.
Higgins, J. (1979) Rainford Ward, Rainhill Hospital. *Bulletin of the Royal College of Psychiatrists.* March: 43.
—— (1981) Four Years' Experience of an Interim Secure Unit. *British Medical Journal* 282: 889–93.
Mandelbrote, B. (1958) An Experiment in the Rapid Conversion of a Closed Mental Hospital into an Open-Door Hospital. *Mental Hygiene* 42: 3–16.
Ministry of Health (1961) *Special Hospitals, Report of Working Party.* London: HMSO.
Orr, J. H. (1978) The Imprisonment of Mentally Disordered Offenders. *British Journal of Psychiatry* 133: 194–99.
Rees, T. and Glatt, M. M. (1955) The Organisation of a Mental Hospital on the Basis of Group Participation. *International Journal of Group Psychotherapy* 5(2): 157–61.
Rollin, H. R. (1963) Social and Legal Repercussions of the Mental Health Act 1959. *British Medical Journal* 1: 786–88.
—— (1966) Mental Hospitals without Bars: A Contemporary Paradox. *Proceedings of Royal Society of Medicine* 59: 701–04.
Royal College of Psychiatrists (1980) *Secure Facilities for Psychiatric Patients: A Comprehensive Policy.* London: Royal College of Psychiatrists.
Scott, P. D. (1974) Solutions to the Problem of the Dangerous Offender. *British Medical Journal* 4: 640–41.

South-East Thames Regional Health Authority (1976) *Secure But Not Secured*. Croydon: South East Thames Regional Health Authority.

Stern, E. S. (1957) Operation Sesame. *The Lancet* 1: 577–78.

Wing, J. K. (1981) How Many Psychiatric Beds? *Psychiatry* 5: 188–90.

Woodside, M., Harrow, A., Basson, J. V., and Affleck, J. W. (1976) An Experiment in the Management of Sociopathic Disorders. *British Medical Journal* 2: 1056–059.

Wykes, T., Creer, C., and Sturt, E. (1982) Needs and the Deployment of Services. In J. K. Wing (ed.) *Long-Term Community Care: Experience in a London Borough*. Cambridge: Cambridge University Press.

3 The special hospitals[1]

John R. Hamilton

Statutory provisions

Special hospitals were constituted by section 97 of the Mental Health Act 1959, later repealed and replaced by section 4 of the National Health Service Act 1977, by which the Secretary of State for Social Services is required to provide special hospitals 'for patients subject to detention' who 'require treatment under conditions of special security on account of their dangerous, violent or criminal propensities'. MacCulloch (1982) says these propensities are interpreted as meaning extremes of behaviour under each category and involving danger to persons more than to property, except perhaps in the case of arson.

Under section 4 of the 1977 Act, the special hospitals are under the direct control and management of the Secretary of State: they are thus not part of the NHS regional administrative structure but rather are in parallel to the NHS in their management by the DHSS. The branch of the DHSS administering the special hospitals is known as MHC (Mental Health Division C) and the management control is exercised through a committee of senior administrators and professional officers whose chairman is the under-secretary of the DHSS's mental health division.

The Mental Health Act 1983 allows for the transfer of patients between special hospitals, and under section 123 the Secretary of State is empowered to direct the transfer of a special-hospital patient into an NHS hospital. It is believed no such direction has been made but such a direction was advocated in 1979 by MIND. MIND asked the Secretary of State to use this power to order the admission of a Broadmoor patient into an NHS hospital which had refused to admit him.

Historical development

There is often confusion in the minds of the public and the medical profession, including psychiatrists, as to the role of the Home Office in the special hospitals, and for understandable reasons, both historically and because of security aspects. Special hospitals are, however, not prison hospitals; there are no prison officers and all patients are detained under mental health legislation. (For further details of the history, see Chapter 1.) Doctors and most staff are employed by the DHSS under similar conditions of service as in the NHS. All members of the staff are civil servants and all must sign the Official Secrets Act. For historical reasons nurses belong to the Prison Officers' Association and in some special hospitals their uniform resembles that of prison officers.

In March, 1984 the four special hospitals had 2,043 beds, of which 370 were vacant. All special hospitals may admit patients detained with any of the four categories of mental disorder defined in section 1 of the Mental Health 1983 (mental illness, psychopathic disorder, mental impairment, and severe mental impairment) but each of the special hospitals has for historical reasons developed differently.

THE CRIMINAL LUNATICS ACTS

When one James Hadfield in 1800 was found not guilty by reason of insanity of high treason following his shooting at King George III, the trial judge commented: 'This unfortunate man should be cared for, all mercy and humanity being shown.' Hadfield was committed to Bethlem and to ensure his detention the Criminal Lunatics Act 1800 was passed, the first use of the term for those acquitted on the ground of insanity or found insane on arraignment, and ordered to be detained in custody 'until His Majesty's pleasure be known'. Criminal lunatics accumulated in Bethlem and in other hospitals and prisons, leaving penal reformists such as Shaftesbury to criticize the mixing together of criminals and lunatics. A select committee of the House of Commons reported in 1860 that such mixing was 'a serious evil' and in the same year was passed the second Criminal Lunatics Act with the purpose of making better provision for their custody and care, and authorizing the building of a special 'asylum' for them. In 1863 Broadmoor opened, the oldest of the special hospitals.

BROADMOOR

Besides the 'pleasure' patients, as they were colloquially known (such as Daniel McNaughton) Broadmoor admitted 'time' patients transferred from prisons when found to be mentally disordered while serving sentence. A few were also admitted after being certified insane while on remand. 'Time' patients, unlike 'pleasure' patients, would usually be free to leave Broadmoor when their prison sentence expired.

The Home Office was not only the manager of Broadmoor but controlled all admissions and discharges. Unlike Rampton, there were until 1960 no transfers from mental hospitals. In 1949 the management of Broadmoor passed to the Board of Control as one of the provisions of the Criminal Justice Act 1948, the Home Office retaining control of admissions and discharges.

With the passing of the Mental Health Act 1959 the administration passed to the DHSS and for the first time it was possible to admit non-offenders. A chronicle of Broadmoor from its foundation until 1953 has been written by Partridge (1953), while Gould (1957) has given an account of clinical practice before modern treatments were available. McGrath (1968), Loucas and Udwin (1974), Hamilton, Tidmarsh, Loucas, Cox, and Black (all 1980) have described more recent aspects of treatment. Broadmoor has always been a hospital for the mentally ill or those with psychopathic disorder and has never admitted more than an occasional patient with mental handicap.

Broadmoor is in the Berkshire village of Crowthorne, ten miles from Reading, and an hour's journey west from London. In March, 1984 the hospital had 584 beds. In recent years Broadmoor has been visited by the Hospital Advisory Service (in November 1974) and the Estimates Committee (1968) of the House of Commons, who referred to 'appalling' overcrowding. (There were then 800 beds.) The hospital is now being rebuilt on site: the first phase of new patient accommodation is due for completion in 1986. Broadmoor is planned eventually to have about 510 beds. Patients have been transferred to Park Lane Hospital (see p. 88) to reduce numbers.

RAMPTON

Rampton Hospital is in the Nottinghamshire countryside near Retford. some fifteen miles west of Lincoln. In March 1984 it had

800 beds and 602 patients. It was opened in 1910 as a criminal lunatic asylum to fulfil the same functions as Broadmoor, but passed in 1920 to the management of the Board of Control under the Mental Deficiency Act 1913 as a state institution for mental defectives with dangerous and violent propensities. Until 1960 patients could only be admitted under the Mental Deficiency Acts 1913–38 and most were transferred to Rampton from other hospitals for mental defectives, whether or not they had previously faced criminal charges. Now Rampton treats patients suffering from all categories of mental disorder. The hospital is divided into a section for the treatment of patients with mental handicap and a section for those with mental illness and psychopathic disorder.

In 1947 the ownership of Rampton was transferred to the Ministry of Health but the Board of Control remained the managers. A description of the functioning of Rampton prior to 1960 has been given by Street and Tong (1960), in which year Rampton passed to the management of the DHSS. Allegations of ill treatment by staff at Rampton were made in a television documentary programme in May, 1979 and repeated in the national press (e.g. *Daily Mail*, 16 May, 1979). The allegations were referred to the Director of Public Prosecutions; subsequently a number of nurses faced prosecution and some were convicted. In September, 1979 the DHSS established a management review team under the chairmanship of Sir John Boynton, whose terms of reference were 'to review the organisation, management and functioning' of Rampton and to recommend any desirable changes. The management review team reported (DHSS 1980) in November, 1980 and in July, 1981 Mr L. Teeman was appointed chairman of the Rampton Hospital Review Board.

In the past Rampton has been visited by the Estimates Committee, by the (then) Hospital Advisory Service in 1971 and was the subject of an inquiry by Mr J. Elliott of the King's Fund Centre in 1973 (see p. 89).

MOSS SIDE

Moss Side, just north of Liverpool, was never a Home Office establishment, but was purchased in 1914 by the Board of Control for the same sort of patients as Rampton. It opened in 1919 and the following year all Moss Side patients were transferred to Rampton, the hospital being leased to the Ministry of Pensions for use as an epileptic colony. In 1933 it was reopened as a state institution for mental defectives and, like Rampton, was managed by the Board of

Control until it became a special hospital in 1960. In March, 1984 Moss Side had 400 beds, of which 264 were occupied.

Park Lane is the fourth and newest of the special hospitals, and is being built adjacent to Moss Side Hospital, with which it shares some facilities. An advance unit with seventy male patients transferred from Broadmoor was opened in 1974 and the first 100 beds in September, 1980. On completion there will be 410 beds for mental illness and psychopathic disorder. There are, as yet, no female patients. In March, 1984 Park Lane had 260 patients.

Management

DHSS AND THE OFFICE COMMITTEE

The Secretary of State exercises direct responsibility for the management and control of the special hospitals through the DHSS. Administration is by a branch of the DHSS's mental health division whose staff (who also have other responsibilities) are London-based civil servants and include senior administrators, doctors, nurses, and social workers. The officers who have direct responsibility for overall policy and management of the special hospitals are known as the office committee for the special hospitals. The office committee acting on behalf of the Secretary of State has a role in relation to the special hospitals similar to that of a health authority. It takes major policy decisions, allocates financial and manpower resources, and makes senior appointments. The chairman of the office committee is the under-secretary of the mental health division and other 'permanent' members of the committee include a senior principal medical officer, a principal nursing officer, an assistant director of social work services, and the assistant secretary in charge of the mental health division. Other departmental officials attend meetings by invitation. The committee visits each of the special hospitals at least twice a year when it meets local management, heads of departments, and the Prison Officers' Association. In Rampton the office committee on their visits meet the Rampton Hospital Review Board.

Aspects of the management of special hospitals have been considered by a number of official reports and discussion documents, in particular the comments of the House of Commons Estimates Committee (1968), the (unpublished) report on Broadmoor Hospital of the Hospital Advisory Service in 1975, a DHSS discussion document of 1975, and the report of the Boynton Committee (DHSS 1980).

The Estimates Committee (1968:xxxii) recommended that it should be possible to have a management committee for each special hospital which would

'have a number of departmental members and a departmental chairman; should have a majority of non-psychiatrically qualified members; should invite psychiatrists from local hospitals and University departments; should include representatives of the Regional Hospital Board, the local authority, and the local community; and within such limits should be constituted to reflect as much specialist knowledge as might be of help in the Special Hospital field. Of course every Management Committee would undertake its task differently, but no doubt the prominence of departmental members on all committees would ensure some degree of uniformity.'

In 1973 the Elliott Report on Rampton Hospital recommended the establishment of a special governing body which would give hospital staff closer access to professional expertise in aspects of treatment and management, enable better links with hospitals, prisons, and community services, and bring about 'visible signs of involvement' by management as desired by many sections of the staff.

After visiting Broadmoor Hospital the Hospital Advisory Service in 1975 advised that the mental health division of the DHSS should consider maximum delegation of decision-making to hospital level and recommended that urgent consideration be given to the establishment of a management committee which would bring advantages in continuity of experience of management, regular contact with NHS personnel, and sharing of responsibility, thereby combating isolation and entrenched attitudes. There was a further recommendation for the provision of a management subcommittee to review the progress and approve the discharge of patients.

A DHSS 1975 discussion paper *Future Management of the Special Hospitals* considered that, whatever system of management was considered best, control of admissions, manpower, and staff pay and conditions should remain with central management. This internal discussion document reviewed different models – direct management by DHSS, management by the local NHS regional authority, by a local governing body, and by a separate central board – and gave the pros and cons of each. In considering management by a local governing body the 1975 paper gave few arguments against and said the arguments in favour were 'it provides a local and more easily identifiable form of management; it associates the local health authority and the local community with the running of the hospital; it more readily provides advice and support to the senior hospital staff.'

The Boynton Report (DHSS 1980) made strong criticisms of the management structure then obtaining at Rampton Hospital, describing the status of the office committee as 'ambiguous and unclear' and as not being a tier of management. This, the report said, led to an unclear distinction 'between management accountability on the one hand and consultation and negotiation with the staff on the other'. The report recommended the establishment, initially for three years, of a review board consisting of five to seven members, the majority of them having local or regional connections and with experience and qualifications in industry, universities, trades unions, and the public services, including the NHS. It was also suggested that the board should have delegated to it all the powers and responsibilities exercised by the Secretary of State except for matters of staffing, admissions, and financial and manpower allocations. The Secretary of State would retain statutory responsibility for managing Rampton but 'means would have to be found of linking the Board to the staff of the DHSS ... so that the Board can have the benefit of their knowledge and experience.' The report recommended that towards the end of the three years 'the Secretary of State should review the way the board had operated and consider whether any of its features should be incorporated on a long-term basis in the management arrangements at Rampton or indeed the other special hospitals.'

Following publication of the Boynton Report the Secretary of State established the statutory Rampton Hospital Review Board to undertake local management functions for Rampton Hospital. The board and the DHSS have not yet published information on how they see their respective roles. The medical director at Rampton is not a member of the review board and although the hospital administrator is the board's nominal secretary he delegates this function to a deputy administrator. It is understood that the medical director attends meetings of the board by invitation. The first report of the board has been submitted to the Secretary of State for Social Services.

Meantime current local management by a hospital management team can include many of the advantages suggested by a management committee such as injection of new ideas, especially in cross-fertilization with other hospitals. Previous medical directors at Broadmoor, for instance, point out that senior staff there have a tradition of active involvement in local and national professional bodies (and similarly these bodies participate in the appointment of the hospital's senior staff), that Broadmoor's management over 120 years has not proved a need for change, that contact with DHSS is easily maintained by telephone and that 'local' management would prove difficult to interpret with such a wide geographical catchment area. It would seem unwise therefore to force a local management committee on a well-functioning special hospital unless there is demonstrable disharmony and widespread lack of confidence in the hospital management team.

It is likely that in 1985 the DHSS will consider whether general managers should be appointed in the special hospitals as elsewhere in the NHS following the government's acceptance of proposals in the Griffith's Report.

Monitoring

The State Hospital for Scotland is visited regularly by the Mental Welfare Commission for Scotland, a central independent authority of medical and lay commissioners whose remit is to exercise general protective functions in respect of patients: that is to enquire into allegations of deficiency in the care and treatment of patients or of ill-treatment or of their improper detention or loss or damage to patients' property. In response to the recommendations of the Royal College of Psychiatrists and the Rampton Hospital management review team, the Government (DHSS, Home Office, Welsh Office, and Lord Chancellor's Department 1981: 11) decided that the new mental health legislation should require the Secretary of State:

'to set up a special health authority to be called the *Mental Health Act Commission* to exercise a general protective function for detained patients and to carry out certain other functions given to the Secretary of State. The Commission will thus be responsible to the Secretary of State, but will be an independent body with members who will be eminent in their different fields; it will be a real safeguard to patients wherever they are detained. The Government intends that the members of the proposed Commission will be lawyers, doctors, nurses, psychologists, social workers and laymen. Their part-time services, as commissioners, will include visiting hospitals where patients are detained with around one visit a month to the four special hospitals. In their visits the Commission members will make themselves available to detained patients who wish to see them and will ensure that staff are helping patients to understand their legal position and their rights. They will look at patients' records of admission and renewal of detention and at records relating to treatment. They will also ensure that detained patients are satisfied with the handling of any complaints they may make.'

Further discussions on the role and functions of the Mental Health Act Commission continue; meantime the proposals are welcomed in general and in particular as they relate to special hospitals, and it is hoped that the commission will play a leading part in giving guidance on, and providing a forum for discussion of, the many issues of concern surrounding the care of detained patients.

Security

Special hospitals have high walls or fences, and patients and visitors have to be escorted everywhere through locked doors. Most patients are not allowed money, matches, or pocket knives, though they do wear their own clothes. The degree of security is such as to prevent patients from absconding: one of the criteria for admission of such patients is that they present a grave and immediate danger to the public.

The House of Commons Estimates Committee (1968) Report on the Special Hospitals and the State Hospital recognized the conflict between the demands of therapy and the protection of the public: 'it is against their solution of this problem that the success of the Special Hospitals will be measured.' The Estimates Committee studied a report of the Ministry of Health working party on security in the special hospitals and entirely agreed with their conclusions, which were that (1) the balance between security and treatment should be a matter for the judgement of the responsible medical officer; (2) security for seriously dangerous patients should be not less than that for the most dangerous prisoners; (3) security should be proportionate to the risks involved and should not be such as to interfere with the needs of treatment; (4) if there was a possibility of an organized attempt at rescue, such offenders should be sent to prison rather than to a special hospital.

The Boynton Report on Rampton Hospital (DHSS 1980) expressed the view that the way a special hospital is run must reflect security and treatment adequately, but recognized that imperfect compromises between both aspects will very often be required. The report said that staff at Rampton seemed sometimes to be tempted to give security priority over virtually all other considerations and concluded that it was wrong to subject patients to a higher degree of security than was clinically necessary: 'if a less rigorous regime could be developed in selected areas of the hospital a more demanding, encouraging and stimulating life could be provided for many patients with greater opportunities for realistic resocialisation programmes and a much more challenging and fulfilling role for the nursing staff.'

In 1981 within a three-week period two patients escaped from Broadmoor, with resultant public concern about security arrangements. The DHSS set up a working party which included Home Office representation to review security policies and procedures including provisions for physical security at all special hospitals. The working party considered that security at Broadmoor should be preserved by a secure perimeter wall, locked wards, the constant vigilance of adequate numbers of well-trained staff, a system of procedures and checks properly communicated and carried out effectively, and the constant review of procedures to ensure that they are at optimum efficiency. The report said that the presence of a secure perimeter wall and locked wards enables the patients to have a greater degree of freedom of association and allows the staff to involve themselves in the many therapeutic activities of the hospital:

'thus, although it was built more than one hundred years ago, Broadmoor Hospital has gradually developed a modern and humane system of care, providing the widest range of treatment within the necessary constraints of security. The medical consultant grade has accepted responsibility for organising the therapeutic milieu and specific treatment programmes within the framework of established security.'

As a consequence of the working party's findings, detailed recommendations were made concerning the hospital's parole system, patients' belongings, instructions to staff, night staffing levels, and other matters.

All hospital staff have a contribution to make to treatment programmes based on their professional expertise and all should have a responsibility for security; there should not be separate non-therapeutic security personnel.

Size and siting

Details have been given on pp. 86–9 of the geographical location and bed numbers in the four special hospitals. Evidence given to the Estimates Committee (1968) was that the ideal total of patients in a special hospital was 450. At that time there were 2,200 patients in the three English special hospitals. The rebuilt Broadmoor will have about 500 patients, Park Lane when completed about 400, and, so far as is understood, Moss Side will continue to have about 300 beds. The Boynton Report recommended an eventual aim to reduce the size of Rampton to 500 or 600 beds. Within a few years then the special hospitals will have a maximum of 1,700 to 1,800 patients, a reduction of about 25 per cent on 1981 figures. It is noteworthy that since the publication of the Boynton Report Rampton has been steadily reducing numbers and, as noted above, at the beginning of 1984 the patient numbers stood at about 600.

There is general recognition that there are patients who are currently in special hospitals who would be better cared for elsewhere if the facilities existed in ordinary psychiatric hospitals or in the community. There are also people who are in prison who perhaps should be in special hospitals. With regard to the annual returns by prison medical officers of prisoners requiring treatment in psychiatric hospitals, it is not known what proportion should be in special hospitals (rather than ordinary psychiatric hospitals). However, there is a group of patients for whom special facilities, including security, are required and for whom the interim or regional secure facilities will not provide.

Historically, psychiatry owes a great deal to the special hospitals, because without them the mental hospitals would not have been able to develop open-door policies. This in turn creates problems because the mental hospitals have lost their expertise in dealing with difficult patients and are now often unable and unwilling to accept them. Such expertise in dealing with the most dangerous patients is concentrated in the special hospitals; if they did not exist this expertise would be scattered or spread among many different places.

So long as special hospitals, or some similar institutions, are needed, they should be as effective and therapeutic as possible, offering the maximum of facilities without being so large as to become impersonal and regimental. It is felt that 400–500 patients would probably be an ideal number, allowing for a full range of medical, social, and recreational facilities. If special hospitals are too large (such as Rampton has been) this implies a very large catchment area with difficulties for patients far from home and relatives seldom able to visit them. Whilst patients with mental impairment traditionally tend to be sent to Rampton, there is much to be said for not separating such patients from those with other forms of mental disorder. Other relevant considerations include the availability of staff and educational facilities, and contact with centres of continuing and postgraduate education.

It is most important that patients, particularly long-stay patients, should receive visitors and this highlights the importance of siting and accessibility. It is also important that other professionals should be able to visit the special hospitals readily and that staff of special hospitals should be able to visit other hospitals, prisons, and universities. Thus the location of special hospitals will have an effect on the quality of the professional staff attracted to work in them. Discussions are currently taking place between the DHSS and the special hospitals on regionalization, so that as far as possible patients can be located in the special hospital closest to their home.

The relationship between special hospitals and secure units is dealt with elsewhere in this work and much will depend on the development of the latter. The Royal College of Psychiatrists (1980) is in favour of the retention of special hospitals. The College said in its policy report on secure facilities:

'The Special Hospitals are situated at one end of the range of secure treatment facilities and should be closely integrated operationally with them. They will continue to provide conditions of maximum security for those exhibiting dangerous, violent or criminal propensities and also require special security as they do at the present time. The College envisages movement between the Special Hospitals and other types of Unit, facilitated by close working co-operation and dependent upon the degree of security and intensive care made necessary by the patient's psychiatric disorder and behaviour.'

In its report on the future of the special hospitals the College (Royal College of Psychiatrists 1983) said:

It is clear that Regional Secure Units will only be able to function effectively with patients who do not need treatment in conditions of maximum security. For other patients Special Hospitals will still be required and they have advantages of providing a range of facilities appropriate for patients requiring more than a short length of stay in hospital.'

Table 3.1 *Staff in special hospitals*

	Broad-moor	Rampton	Moss Side	Park Lane
medical				
consultant psychiatrists	9	11	5	7
consultant psychotherapists	2	0	0	1
training-grade psychiatrists	3	0	1	. 3
other medical staff	4	6	0	0
nursing				
senior nursing staff	10	8	5	7
total in post	576	697	330	364
psychologists	7	4	6	7
social workers	12	13	8	8
occupations officers	71	105	57	25
administrative and clerical	49	51	30	21

others include teaching staff, librarians, chaplains, dentists, physiotherapists, radiographers, speech therapists, transport, catering, domestic, and other staff

	Broad-moor	Rampton	Moss Side	Park Lane
total staff in post	872	1054	538	500
patient numbers	591	629	285	209

Staffing

Table 3.1 gives the latest available details of the staff (given in whole-time equivalents) of the special hospitals though vacancies will have been filled or created and posts otherwise changed since.

MEDICAL STAFF

Table 3.1 gives an indication of staffing levels for psychiatrists and other disciplines in each special hospital. In some areas the medical staffing has been poor; the Ministry of Health (1961) working party on the special hospitals said more than twenty years ago that 'a relatively large medical establishment is needed if the special hospitals are to be able to do all that is expected of them.' Besides purely clinical work in assessment and treatment of patients, consultants have much other work, including providing annual reports on patients, mental health review tribunal reports and appearances, preparation of reports for conditional discharge and transfer, reports recommending or advising against admission, court reports and appearances, as well as time needed to see patients outside, conducting follow-ups, for research, teaching and training others, continuing medical education, attending conferences and courses, and administrative meetings. All patients in special hospitals deserve the best of medical attention with regular review of their cases, and this cannot be provided properly when each consultant has over 100 patients to treat. One full-time consultant for sixty-five patients should prove a maximum case-load.

There is often a problem in filling vacant consultant appointments in the special hospitals; several consultants are locums and past the normal retirement age. Advisory appointments committees have sometimes been in difficulties because they adhere rigidly to the concept that such appointments should be restricted to those with experience in forensic psychiatry. In 1980 the Royal College of Psychiatrists issued a policy statement which said: 'While most consultants in Special Hospitals will be fully trained forensic psychiatrists, those trained in general psychiatry or in mental handicap with a special interest in forensic psychiatry could well contribute to the work of the Special Hospitals.'

All special hospitals should have a designated clinical tutor appointed by his peers with ratification by the local university. Special hospitals are more suited to the training of senior registrars than registrars, though Moss Side and Rampton have registrar posts as part of the Liverpool and Nottingham registrar rotation schemes. Broadmoor has two senior registrar posts, both of which have full approval from the Joint Committee on Higher Psychiatric Training and which in 1983 were amalgamated with the Maudsley Hospital/ Institute of Psychiatry forensic psychiatry senior registrar rotation scheme. Park Lane also has a comprehensive training scheme for senior registrars, and Rampton is making attempts to regain approval for its senior registrar post. Joint appointments between special hospitals and universities are referred to on pp. 122–23 but besides these it is interesting to note that in Scotland the State Hospital, Carstairs, has successfully tackled its recruitment problems by making joint consultant appointments with NHS hospitals.

The care of the physical health of patients in each special hospital varies according to local circumstances. In some cases this work is undertaken by associate specialists who have had varying amounts of psychiatric experience. In addition to the associate specialists who care for the general health of patients at Broadmoor and Rampton, there are also visits from various specialists as needed. Park Lane has developed an effective service using a local general practitioner. Associate specialists are not regarded as responsible medical officers, and it has been suggested that they should perhaps be replaced by consultants.

NURSING STAFF

Broadmoor, Moss Side, and Park Lane hospitals were all recognized by the General Nursing Council (GNC) as training schools for learner nurses. In 1981 permission to train nurses in mental subnormality was withdrawn from Rampton, although it is hoped to re-establish training there as soon as possible. GNC inspectors had been critical of some aspects of education and training which led the mental nurse committee of the GNC to express a view about the longer-term suitability of the special hospitals to provide a basic nursing training: this view is the subject of discussion between the DHSS and the UKCC which has now replaced the GNC.

Nurses at Rampton in particular feel that medical staffing problems have contributed towards a lack of leadership and this has been accentuated by an atmosphere of dissent and disunity within the medical team. The nursing shift system at Rampton has been thought to be against the best interests of the care of patients by failing to provide continuity of care. Mr L. Teeman, chairman of the Rampton Review Board, has said that about 100 more nurses were required at Rampton to end the 'long-day' shift system (which has now been abandoned at Carstairs), the problem being accentuated by difficulties in recruitment following the withdrawal of recognition of the nurse training school by the GNC. There are problems in attracting experienced nurses to special hospitals because of agreements made between the Prison Officers' Association and management, for example that no nurse is eligible to apply for the position of charge nurse until he or she has served as a staff nurse in that special hospital for at least four years.

The Boynton Committee commented that nursing staff uniforms give an inappropriate and unhelpful expression to the custodial aspects of nurses' role. It is argued that there is a need for a distinctive uniform for security reasons, but this can perhaps be modified to something more appropriate in a therapeutic environment. There have been discussions as to whether the special hospitals branch of the Prison Officers' Association (POA) should become a specialist independent body: encouragement is given to any attempt to ensure that special-hospital nurses are held in the public eye with the same professional respect as their counterparts in the NHS. Nurses in Park Lane have at present less strong allegiance to the POA than in the other special hospitals.

CLINICAL PSYCHOLOGISTS

Clinical psychologists in special hospitals work in the fields of assessment, treatment, research, and teaching. Some treatment programmes in which they are involved are difficult if not impossible to administer in the artificial conditions of special hospitals, particularly behaviour therapy for sex offenders when there is only minimal integration of the sexes. Some clinical psychologists feel there are ethical problems in starting treatment programmes (some of which, such as psychophysiological treatments, are of unestablished validity) which cannot be carried through in more natural conditions. There are clearly advantages in psychologists involving their NHS colleagues in treatment and assessment while the patient is in a special hospital to facilitate continuity of appropriate treatment when the patient is transferred or discharged: such a policy would more easily be realized if each special hospital had a clearly defined catchment area.

Psychologists have a not unreasonable claim to be consulted when a decision is being made on the admission of a patient whom they will be asked to treat. Difficulties in recruitment of psychologists caused by geographical isolation and fears of 'super-specialization' affecting career prospects of junior grades can be helped by rotational schemes and joint appointments.

If clinical psychologists are to participate in consent to treatment consultations it is important that they should be of an adequate level of training and experience. There will be a further demand for psychological services when remands for reports and assessment come into operation. For all these reasons there is probably a need for a modest expansion of clinical psychology departments.

SOCIAL WORKERS

Because of the widespread catchment areas of special hospitals social workers have less direct contact with patients' relatives than their counterparts in the NHS. Relatives are, however, frequently seen on visits and full reports on the family background are carried out following a patient's admission. During the patient's stay in hospital social workers assist with many diverse problems, including helping the patient manage his affairs and giving advice in connection with appeals to mental health review tribunals. They co-operate closely with Leagues of Friends and organize regular visitors for patients who would otherwise have few or no contacts outside the hospital. In the clinical team social workers have a valuable role in helping devise resocialization and rehabilitation programmes. At the time of transfer, and particularly discharge to the community, they have the important tasks of finding hostels and liaising with other social workers and the probation and after-care service.

OCCUPATIONS OFFICERS

There are about 250 occupations officers in the special hospitals, providing a range of work placements for patients ranging from those teaching basic craft skills and allowing patients to practise hobbies, to more advanced subjects such as tailoring, printing, and electronics. Discussions are taking place on how occupational therapists are best deployed in these areas to facilitate rehabilitation programmes.

Admissions

LEGAL CATEGORIES

As stated above, all patients in special hospitals are detained patients, mostly under the provisions of the Mental Health Act 1983. Direct admission to special hospitals under Part II of the Act are possible, but extremely rare; more common are transfers from NHS psychiatric hospitals of patients already detained under section 3. Patients may similarly be transferred when already detained under Part III. Both groups of patients have usually constituted management problems in their hospitals and have invariably behaved dangerously to either staff, fellow patients, or the public.

The most common means of admission to special hospitals generally is through a hospital order under section 37, with or without a restriction order under section 41, which nowadays is almost always without limit of time.

Under section 5 of the Criminal Procedure (Insanity) Act 1964, accused persons found under disability in relation to trial (unfit to plead) must be admitted to a hospital specified by the Home Secretary:

some such patients are admitted to special hospitals where they are detained as though admitted under sections 37 and 41 without limit of time.

A small group of patients are transferred each year to the special hospitals in terms of section 47 of the Mental Health Act – prisoners serving sentence and found to be suffering from a mental disorder of a nature or degree requiring detention in hospital for treatment. Such prisoners may be transferred to hospital (often a special hospital) on the direction of the Home Secretary. In most cases the Home Secretary appends a section 49 order, equivalent to a section 41 restriction order without limit of time. On expiry of the prison sentence (taking into account any remission), if the offender is still in hospital, he is detained as though admitted on a section 37 order alone (a 'notional section 37').

Patients detained under sections 41 or 49 or under the Criminal Procedure (Insanity) Act may not be transferred or discharged without the consent of the Home Secretary. Responsible medical officers agree in their contracts not to discharge or transfer any patient whom they have the power to discharge or transfer without first informing the DHSS as managers. In Rampton the review board must similarly be informed.

ADMINISTRATIVE ARRANGEMENTS

The method of obtaining a bed in a special hospital is for an application to be made to the DHSS, this usually being by the prison medical officer for a mentally abnormal offender on remand (or serving sentence), or by a consultant in an NHS hospital when a request is made for the transfer of a section 3 patient (or a section 37 patient already detained in that hospital). Every case is considered on its merits by a DHSS admission panel consisting of senior officers including a psychiatrist. The case is considered by reports and the patient is not seen by those making the decision. However, the DHSS does in most cases seek the opinion of a special hospital consultant on the suitability or otherwise of the patient for admission to a special hospital. Even if the special hospital consultant's opinion is against admission he may be able to offer some advice on the management of the case, which might be of benefit to prison medical officers and NHS consultants.

As far as possible the doctor who is to treat the patient in his special hospital should be involved in the decision-making about his admission. Sometimes it might be useful for the RMO to have with him one of the nursing staff, particularly when assessing a 'management problem' in another psychiatric hospital. The Broadmoor system of a weekly meeting of all medical staff to discuss potential admissions is commended for its aims of striving to obtain consistency in admissions policy, as well as serving a useful forum for teaching and peer review.

There are welcome new statutory provisons in the Mental Health Act 1983 to allow remands to hospital for assessment and for treatment, and also for the making of interim hospital orders. Remands for assessment and interim hospital orders should prove valuable in determining the treatability of those suffering from psychopathic disorders and mental impairment. Remands for treatment will solve some of the problems which arise from those who are currently found 'unfit to plead' but it is regretted that those charged with murder will be excluded from this provision. Staff in the special hospitals are discussing how to implement the new proposals when they come into force.

WAITING LIST

From time to time there is a small waiting list for admissions to special hospitals. Patients made subject of a section 37 hospital order have to be admitted within twenty-eight days, and where a section 47 order is made the prisoner must be transferred within fourteen days. Nevertheless there are many mentally disordered prisoners waiting at any one time for section 47 applications to be processed.

PRISON TRANSFERS

On section 47 transfers from prison, Orr (1978), then the director of the Prison Medical Service, commented on the falling numbers of transferred mentally ill prisoners, noting that in 1931 (when the prison population was 12,000) 105 prisoners were transferred to hospital; in 1976 (prison population 42,000) more than double that number were found to be suffering from mental illness, but less than half were transferred. In recent years prison medical officers have probably put forward fewer cases for consideration for transfer under section 47 because of their experiences of cases not being accepted.

During the 1970s, concern was expressed in the annual reports on the work of the prison department about a marked decline in the effectiveness of those provisions of the 1959 Act (72–4) which enable the transfer of mentally disordered prisoners to hospital, particularly because at that time the size of the prison population had risen to unprecedented levels. In 1976 the Home Office instituted a six-monthly survey of the number of prisoners who were considered by their respective prison medical officers to be suffering from mental disorder to an extent which would justify their transfer to hospital. Since these returns were first instituted, the numbers revealed have consistently fallen: the latest figures relate to 30 September, 1982, when there was a total of 286, including 37 female prisoners. Of the total, 160 were remand prisoners, in respect of whom the court would therefore have the opportunity to make a psychiatrically orientated order if they were convicted. Of the 126 sentenced prisoners, 68 were thought to suffer from mental illness, 13 from mental handicap, and 44 from psychopathic disorder. No estimate has been made of how many such prisoners would require treatment in the conditions of security of a special hospital. This decline appears in part to reflect a greater measure of success recently in the operation of sections 72–4 of the 1959 Act. The number of prisoners transferred under section 72 (with and without restrictions under section 74) increased from fifty-six in 1977 to eighty-six in 1981.

Most (81 per cent in 1981) of those transferred from prison have a restriction order added. The proportion of prisoners transferred to special hospitals rather than NHS hospitals is rising (from 25 per cent in 1966 to 33 per cent in 1976) (DHSS, Home Office, Welsh Office, and Lord Chancellor's Department 1978). In 1981 the proportion was 42 per cent with thirty-six prisoners transferred to a special hospital and fifty to a local hospital.

'UNDER DISABILITY' CASES

Only a minority of persons found under disability in relation to trial (unfit to plead) are admitted to special hospitals. In 1981 in England and Wales there were thirty-three such cases and twenty-six were admitted to local hospitals.

APPLICATIONS FOR ADMISSION

Of the 288 applications for admission to special hospitals in 1983, 187 (65 per cent) were accepted and 101 (35 per cent) were rejected by DHSS (see *Table 3.2*). In addition a small number of potential cases may have been examined by special hospital consultants who

Table 3.2 *Applications for admission to special hospitals 1983*

	accepted	rejected	total
mental illness	118	53	171
psychopathic disorder	49	33	82
mental impairment	17	11	28
severe mental impairment	3	4	7
all mental disorders	187	101	288

advised against formal application being made to the DHSS. Taking these figures together with those for 1982, roughly two out of three applications on behalf of the mentally ill were successful, while those with psychopathic disorder or mental impairment had an even chance of being accepted.

The acceptance rate has remained steady over the last five years at about 200 per annum. The number of applications received has been falling from about 530 per year in the mid-1970s, through about 350 per year in the late 1970s, to currently less than 300 per year, probably reflecting recognition by applicants of the strict criteria used by the DHSS in agreeing to admission.

ADMISSION RATE

Of the 172 admissions in 1983 the distribution per special hospital was Broadmoor fifty-nine, Rampton fifty-eight, Moss Side twenty-nine, and Park Lane twenty-six. For those being readmitted to a special hospital in 1983 eight patients were recalled from conditional discharge in the community, thirteen were readmitted from an NHS hospital (two from the Eastdale Unit), nine were readmitted on a court order, and three readmitted from prison. Thus 35 of the 172 admissions in 1983 were readmissions or 20 per cent, the mean for the previous three years being 21 per cent.

Although the number of offenders made subject of restriction orders in England and Wales has steadily decreased over the last decade, the proportion (just over half) entering special hospitals rather than ordinary hospitals has remained the same (Home Office 1982). In 1981, 114 patients on restriction orders entered local hospitals and 130 entered special hospitals. Of all the offenders made subject to sections 60 and 65 of the Mental Health Act 1959, 73 per cent entered special hospitals in 1981.

Patients in special hospitals

The following series of tables (*Tables 3.3–3.11*) give details of the characteristics of patients admitted to and resident in the special hospitals.

Table 3.3   *Sex and age on admission of all patients admitted to special hospitals 1977–79 inclusive*

	males		females		both sexes	
	N	%	N	%	N	%
17 or under	34	7	3	3	37	7
18–20	61	13	12	12	73	13
21–29	150	32	35	35	185	33
30–39	136	29	34	34	170	30
40–49	53	11	10	10	63	11
50+	31	7	7	7	38	7
all ages	465	100	101	100	566	100

The mentally ill tend to be older than those with other diagnoses, the mean ages being for mental illness 32 years, psychopathic disorder 24, mental impairment 25, and for severe mental impairment males 24, females 29.

Table 3.4   *Patients admitted to the special hospitals in 1977–79 directly from courts*

	N	%
homicide	59	21
other violence against the person	126	44
sexual offences	19	7
arson	38	13
criminal damage	18	6
theft, burglary	16	6
other offences	9	3
total	285	100

The proportion of those convicted for homicide is twice as common in men as in women. Offences against property (as the admission offence) are commoner among women, with 40 per cent having been convicted for arson or criminal damage.

Table 3.5   *Admissions from courts to all special hospitals 1977–79 by offence and Mental Health Act classification (males only)*

	mental illness (N = 147)	psychopathic disorder (N = 73)
	%	%
homicide	29	12
other violence	51	40
sexual offences	2	12
arson	7	15
criminal damage	3	10
theft, burglary	5	8
other	3	3

For men admissions from courts following a main offence of homicide or violence are more common among those with mental illness than among those with other diagnoses. Sexual offences and arson are more commonly found with psychopathic disorder and mental impairment. (Data for females and for those with a Mental Health Act 1959 classification of mental subnormality or severe mental subnormality are not included as numbers are small, making comparison by percentages potentially misleading.)

Broadmoor has by far the biggest proportion of those convicted for homicide. Sexual offences and arson are associated with mental handicap and more of these patients find their way to Rampton and Moss Side.

Patients transferred to special hospitals under section 3 are most likely to have a diagnosis of mental illness or severe mental impairment. Most of those transferred from prison have a classification of mental illness.

Broadmoor and Park Lane have virtually no patients with mental impairment and three-quarters have mental illness. In Rampton and Moss Side two-thirds of the patients have a main category of mental illness or psychopathic disorder. In very rough figures just over half the patients in the special hospitals have mental illness, a quarter

Table 3.6   *Admissions directly from courts to special hospitals 1977–79 by offence (males and females)*

	Broadmoor (N = 146)	Rampton (N = 93)	Moss Side (N = 43)
	%	%	%
homicide	30	13	7
other violence	47	40	44
sexual offences	3	12	9
arson	10	17	16
criminal damage	5	7	9
theft, burglary	3	6	9
other	2	4	5

Table 3.7   *Resident patient numbers – 1 March, 1984*

	males	females	total
Broadmoor	477	107	584
Park Lane	223	0	223
Rampton	443	159	602
Moss Side	207	57	264
total	1350	323	1673

Table 3.8   *Percentage of resident patients by Mental Health Act 1983 section – 31 December, 1983*

	Broad-moor	Rampton	Moss Side	Park Lane	all special hospitals
unrestricted					
s. 3	9	24	32	7	18
s. 37	11	12	15	7	11
other	0	8	3	1	4
total unrestricted	20	44	50	15	33
restricted					
ss 37 and 41	62	44	40	64	52
s 46–8	13	6	5	15	9
other	5	6	5	6	6
total restricted	80	56	50	85	67

Table 3.9   *Patient numbers at 31 December, 1983 in all special hospitals according to Mental Health Act 1983 section and type of mental disorder*

	mental illness	psychopathic disorder	mental impairment	severe mental impairment	total
unrestricted					
s. 3	191	12	29	75	307
s. 37	105	56	27	1	189
other	11	4	7	35	57
					553
restricted					
s 37 and 41	430	308	86	6	878
s 46–8	111	26	5	2	159
other	65	5	14	6	96
					1686

Table 3.10   *Mental disorder of patients in special hospitals – 31 December, 1983*

	Broadmoor	Rampton	Moss Side	Park Lane	total
mental illness	437(75%)	278(46%)	98(36%)	169(75%)	982(58%)
psychopathic disorder	146(25%)	130(21%)	79(29%)	56(25%)	411(24%)
mental impairment	2	107(18%)	59(22%)	0	168(10%)
severe mental impairment	0	90(15%)	35(13%)	0	125(7%)
total	585	605	271	225	1686

psychopathic disorder, and the remainder are equally divided between those with mental impairment or severe mental impairment.

Some patients have two diagnoses, that is some of those detained in e.g. Rampton with a classification of mental illness will also be mentally impaired.

In all the special hospitals, besides personality disorders and

Wildy & Sons Ltd.
LAWBOOK SPECIALISTS

Lincoln's Inn Archway, Carey Street, London WC2A 2JD.

TEL. 01-242-5778

CASH SALE RECEIPT

VAT No. 233 5262 84

DATE 16/9/85

AUTHOR	TITLE	DATE	new	s/h	£	p
S.				✓	5	05

PAID
16 SEP 1985

per

TOTAL

mental handicap, the psychiatric conditions most frequently found are schizophrenia and paranoid states. Less than 10 per cent of patients (in each case) suffer from manic–depressive illness, organic disorders, neurosis, epilepsy, alcoholism, or drug addiction. In the latter three cases the patient would of course suffer an additional mental disorder.

In Broadmoor the unrestricted patients comprise 20 per cent of the hospital population, half of them have been transferred from NHS hospitals, and half are on a hospital order. Ninety per cent of them have mental illness. Of the restricted patients one in seven have been transferred from prisons; of these only a handful have psychopathic disorder. Thirty-five per cent of those detained under sections 37 and 41 have psychopathic disorder. Sixty per cent of the patients with mental illness have come from the courts and 10 per cent from prisons, and this is the most likely diagnosis for section 47 transfer. All those with psychopathic disorder are offender patients.

Of the patients in Rampton with mental illness, who comprise 46 per cent of the total, 58 per cent are restricted and 42 per cent unrestricted. Of these same patients with mental illness one-quarter have been transferred from NHS hospitals and are non-offenders, half have come from the courts, and about 8 per cent from prisons. Eighty per cent of those with psychopathic disorder have come from the courts and only a handful have been transferred from NHS hospitals or prisons. Half of those with mental impairment are on a hospital order and restriction order, and 13 per cent have been transferred from other hospitals. There are very few restricted patients with severe mental impairment, most of whom have been transferred from other hospitals.

About a third of the patients in Moss Side have been transferred from other hospitals and half are on hospital orders. Half the patients with mental impairment have come from the courts and 25 per cent are from other hospitals. Sixty per cent of the patients with severe mental impairment have been transferred from other hospitals: the vast majority of these patients are unrestricted, as are more than half of those with mental illness. In the hospital as a whole there are equal numbers of unrestricted and restricted patients.

In Park Lane, three-quarters of the patients have mental illness, the rest psychopathic disorder. Eighty-five per cent are on restriction orders.

The special hospitals have a lower proportion of long-stay patients than NHS mental hospitals. Data are not available on the average length of stay in each of the special hospitals but Tidmarsh (1980)

Table 3.11   *Length of stay of patients resident in the special hospitals – 1 January, 1977*

	Broadmoor (N =768)	Rampton (N = 959)	Moss Side (N = 385)	all special hospitals
	%	%	%	%
less than 5 years	52	69	48	49
5 years or more	48	52	52	51
8 years or more	28	31	34	30
10 years or more	21	22	20	21
16 years or more	9	11	6	9
20 years or more	6	6	3	5

has shown that in Broadmoor the mean length of stay of the resident population in 1979 was 6.5 years.

Treatment issues

The management of patients in special hospitals is and should be, as far as possible, on the same lines as in ordinary psychiatric hospitals although there are limitations imposed by security provisions and the dangerousness of special hospital patients.

As in other psychiatric hospitals there are from time to time criticisms of treatment methods, sometimes without recognition of the exceptional problems posed by patients who have arrived in special hospitals partly because their conditions have failed to respond to conventional treatments. There is no evidence that special hospital patients receive higher doses of medication or more electroconvulsive therapy than similar patients elsewhere. On the contrary it can be expected that those who are not mentally ill (e.g. those with psychopathic disorder) will receive little or no medication, and with proportionately fewer depressive patients ECT will be used less often than in other psychiatric hospitals. There was however a well-publicized case of unmodified ECT being given in Broadmoor on a small number of occasions which led the Royal College of Psychiatrists to declare that this should not happen except in rare cases of extreme necessity. There have also been criticisms of the use of psychosurgery at Rampton, though many years have elapsed since such operations have been carried out in any of the special hospitals. The Mental Health Act 1983 has clarified the law on consent to treatment and it remains to be seen how the new provisions will work out in practice in hospitals where each and every patient is compulsorily detained.

The issue of 'treatability' of patients has again been raised by the Mental Health Act 1983. In general no patient should be admitted to a special hospital unless there is a prospect of the patient benefiting from the treatment available in that hospital, though there are important issues of custody and public protection. Milieu therapy is often criticized as being 'no treatment' or 'treatment just by being there', but its advocates firmly believe it to have beneficial effects on retraining and resocialization of all patients exhibiting anti-social behaviour: such treatment is in the patients' own interests as well as in the interests of the community at large. For some mentally ill patients, for instance those with irreversible organic brain disease, medical treatment might be of limited usefulness but it is more humane for such offenders to be managed in hospital rather than prison. For those with personality disorders and those who have committed sexual offences, it is necessary to have on the staff psychotherapists and clinical psychologists to assist in their assessment and treatment. As mentioned earlier, interim hospital orders as proposed in the new mental health legislation will be of great value in assessing the treatability of those with psychopathic disorders and mental impairment. In the meantime many consultants prefer not to recommend a hospital order but to suggest that treatment could be attempted by means of a transfer under section 47 of the 1983 Act. Blackburn (1982) has made the point that, where clinical psychologists are being asked to treat patients with certain disorders, it is reasonable for them to be associated with admission and assessment procedures.

Rehabilitation and resocialization policies continue to attract considerable comment. The length of stay of patients is given above, and shows that the hospitals function on a medium- to long-stay basis. Criticisms made by the Elliott Report on Rampton in 1973 and the Hospital Advisory Service of Broadmoor in 1975 of the lack of effective rehabilitation policies have been answered by each special hospital reviewing its rehabilitation policies and procedures and adapting them to the changing picture in the NHS and the community. The Boynton Report (DHSS 1980: 90) commented on the need for increased multi-disciplinary co-operation and co-ordination of the various resocialization departments in Rampton. Considerable progress has been made in all the special hospitals in improving rehabilitative resources since 1974, in which year the Eastdale Unit at Balderton Hospital was opened for male patients discharged from the special hospitals. The unit aims to provide rehabilitation facilities for patients at an interim stage between special hospital care and that provided in an ordinary psychiatric hospital or the community, and has been commended as a 'valuable resource'. A recently published report on the working of the unit (Trent Regional Health Authority and Central Nottinghamshire Health Authority 1982) has recommended that 'encouragement be given to all the Special Hospitals, but particularly Rampton, to develop more sophisticated and extensive programmes of rehabilitation'. The report noted that the unit was used mainly by Rampton, whereas Moss Side and Park Lane tended to use the interim secure units in Liverpool and Manchester. The report added that 'the rehabilitation programme at Broadmoor Hospital does not appear to offer sufficient programmes' and suggested that serious consideration be given to Broadmoor having a similar unit to that at Balderton. Considerable changes have taken place in Broadmoor Hospital since publication of that report and a comprehensive range of resocialisation programmes are now available to patients.

Issues of special concern

Because of the very nature of special hospitals certain other matters to do with management and the interests of patients will always be problematical and many issues will require time and extended discussion before they can be resolved.

All special hospitals should have ethical committees which consider not only research proposals but also treatment issues affecting the interests of patients. Progress is being made towards improving the constitution and procedures of these committees – in Broadmoor for instance the ethics committee is now chaired by an experienced and eminent lay person from outside the hospital.

Complaints procedures in the special hospitals are not yet wholly satisfactory and difficulties are being encountered on reaching nationally agreed procedures acceptable to the management and the Prison Officers' Association. The policy of the POA is that all allegations by patients of assaults by members of staff should be referred to the police. It is hoped that agreement will be reached as soon as possible on a set of procedures which will be clearly understandable to patients, that a register of complaints be kept in each hospital, and a record of the action taken be open to inspection by the Mental Health Act Commission which has a duty to ensure that complaints are being properly handled. Further detailed comment on complaints procedures is available in the Boynton Report (DHSS 1980).

Seclusion of patients is inevitably practised more often in special hospitals than elsewhere because of the types of patients and the reasons for their being detained in maximum-security institutions. Patients are more violent: in 1981 in Broadmoor Hospital alone there were recorded 173 assaults by patients on staff and a further 195 assaults by patients on other patients. While seclusion might sometimes be necessary as a preventive measure, it should never be used without the authorization of a responsible medical officer. As a result of a judgement by the European Court of Human Rights, seclusion instructions have been more stringently defined in each special hospital including detailed recording of hours spent in seclusion for each patient and facilities provided for the patient.

Integration of female and male patients poses considerable problems, understandable perhaps given the limitations imposed by considerations of structural facilities, security, and staff attitudes. While there are no mixed-sex wards there is mixing of female and male patients in all special hospitals (except Park Lane which has no female patients) in work and recreational areas. Moss Side Hospital has recently been experimenting with an integrated pre-discharge ward. Marriage of patients to outside partners has recently been a subject of discussion but conjugal visits appear to be a long way off.

CONFIDENTIALITY AND THE OFFICIAL SECRETS ACT

Staff in special hospitals are required to sign the Official Secrets Act. Many of the staff think this to be unnecessary and it is sometimes seen, rightly or wrongly, as a barrier to more open discussion of the problems special hospitals face. Staff of the State Hospital in Scotland are not asked to sign and there are no problems there in that respect. In any case it is recognized that staff should never discuss important matters of security, and professional ethics preclude the discussion of patients, as elsewhere in medicine. The policy of the DHSS since June, 1981 has been to encourage informed discussion of the work done by the special hospitals and not to suppress such discussions by reference to the Official Secrets Act.

Case notes of patients are generally made available to visiting doctors and the Mental Health Act 1983 requires medical records to be produced at the request not only of the medical member of the

Mental Health Review Tribunal (MHRT), but of any doctors providing a separate report for the MHRT, and to the Mental Health Act Commission.

VISITING ARRANGEMENTS

Facilities and arrangements for visiting patients by relatives and friends are generally satisfactory. Thre is financial assistance for travelling, and Leagues of Friends help with transport to and from hospitals, and with accommodation. Many patients have no visits from relatives or friends, often because their offence has alienated them from their family, and Leagues of Friends again have a valuable role here in providing visitors. These are local interested people whose selection and visiting is monitored by the hospitals' social work departments.

Mental Health Review Tribunals

Patients in special hospitals are usually discharged or transferred on the initiative of the responsible medical officers but have the same right to apply for their continued detention to be reviewed by mental health review tribunals as patients in ordinary psychiatric hospitals. Under the 1959 Mental Health Act patients on restriction orders could not be discharged or their transfer ordered by a MHRT; instead the MHRT advised the Home Secretary on whether the patient should remain in a special hospital or be transferred or conditionally discharged. *Table 3.12* shows the results of these hearings in the last full year of the 1959 Act.

Where the Home Office had come to a decision on the tribunal's advice, in 88 per cent of cases the advice was accepted. Excluding advice given and accepted that the patient remain in a special hospital, advice that the patient be transferred or conditionally discharged was accepted in 60 per cent and rejected in 40 per cent, compared with 70 per cent and 30 per cent respectively in the previous year.

Overall in the special hospitals in the last full three years under the 1959 Act just less than 10 per cent of applications to MHRTs of unrestricted patients resulted in their discharge, the rate being higher in Rampton than in the other hospitals. An explanation might be that RMOs in Rampton used MHRTs to confirm or decide for them on patients' suitability for leaving Rampton but consultants there deny that this is still the case. Some special hospital consultants see

Table 3.12   *MHRT advice to Home Secretary (restricted patients) special hospitals 1982*

	Broad-moor	Rampton	Moss Side	Park Lane	total
remain in special hospital:					
accepted	57	44	11	9	121
rejected	0	0	0	0	0
transfer to NHS hospital:					
accepted	1	19	3	1	24
rejected	9	9	0	0	18
conditional discharge:					
accepted	0	5	1	0	6
rejected	0	2	1	0	3
decisions pending	20	38	17	7	82
other	2	7	0	0	9
total referrals by Home Secretary	89	124	33	17	263

advantage in this sharing of responsibility, while others disapprove of what they see as a misuse of MHRTs.

The huge increase in the number of MHRTs in 1983 was a result of referral of cases by hospital managers to MHRTs in anticipation of the provisions of the Mental Health Act 1983. These 'automatic' MHRTs resulted in very few discharges, though interestingly two patients have remained in hospital as informal patients.

EFFECTS OF NEW LEGISLATION

The Mental Health Act 1983 provides for a doubling of the number of opportunities for MHRTs for all patients and this will result in a large increase in the workload of RMOs. Without an increase in staff, the time spent in justifying detention will have to be taken at the expense of time treating patients. The Mental Health Act 1983 provides, in response to a decision of the European Court on Human Rights, that MHRTs will have the power to order the conditional or absolute discharge of restricted patients; such tribunals will be enhanced by having as chairman a senior judge. The Act also means that patients who do not exercise their rights to a tribunal hearing should have their cases referred automatically by the managers every

Table 3.13   *MHRT hearings (unrestricted patients) special hospitals 1979–82 (average per year) and 1983*

	Broadmoor		Rampton		Moss Side		Park Lane		total	
	1979–82	1983	1979–82	1983	1979–82	1983	1979–82	1983	1979–82	1983
applications	39	241	108	132	60	67	8	7	215	447
discharges	2	3	18	5	5	7	1	4	26	19
total	41	244	126	137	65	74	9	11	241	466

three years (and for unrestricted patients during their first year of detention). This is doubtless considered useful for the apathetic, withdrawn, and institutionalized patient but in a few cases might be unsettling to patients who deliberately do not appeal against detention, being content to continue with their treatment programme rather than have their offence and detention discussed by others. There is an increasing trend for patients to be represented at MHRTs by solicitors or barristers, and RMOs are often questioned on side-issues such as treatment rather than the central issue of need for continued detention. Furthermore the new legislation gives patients more opportunity to be legally represented when they appear before a MHRT.

Discharges

In special hospitals the duty of the responsible medical officer, when he considers that a patient no longer requires treatment in the conditions of security of a special hospital, is: (1) when it is a non-restricted patient, to discharge him or transfer him to an NHS hospital; (2) for a patient on a restriction order, to recommend to the Home Secretary his conditional discharge or transfer; (3) for an offender still liable to a prison sentence, to recommend to the Home Secretary the patient's return to prison. In the case of the transfer of a restricted patient the DHSS as manager of the special hospital give its approval in principle before the papers are sent on to the Home Office to obtain the Home Secretary's consent. When approval is given the RMO can then either ask the DHSS to find a bed in a hospital for the patient (the 'formal' approach), which involves a procedure passing from the DHSS to the region to the area to the catchment area hospital; or, alternatively, the RMO can do this himself by asking a colleague in the catchment area hospital to admit him (the 'informal' approach). RMOs in Broadmoor almost always use the 'informal' approach and tend to start looking for a bed at the same time as making their recommendation to the DHSS and Home Office. RMOs in Rampton in the past and Moss Side have tended to use the 'formal' procedure. In all hospitals use of the 'informal' approach considerably shortens the waiting time before transfer. A diagnosis of mental impairment and particularly severe mental impairment usually means a longer wait, whichever procedure is used. The chances of success in transferring a patient are considerably increased if the NHS consultant and nursing staff come to see the patient in the special hospital.

There is no doubt as to the importance of RMOs establishing personal relationships with other hospitals in relation to admission, continuing care, and transfer of patients. Successful placement after treatment in a special hospital often depends on the reality and warmth of contact between special-hospital staff and area of domicile concerned. Close contacts are essential in terms of a proper understanding of the problems, of optimum placement and care, and of educating professionals who, without close experience or knowledge or interest, can be hostile to providing further help for patients who are fit for discharge from special hospitals.

Apart from contacts before discharge from special hospitals and other elements of professional contact and discussion, long-term follow-up provides a measure of support and even security for those who have undertaken the placement and also provides interest for and elicits concern from those who have responsibility in the special hospitals for advising the next stage of care.

Table 3.14　*Discharges and transfers from special hospitals 1983*

	Broad-moor	Rampton Side	Moss Lane	Park	total
transfer to NHS hospitals	28	62	32	10	132
conditional discharges	17	24	14	16	71
total	45	86	46	26	203

In addition twelve patients were transferred to the Eastdale Unit at Balderton Hospital in 1983, mostly from Rampton and Moss Side. Altogether 215 patients left special hospitals, one in six of the resident population, about one-third by conditional discharge and two-thirds by transfer to an NHS psychiatric hospital.

Over the last seven years the special hospitals have consistently discharged more patients than they have admitted with a net 'loss' of over sixty patients per year. 1981 was especially noteworthy in this respect, mainly due to Rampton, which discharged or transferred twice as many patients as Broadmoor, mainly as a result of the special procedures resulting from the Dell (1980) report where the Secretary of State dealt directly with regional health authorities in the cases of patients awaiting transfer to NHS hospitals.

Table 3.15   *Turnover of patients in special hospitals*

	admissions	transfers and discharges
1979	191	228
1980	194	226
1981	175	300
1982	185	222
1983	172	215

Table 3.16   *Patients waiting to leave special hospitals on 31 December, 1983*

	awaiting transfer	awaiting conditional discharge	total
Broadmoor	36	6	42
Rampton	119	20	139
Moss Side	48	4	52
Park Lane	25	13	38
total	228	43	271

Sixteen per cent of the patients in the special hospitals are waiting to go, their discharge or transfer having been agreed. The number and, more important, the proportion of special hospital patients has increased in the last two years, despite attempts to deal with the 'national scandal' of Dell's (1980) report. Even over the last year the proportion of patients waiting to leave has worsened from one in eight to one in six.

Dell (1980) showed that in 1979 more than one in three of the patients awaiting transfer had been waiting for over two years compared with less than one in ten three years previously. The number of patients waiting for less than a year had dropped over the same period from 70 per cent to 40 per cent. At that time then the number of patients awaiting transfer was increasing (from 146 in 1976 to 197 in 1979) and the waiting period was getting longer. Seventeen patients (most with severe subnormality) had been waiting for more than four years, as shown in *Table 3.18*.

Since Dell (1980) published her work, the position of those awaiting transfer has eased slightly in terms of length of wait but the numbers continue to grow. Since that time the DHSS has held a

Table 3.17 *Length of wait for patients awaiting transfer to NHS hospitals on 31 December, 1983 (excluding Eastdale Unit)*

	under 1 year	1–2 years	2–3 years	over 3 years	total
mental illness	66	21	8	3	108
psychopathic disorder	28	5	4	0	40
mental impairment	11	11	4	0	31
severe mental impairment	13	9	5	11	44
total	118	46	21	21	223

Table 3.18 *Numbers and waiting time for transfers from special hospitals*

	1976	1979	1982
under 1 year	102	79	80
1–2 years	30	49	42
over 2 years	14	69	57
total	146	197	179
total special hospital patients	2185	1995	1744
% awaiting transfer	6.7	9.9	10.3

special conference of representatives of all special hospital staff and the Secretary of State has personally dealt with a list of cases with the chairmen of regional health authorities. Advice has been given on the preferred method of arranging transfers, and the DHSS has agreed that it will give an unconditional undertaking to readmit a patient if, within the first few months after transfer, he does not settle and in any case where a receiving hospital asks for such a guarantee. There is obvious value in offering continued interest in the patient and participating in decisions on after-care, for instance by the RMO, nursing staff, or social worker attending case conferences at the receiving hospital. Similarly there is value in 'trial leave' for appropriate patients either as a preparation for transfer or discharge, or for testing the patient's readiness or acceptability for transfer or discharge.

While the RMO in the receiving hospital takes over the charge of the patient (and this is also the norm for patients being conditionally discharged), some RMOs, particularly in Broadmoor, continue as the supervising psychiatrist for some conditionally discharged patients, sometimes through choice and sometimes because another psychiatrist cannot be found. For all patients leaving special hospitals there is a need for close contact between special hospital staff and those in the receiving facility. There is an invaluable guarantee that patients on restriction orders will be supervised by the Probation and After-Care Service; accordingly probation officers or social workers should always see the patient before he leaves hospital and receive full information on the patient. Special hospital consultants consider their relationship with the Home Office works well and few cases are referred to the advisory board on restricted patients.

Research

Research is carried out in each of the special hospitals by different disciplines, by individuals and through the Special Hospitals Research Unit. The latter was established in 1969 following the recommendation of the Estimates Committee (1968) Report. It decided initially that its strategy would be to define the special hospital population in order to follow up discharged patients to enable evaluative studies to be conducted. A case register has been developed (Special Hospitals Research Unit 1979) and a list of the publications as Special Hospitals Research Reports is given in that report.

Among follow-up studies of special hospital patients the Aarvold Committee (1973) asked the Home Office Research Unit to find out what happened to all the 180 patients subject to restriction orders who left hospitals in 1966 and 1967. Forty-three per cent had received the hospital and restriction orders because of offences involving homicidal assault. In a four-year period, 84 per cent had no convictions and 12 per cent had convictions for property offences alone.

Acres (Home Office and DHSS 1975) in 1974 followed up all the ninety-two patients (seventeen women) transferred or conditionally discharged from the special hospitals in 1971. They had had an average length of stay of four years ten months; twenty-eight had mental illness and forty-three psychopathic disorder. When followed up two years after release, 17 per cent were back in a special hospital,

13 per cent were in prison, 2 per cent were in an NHS hospital and 58 per cent were living in the community. Fifty-four per cent had not been reconvicted in that period, 22 per cent had one conviction, 10 per cent two convictions and fewer than 10 per cent had four or more convictions. Two-thirds of the convictions were for acquisitive offences; there was one murder, one rape, two other sexual assaults, and thirteen offences of violence.

Tong and Mackay (1959) in 1957 followed up 423 patients discharged from Rampton between 1945 and 1956. Fourteen per cent had been readmitted to Rampton and another 14 per cent had entered the penal system. In general they found the anti-social behaviour the second time round less serious than the offence leading to the original admission. Tong and Mackay thought that aggression and/or attempts to escape while in Rampton were significantly related to the probability of relapse. Other follow-up studies include Gathercole et al. (1968), following up seventy-two patients who left Moss Side in 1961, and Walker and MacCabe (1973), studying reconvictions of a very large group of patients on hospital orders, including those admitted to special hospital.

Black (1982) followed up 128 men discharged from Broadmoor between 1960 and 1965. Half the group had originally been admitted following a homicide. The mean length of stay in Broadmoor was seven and a half years. In the five-year follow-up thirteen committed assaults; there were no homicides in the five years but there were two later. Patient factors relating to reconviction and readmission to hospital are given. The results are soon to be published as a research project (by Dr M. Norris of the University of Surrey) which investigated social factors associated with the successful reintegration into the community of male Broadmoor patients.

Bowden (1981) reviewed the progress of patients leaving special hospitals and concluded that about one in five return to a special hospital, about one in two are subsequently convicted, but usually of trivial acquisitive offences, and perhaps one in ten are involved in serious or homicidal acts of violence. Tidmarsh (1982) has since reported that in the eighteen years since the implementation of the 1959 Mental Health Act, of some 2,000 patients who left Broadmoor, twenty committed homicide (of whom four had killed before admission to Broadmoor), giving a post-Broadmoor homicide rate of about 1 per cent. Tidmarsh's work is quoted in a publication (Hamilton and Freeman 1982) of the proceedings of one of the hospital's biennial conferences. In the 1979 conference

Broadmoor psychiatrists pooled their knowledge with that of other forensic psychiatrists, criminologists, and others to present a British view on the psychiatric assessment and management of dangerousness.

These are only a fraction of many pieces of research into the functioning of the special hospitals. Such research is necessary and of much value in raising the prestige of special hospitals, as well as providing guidance on how they can improve their functioning. In recent years an academic unit at Broadmoor has been developed in association with the forensic psychiatry unit at the Institute of Psychiatry. Two consultants were appointed jointly to the two establishments with responsibilities to develop research proposals, and one is currently under way in the treatability of psychopaths. Similarly a joint appointment has been advertised between Park Lane and the University of Liverpool, and Rampton is investigating links with the University of Sheffield/Nottingham/Leicester. There are plans to set up a committee to co-ordinate research in the special hospitals.

Note

1 Some of the material in this chapter is derived from the proceedings of a special committee of the Council of the Royal College of Psychiatrists, but the views expressed are not necessarily those of the Royal College and they do not in any way commit the Department of Health and Social Security.

References

Aarvold Committee (1973) *Report on the Review of Procedures for the Discharge and Supervision of Psychiatric Patients Subject to Restrictions.* London: HMSO.

Black, D. A. (1980) Advances in the Psychological Assessment of Offender Patients. *Bulletin of the Royal College of Psychiatrists* 4: 139–40.

—— (1982) A Five-Year Follow-up of Male Patients Discharged from Broadmoor Hospital. In J. Gunn and D. F. Farrington (eds) *Abnormal Offenders: Delinquency and the Criminal Justice System.* Chichester: Wiley.

Blackburn, R. (1982) Are Personality Disorders Treatable? Paper read at a British Psychological Society Conference, Oxford, on the Mental Health Amendment Act 1982, 1 October 1982.

Bowden, P. (1981) What Happens to Patients Released from Special Hospitals? *British Journal of Psychiatry* 138: 350–45.

Cox, M. (1980) The Contribution of Dynamic Psychotherapy to Forensic

Psychiatry and Vice Versa. *Bulletin of the Royal College of Psychiatrists* 4: 137–38.

Dell, S. (1980) *The Transfer of Special Hospital Patients to the NHS Hospitals.* Special Hospitals Research Unit Report No. 16, London.

DHSS (1980) *Report of the Review of Rampton Hospital.* Cmnd 8073. London: HMSO.

DHSS, Home Office, Welsh Office, and Lord Chancellor's Department (1978) *Review of the Mental Health Act 1959.* Cmnd 7320. London: HMSO.

—— (1981) *Reform of Mental Health Legislation.* Cmnd 8405. London: HMSO.

Estimates Committee (1968) of the House of Commons. *Second Report: The Special Hospitals and the State Hospital.* London: HMSO.

Gathercole, C. E., Craft, M. J., McDougall, J., Barnes, H. M., and Peck, D. F. (1968) A Review of 100 Discharges from a Special Hospital. *British Journal of Criminology* 87: 419–24.

Gould, J. (1957) Clinical Observations on Broadmoor Patients. *British Journal of Clinical Practice:* 129–36.

Hamilton, J. R. (1980) The Development of Broadmoor 1863–1980. *Bulletin of the Royal College of Psychiatrists* 4: 130–33.

Hamilton, J. R. and Freeman, H. (eds) (1982) *Dangerousness: Psychiatric Assessment and Management.* London: Gaskell.

Home Office (1982) *Statistical Bulletin* 19/82.

Home Office and DHSS (1975) *Report of the Committee on Mentally Abnormal Offenders.* Cmnd 6244. London: HMSO.

Loucas, K. (1980) Broadmoor's Relationship with the NHS Psychiatric Hospitals. Bulletin of the Royal College of Psychiatrists 4: 133–35.

Loucas, K. and Udwin, E. L. (1974) The Management of the Mentally Abnormal Offender. *British Journal of Hospital Medicine* 12: 285–94.

MacCulloch, M. (1982) The Health Department's Management of Special Hospital Patients. In J. R. Hamilton and H. Freeman (eds) *Dangerousness: Psychiatric Assessment and Management.* London: Gaskell.

McGrath, P. G. (1968) Custody and Release of Dangerous Offenders. In A. V. S. de Reuk and R. Porter (eds) *The Mentally Abnormal Offender.* Ciba Foundation Symposium. London: Churchill.

—— (1982) The Psychiatrist's View. In J. R. Hamilton and H. Freeman (eds) *Dangerousness: Psychiatric Assessment and Management.* London: Gaskell.

Ministry of Health (1961) *Special Hospitals: Report of Working Party.* London: HMSO.

Orr, J. H. (1978) The Imprisonment of Mentally Abnormal Offenders. *British Journal of Psychiatry* 133: 194–99.

Partridge, R. (1953) *Broadmoor.* London: Chatto & Windus.

Royal College of Psychiatrists (1980) *Secure Facilities for Psychiatric Patients: a Comprehensive Policy.* London: Royal College of Psychiatrists.

—— (1983) *The Future of the Special Hospitals.* London: Royal College of Psychiatrists.

Special Hospitals Research Unit (1979) *Special Hospitals Case Register: The First Five Years.* Special Hospitals Research Report No. 15.

Street, D. R. K. and Tong, J. E. (1960) Rampton – a Special Hospital. *The Lancet* 2: 143–45.

Tidmarsh, D. (1980) Trends in Length of Stay at Broadmoor. *Bulletin of the Royal College of Psychiatrists* 4: 135–36.

—— (1982) Implications from Research Studies. In J. R. Hamilton and H. Freeman (eds) *Dangerousness: Psychiatric Assessment and Management.* London: Gaskell.

Tong, J. E. and Mackay, G. W. (1959) A Statistical Follow-up of Mental Defectives of Dangerous or Violent Propensities. *British Journal of Delinquency* 9: 275–84.

Trent Regional Health Authority and Central Nottinghamshire Health Authority (1982) *Report of a Joint Subcommittee to Review the Working of the Eastdale Unit, Balderton Hospital.*

Walker, N. D. and MacCabe, S. F. (1973) *Crime and Insanity in England.* Vol. 2. Edinburgh: Edinburgh University Press.

Acknowledgements

Grateful acknowledgement is made to the DHSS and the Home Office for permission to quote from their annual statistics and unpublished documents. Thanks are also due to Mrs Elizabeth Parker for providing the most recent statistics from the Special Hospitals Case Register, and to Mrs Jean Pym for preparation of this manuscript.

4 Psychiatry and the Prison Medical Service

John Gunn

Prisons vary from country to country and this is even true within the United Kingdom. This article will be concerned with the largest prison system in the UK, that of England and Wales, which is the only prison system in the Western world to have a large, complex, self-contained prison medical service.

The development of the Prison Medical Service

The impetus for providing doctors for prisoners came partly from a need to prevent typhus spreading to communities surrounding prisons (Dubler 1980). Under the 1774 Act 'for Preserving the Health of Prisoners in Gaol' local justices were obliged 'to appoint an experienced surgeon or apothecary'. He was required to be resident and to have no practice outside the prison. However, right from the beginning there has been a tension within prisons between the need for punishment and the need for humane care. One eminent prison official of the time, Sir George Onefiphorous Paul, persuaded prison officials to allow the shaving of prisoners' heads, and thus control the head louse, on the grounds that the head shaving would also be salutary humiliation (Ignatieff 1978: 101)!

An organized full-time medical service began in 1877 when the Prison Commission was established. The hospital officer (male) grade was established in 1899. It was in the context of new developments in mental health care, especially the County Asylum

Acts, that prison doctors first began to take an interest in what we now call psychiatry. Legislation empowered the Home Secretary to transfer offenders from prisons to asylums, provided that insanity had been certified by two justices and two doctors. Later the prison doctor became involved in two other mental health issues: the certifying of prisoners as sufficiently sound in mind and body to withstand punishments, and giving evidence to courts about the insanity or otherwise of accused prisoners.

When the strict rules of silence and solitary confinement were introduced doctors became concerned about the effect of this kind of regime on mentally vulnerable prisoners. Doctors such as William Baly allowed association for the mentally infirm (Baly 1852) and one of the hulks in the Thames was set aside as an 'invalid depot' partly for the 'weak minded'. When Dartmoor came into use in 1852 it too was designated as an invalid depot. By the end of the nineteenth century Parkhurst Prison was designated as the establishment for prisoners who were 'unfit for ordinary penal discipline because of some mental instability other than insanity', and in 1895 the Gladstone Committee was recommending that all prison doctors should have special experience in the subject of lunacy (Home Office 1895).

The early years of the twentieth century brought special concern for the mentally defective, and for 'inebriates'. The Inebriates Act passed in 1898 had enabled courts to send inebriate offenders to special reformatories for up to three years. Two such reformatories were established in 1901, one for women at Aylesbury and another for men at Warwick. But by 1921 the system had been abandoned and the drunkenness offender remains a mainstay of the prison population despite the widely accepted view that this is inappropriate and despite two Acts (the Criminal Justice Acts of 1967 and 1972) giving powers to the Home Secretary to try other methods. Mental defectives fared better, although many are still to be found in prison and there is an increasing pressure to allow them the 'right to punishment'. The Mental Deficiency Acts of 1913 and 1927 required local authorities to set up special institutions for the mentally defective; the idiots, imbeciles, and feeble-minded persons were largely diverted from prisons to hospitals, although it is possible that now these institutions are being dismantled such patients will be directed back to prisons again.

The years between the two world wars were a remarkable phase in the history of criminology. This was the period of positivism and Freudian psychoanalysis. It was widely believed that criminals should be treated and treated medically rather than punished (see for example Commissioners of Prisons 1921). A humane and influential voice of this period was Dr M. Hamblin-Smith of Birmingham Prison (Hamblin-Smith 1922 and 1934). He recommended special treatment units within the prisons. In 1922 a unique medical postgraduate course in the University of Birmingham was held on The Medical Aspects of Crime and Punishment, and lectures and demonstrations were held in the prison. In 1924 Birmingham Prison became a centre for the psychotherapy of prisoners but Hamblin-Smith eventually concluded that prisons were not suitable for this kind of treatment because of their punitive ethos.

Norwood East, an influential prison doctor, talked of 'non-sane non-insane' prisoners, that is prisoners who could not legally be transferred to mental hospitals, but who were unsuitable for prison because of their psychological difficulties and weaknesses. He believed that there were three types – subnormals, psychopaths, and neurotics (East 1949). However, he was sceptical about the more extravagant claims that were being made about curing some of these criminals and he was a member of the 1931–32 Departmental Committee on Persistent Offenders (Home Office 1932) which decided that the results of such treatment were inconclusive.

Dr W. de Hubert from St Thomas's Hospital was appointed in 1933 to carry out psychological treatment on selected prisoners at Wormwood Scrubs. He used both discussions and analysis. Two hundred and fourteen prisoners were treated. Although no follow-up was conducted, ostensibly because the prisoners had only been at liberty for four years at the most, Hubert concluded (East and Hubert 1939) that 'psychotherapy as an adjunct to an ordinary prison sentence appears to be effective in preventing or in reducing the chance of future antisocial behaviour' in a small highly selected group of cases. East and Hubert went on to recommend the building of a special kind of penal institution to serve three functions: (1) as a clinic for medical investigations and criminological research; (2) as a treatment centre for selected prisoners; and (3) as a colony for offenders who could not adapt to ordinary social life but for whom reformative measures seemed useless. It was further recommended that the medical staff should be psychiatrically trained and that the superintendent should be a prison psychiatrist. Grendon Prison (although not built until well after the second world war) was the direct result of the East–Hubert Report.

The second world war helped to develop the new technique of group psychotherapy, and Maxwell Jones's idea of therapeutic community treatment for psychopaths followed on. These new ideas were imported into the prisons, so much so that the main therapeutic tool for the new psychotherapeutic institution became group psychotherapy instead of individual psychotherapy.

When the National Health Service was introduced in 1948 the Prison Medical Service (PMS) continued separately within the Home Office, its full-time medical officers being civil servants. However, it expanded its psychiatric services and by 1950 it was being acknowledged by the commissioners that 'while medical practice affords considerable opportunity for experience in physical medicine, it is recognised that the greater part of the work lies in the psychiatric field' (Commissioners of Prisons 1951). Most of the work however was diagnostic rather than therapeutic. In 1957, for example, when there were 16,000 sentenced men in prison, the number receiving psychotherapy was about 200, while over 5,000 men were remanded in custody for psychiatric reports in that year (Commissioners of Prisons 1958).

At this time visiting psychotherapists were introduced from local hospitals. The original idea was that short-term prisoners in need of treatment would continue to visit the same therapist after release. In practice this has rarely happened. Standard psychiatric treatments of other kinds were also introduced, for example ECT. These have tended to wax and wane in popularity in line with the fashions in the rest of psychiatry.

How many psychiatric cases?

A background question that has to be addressed if the modern problems of the Prison Service are to be put into perspective is the number of psychiatric cases within the prisons. Very few research enquiries of this issue have been conducted anywhere. Roth (1980) tells us that in the few studies carried out in the USA estimates of the number of prison inmates manifesting sufficient psychiatric pathology to warrant medical attention or intervention vary between 15 and 20 per cent. However the number of prisoners manifesting severe psychiatric disturbance is of the order of 5 per cent and Guze (1976) has estimated that 1 per cent of released male felons are schizophrenic. In their own survey of prisoners Roth and Ervin (1971) estimate that alcoholism, drug abuse, epilepsy, and schizophrenia are over-represented within the prison population. There is in fact broad agreement between authors from various countries that the most numerous mental disorders to be found among sentenced prisoners are personality disorders and substance abuse, especially alcoholism. A recent study of prisoners remanded into custody has shown that about 9 per cent of them are psychotic, 4 per cent alcoholic, and 5 per cent drug-dependent (Taylor and Gunn 1984.)

In 1972 the Home Office Research Unit was conducting a 10 per cent census survey of the prisoners in the south-east prison region. The forensic unit at the Institute of Psychiatry joined in with some health questionnaires and obtained data about previous psychiatric history, desire for treatment, and levels of neurotic symptomatology (Gunn et al 1978). We then (blindly) interviewed 10 per cent of the census sample (i.e. 1 per cent of the prisoners) to see which combination of these factors would correlate with a clinical assessment of being a psychiatric case, and a simple weighted formula was devised and applied to the questionnaire data. It turned out that about a third of the prisoners could be designated as psychiatric cases by the quite conservative methods we were using. Using ICD criteria the interviewed men revealed the following diagnoses: 21 per cent were personality disordered, 12 per cent were alcoholic, 9 per cent neurotic, 3 per cent sexually deviant, 3 per cent drug-dependent, 2 per cent psychotic (we were unable to estimate the number who were mentally handicapped). None of the 106 prisoners interviewed on this particular occasion was epileptic but a previous prison survey (Gunn 1977b) showed that about 7 or 8 in every 1000 British prisoners are epileptic and there is evidence that the figure is nearer 3 per cent in the USA (Whitman, Hermann, and Gordon 1984). If given the opportunity 38 per cent of the prisoners would like to have psychiatric treatment, and 28 per cent would like to go to Grendon Prison.

Transfers from prisons to hospitals

The number of prisoners who require transfer from prison to hospital is debatable and the number actually transferred depends upon the prevailing philosophy of imprisonment, the prevailing philosophy of hospitals, and the facilities provided in the two systems. For many years there has been a decline in the availability of mental hospital beds and this has been accompanied by a decline in the use of security. By the time of the introduction of the Mental Health Act 1959 there was a general belief that most psychiatric patients could be dealt with in open-door conditions in district general hospitals, and the Victorian mental hospitals were under threat of closure. Reality has been different. Prisons have no choice in whom they care for, only a choice in the services they provide within their walls. They have developed a number of psychiatric services, e.g. visiting psychiatrists, psychotherapy, Grendon Prison. The number of cases flowing into prison psychiatric facilities is controlled by courts and pressures from the NHS. In 1978 the then director of the Prison Medical Service, Dr J. Orr, blamed the hospitals for divesting themselves of their asylum role, suggesting that this had increased the number of mentally abnormal people being cared for in prisons (Orr 1978). The Mental Health Act 1959 should have assisted the prisons by making it easier for mentally abnormal offenders to be treated in hospital. In fact the position deteriorated between 1961 and 1976. In 1961 there were 179 sentenced men transferred from prison to hospital (39 of these were to special hospitals) whereas in 1976 there were only 30, and 19 of these went to special hospitals. This is in spite of a rise in the prison population (Robertson and Gibbens 1980). The fall was in line with a more general fall in the use of hospital orders for mentally abnormal offenders. The figures have started to improve since 1976, partly as a result of the campaign waged by the PMS, which resulted in ministerial discussions about the difficulties of placing mentally abnormal offenders in the NHS.

Psychotherapy in prison

Wormwood Scrubs is one of the largest prisons in Britain and has a strong medical tradition. In 1971 it was investigated as part of a series of enquiries into some of the psychiatric aspects of imprisonment (Gunn et al. 1978). When the research started there were 1,300 prisoners. As in many other English prisons, much of the basic medical work was done by visiting GPs, who conducted a sick parade. The GPs and senior prison staff sometimes referred men to a full-time medical officer for a psychiatric assessment. Some prisoners were kept in the prison hospital as in-patients. At the time of our study there were twenty-eight psychiatric beds available and an average bed occupancy of twenty-one. A few of the hospitalized men were transferred to mental hospitals under the Mental Health Act but the majority were treated and returned to ordinary locations. The average length of stay in the prison hospital was twenty-five days. Less severe cases were dealt with by conventional out-patient care (i.e. support plus medication) within the prison or by referral to a visiting psychotherapist. A few were transferred to Grendon Prison. In 1971 there were seven visiting psychotherapists. Most were consultant psychiatrists in the NHS and they normally worked two half-day sessions each week. Five practised psychotherapy on an individual basis, one specialized in the group treatment of substance-abusers, and the seventh ran a clinic for men with sexual problems, the treatment consisting mainly of hormone implants given shortly before discharge.

During a twelve-month period four of the five individual psychotherapists took on forty-four new patients at Wormwood Scrubs (the fifth doctor took on no new patients as his books were full!). We studied twenty-nine cases treated individually and thirteen men treated in groups. The individual treatments lasted from four months (sixteen men) to nine months or longer. The group-treated men tended to improve their self-esteem whilst the individually treated men reduced theirs; this is a finding of some importance for it suggests that the support afforded by group treatment may help to counteract the ordinary demeaning experience of imprisonment. Both group- and individually treated men improved in terms of psychiatric symptomatology. However, there was little evidence in the sample of changes in motivation towards either crime or treatment or of changes in attitude towards authority figures. The only hint of improvement came from the group-treated men. They had initially expressed exceptionally low opinions of police and magistrates, but they later rated those figures in the same way as the rest of the sample. The group-treated men showed some increase in positive motivation towards treatment.

We also studied Grendon Prison, where treatment was different. The prison evolved from the East–Hubert report of 1939 but became a psychotherapeutic institution taking personality-disordered, neurotic prisoners of average intelligence or above (see Gunn *et al.* 1978, and Gunn and Robertson 1982 for full details). The prison in 1971/2 housed 150–200 men and boys in five separate wings. Unlike all other prisons it was governed by a doctor who was a trained psychiatrist. Our research was concerned only with the three wings containing adults. Each wing consisted of thirty to forty inmates, some ten prison officers and two therapists (doctors or psychologists usually). No individual treatments were given, drugs were eschewed, and the whole system was run as democratically as is possible in a maximum-security institution. This meant that all decisions were discussed, there was open and free communication between the staff and the men, and formal group meetings of all kinds were held regularly. The courts have no powers to send offenders to Grendon. The prisoners who went there were chosen from the general prison population by the prison medical staff. Nobody was forced to go to or stay at Grendon and a period at Grendon did not have much influence on the eventual date of release from prison. Men with psychoses or with mental handicap were excluded.

We studied a consecutive sample of admissions comprising 107 men, 27 of whom left prematurely (often at their own request). To summarize a great deal of data we found that the men showed a significant reduction in neurotic pathology, an increase in social self-confidence, and an improvement in attitude towards authority figures. Embittered neurotic men damaged by institutionalization were improved in mental health and social attitudes. Sex offenders and violent men who had proved difficult to manage in other prisons became manageable in Grendon. What we could *not* show was a lowered reconviction rate compared with similar prisoners after leaving prison, but it seems unreasonable to expect one prison to differ from another in criminological terms. As our data showed, criminality and neuroticism are independent variables. Offending in the community is much more likely to be influenced by community factors such as support, opportunity, peer-group pressure, police activities, and the like than by what happens during a period of imprisonment (see Gunn *et al.* 1978 for a discussion).

Although Wormwood Scrubs and Grendon Prisons were catering for dissimilar groups (e.g. Grendon dealt with recidivists – old hands – and Scrubs with first-time prisoners – 'stars'), there seemed some evidence from the research to suggest that individual psychotherapy in prison is of limited value, group psychotherapy within an ordinary prison brings some benefits, but the best prison results (in terms of psychiatric improvement and attitude change) come from a total therapeutic community.

It has to be remembered of course that these studies were conducted twelve years ago. Since that time a number of changes have taken place, particularly at Grendon. In 1975 the governor/medical director changed, but this did not alter the basic medical philosophy. A new development has been the introduction of a ten-day induction period. Now candidates are assessed within the hospital area of the prison before they are allowed on the wings and quite a lot are rejected at this stage. The assessment service is also used to provide the PMS with information about prisoners who are not going into the therapeutic community at Grendon. Grendon is also taking more prisoners than it did in 1971 because a sixth wing (making four adult wings in all) has been opened. Our research findings have been used to consolidate the work the prison is doing with violent offenders and sexual offenders. More men in each of these categories are now being taken. At the time of writing the future of Grendon is in some doubt and there has been some slippage of medical control. When the medical director died in 1983, his temporary replacement was a non-medical governor and the advertisement for his successor asked for both doctors and non-medical governors to apply.

Independence or amalgamation

In 1962 the Home Secretary established a working party under the chairmanship of Mr E. H. Gwynn to look at the organization of the PMS (Home Office 1964). At that time there were 140 doctors in the PMS, 62 whole-time and 78 part-time. It was apparent that the service had been having difficulty for many years in attracting sufficient recruits of suitable calibre and qualifications. It was felt that the number of doctors at that time was inadequate to meet the growing needs of the prison service, especially as the working party believe that it was 'highly desirable that a thorough psychiatric appraisal should be made of every offender received into custody for the first time'. A need to specialize within the PMS was seen, and very serious consideration given to a suggestion that the service should be fully amalgamated with the NHS. However the working party stopped short of that recommendation.

Instead fifteen new developments were proposed. The best-known recommendation was the establishment of psychiatric posts held jointly between the PMS and the NHS. This proposal was taken up, and at one point eight psychiatrists held such posts, but the arrangements were not a success. Following the deliberations of a special committee within the Royal College of Psychiatrists, almost all have been discontinued.

The Royal College of Psychiatrists, having recommended the cessation of joint appointments, then went further and recommended that the PMS should be abolished and that medical services to prisoners should be provided wholly by the NHS (Royal College of Psychiatrists 1979). The College identified several categories of medical practitioner required in prisons – general practitioners for primary health care, community physicians to deal with the public health aspects of prisons and to carry out the statutory non-clinical functions of prison medical officers, and administrative doctors to co-ordinate the other doctors, including visiting specialists. In this new framework the College envisaged that the NHS would be responsible to courts for providing psychiatric reports. It was also envisaged that occupational therapy, social work, nursing, and psychology would be developed alongside the medical services.

The occasion for this radical proposal was the giving of evidence to the Prison Services Inquiry (Home Office, Scottish Office, Northern Ireland Office 1979). In the event the May Committee (as it came to be called) said the Royal College view was beyond its remit and reiterated the Home Office complaints, especially the growing number of mentally disordered offenders in prison (although the May Committee regarded this as peculiar to England and Wales). It rejected the idea of offenders being sent to prison because of no alternative placement, and took to task those prison doctors who would accept such people as a permanent part of the prison population. It also attacked the NHS for overemphasizing the convenience of not disturbing its current structure and for failing 'to measure up to its responsibilities towards mentally disordered offenders', holding up Scotland as a model system.

In response to the Royal College evidence to the May Committee and to a call by Lord Donaldson in Parliament for the abolition of the PMS, the 1981 prison department report (Home Office 1982) contained a long piece entitled 'Prison Medical Service and the National Health Service'. It described how the number of out-patient attendances and admissions of inmates to NHS facilities had increased to 16,827 and how GPs provided the basic medical care at all 112 establishments. It argued that the PMS is not self-sufficient and does not duplicate services better provided by the NHS. The report attacked the proposal for merging the PMS and the NHS. It talked of accountability of the Home Secretary to Parliament, and the supervision of the prison inspectorate. The main argument seemed to be that as a prisoner cannot have the same freedom of choice of medical services as other people, then central control of medical services and ministerial accountability provides an essential safeguard for those in custody. The report then went on to outline the tasks of the PMS – e.g. examination of all inmates on admission and discharge, the provision of reports to court and to the Parole Board, the regular review of prisoners serving life imprisonment, the examination of prisoners charged with offences, the hygiene of the establishment as a whole, and the total well-being of its inmates (and in this capacity occasionally acting as an independent referee of the system). The report is at pains to explain that a prison doctor's duties go well beyond those of a general practitioner or a psychiatrist. The section concluded with the view that if the NHS took over prison medicine the current duties of the prison medical officer would be divided between various agencies, removing the concept of one individual in a prison ultimately being responsible for all medical matters, thus producing the possibility of conflict and contradictory advice.

Fundamental problems of the Prison Medical Service

There are many problems for the PMS (e.g. overcrowding, lack of resources, too many mentally abnormal prisoners), but we must first discuss the fundamental problems. Clearly which problems are fundamental is a matter for debate. I have chosen five: (1) recruitment and training, (2) compulsory treatment, (3) the production of court reports, (4) ethical questions, and (5) numbers of prisoners.

RECRUITMENT

Recruitment to the PMS has received less attention than it deserves. It was discussed by the Gwynn Committee but it is hardly ever mentioned in the annual prison department report. Nevertheless at an informal level it is a constant anxiety for senior prison doctors, not only in terms of numbers but also in terms of quality; the size of the advertisements in the medical journals gives a clue to the difficulties being encountered. There is certainly a strong belief that prison medicine is rarely a first-choice career.

The Gwynn Committee said that young doctors see the PMS as isolated and they also made the important point that recruitment and training are intimately linked. The policy of the prison department seems to be that large quarter-page advertisements will attract doctors to the lower ranks of the PMS (psychiatric experience usually being regarded as 'an advantage') and thereafter the new recruit learns his tasks on the job and if successful and/or persistent steadily gains promotion; this in spite of the specialized role which the prison department claims the prison doctor has.

The Butler Committee (Home Office and DHSS 1975) suggested that if training grades were introduced into the PMS the movement of medical officers into and out of prisons would be encouraged; one result of this being that experience in the PMS would be more attractive to doctors who do not wish to adopt it as a life-long career.

COMPULSORY TREATMENT OF MENTALLY ABNORMAL OFFENDERS

The ordinary basis on which a doctor carries out treatment is that a patient seeks advice, a treatment is prescribed, the patient agrees to have it, and someone (usually a doctor or a nurse) administers it. This is a free relationship under the common law (see Chapter 8). If however the patient cannot give consent in the usual way this does not mean that he should necessarily be deprived of treatment. For example in emergencies (e.g. if the patient is unconscious) the medical personnel are protected against an action for battery if they act skilfully in the best interests of the patient. Children are able to give consent through their parents or even on occasion through the courts. The patient who is too mentally impaired or mentally ill to be able to give consent on his own behalf has separate legislation to deal with his/her problems in the form of the Mental Health Acts, but these apply only to psychiatric treatment. The prison department takes the view that the Mental Health Act 1983 does not apply to prison hospitals because they are not included under section 145 of the Act; therefore they will not give medical treatment to an inmate against his/her will except in an emergency.

Lord Elton, the minister responsible for prisons, recently expounded this view in Parliament:

'Doctors working in prisons have no statutory authority to administer treatment against the wishes of their patients. It would thus be defensible to treat a prisoner against his wishes only if otherwise his life would be endangered, serious harm to him or to others would be likely or there would be an irreversible deterioration in his condition. Such emergencies are in practice very rare.' (*Hansard* June 1982)

Nevertheless attacks are made by the press and by prisoners' rights organizations on the PMS. The argument is something along these lines. Prisons are a form of social restraint, most of the activity that goes on within prisons is restraining and this includes medical activity. Staff who are under the control of the Home Secretary (and this includes doctors) are necessarily part of the restraining system and will inevitably do as they are told by senior government officials. It is possible, therefore, for doctors to abuse their medical techniques, especially their drugs, in order to assist the prison system to maintain order, so that doctors may give sedatives (for example) to prisoners who are quite mentally healthy but who are being a nuisance by continual protests or breaking of prison rules. The argument seems to be given credence by ex-prisoners telling stories of how they were drugged against their will while in gaol, and by stories of large quantities of drugs being used by the PMS.

The argument, however, neglects many important points. Whenever prison doctors have taken individuals to court for making such allegations against them they have won damages. Ex-prisoners' stories may be unreliable and need careful checking. A proportion of psychiatric patients in any setting complain about drugs given to them – it is far too frightening to admit that they need the drugs. Prisoners, like other citizens, are often taking quite large quantities of sedation at the time of their arrest, e.g. tobacco, alcohol, illegal drugs, prescribed sedatives (such as Valium). All these, except a small tobacco allowance, are withdrawn abruptly when the prisoner goes into custody and yet this is a moment of great stress. Prison doctors therefore come under a continual barrage of requests from prisoners for the prescription of sedatives.

A recent decision in the High Court (*Freeman v. Home Office*) has complicated this matter. It has been held that doctors in prison are not only doctors but also 'prison officers' and therefore disciplinarians as well – this in spite of established practice and Home Office pronouncements to the contrary (e.g. the statement in para. 177 of the prison department report for the 1979 – Home Office 1980). By and large prison doctors do not see themselves as entirely subservient to the civil service and they have on occasions refused to do as they are bid by higher authority, e.g. by refusing to force-feed hunger strikers, or by refusing governors' access to prisoners' case notes. The *Freeman* case also established the principle that a prisoner's consent was valid even though he claimed to have been under severe 'institutional' constraints to accept drug treatment.

One of the results of the press campaign against the PMS has been a statement about the use of drugs in prison and the introduction of a new set of tables in the annual prison department reports. In the 1979 report (Home Office 1980) a new section appeared entitled 'Use of Medicines', but unfortunately it is largely meaningless (Gunn 1981).

COURT REPORTS

A peculiarity of the British penal system is that it is called upon to make psychiatric assessments for courts. This means that accused people who have or appear to have some form of mental abnormality are remanded into custody, sometimes even when it is unlikely or indeed impossible for them to get a prison sentence if they are found guilty. This is very harsh, for a remand into custody is in effect a prison sentence. It may be possible for a prisoner to continue to wear his own clothes and it may be possible for his mother or his wife to bring his meals in six days a week, but he is still a prisoner with his job and domestic life in jeopardy, and this prisoner status may last many months before he is brought to trial. There is also evidence that the context in which court reports are written influences the opinions given in the report (Zusman and Simon 1983).

For the PMS the provision of numerous medical reports is a considerable burden. They provide between 8,000 and 9,000 reports each year, including several hundred so-called voluntary reports (i.e. reports unsolicited by courts) and between 100 and 200 reports on bail. Admittedly the numbers of such reports have been falling steadily since the mid-1970s (for example, the 1982 figure of 8,755 reports was only 68 per cent of the 1975 figure of 12,964) but they constitute a vast volume of work which has to be resourced. The system of courts remanding prisoners to the PMS on bail has never really caught on, and only 119 prisoners were dealt with like this in 1982. The vision of a mentally distressed accused man knocking on the prison gate asking to see the doctor for a report seems incongruous!

In an important study Bowden (1978a and 1978b) looked at the medical remand process at Brixton prison. He found that, over a three-month period in 1975, 634 men were remanded into custody into this one prison for medical reports. Eighty-seven received recommendations for psychiatric treatment, eighty-two actually getting to hospital. Fourteen months later nearly three-quarters of these men had been discharged. Sixty-two percent of the eighty-two cases were regarded as receiving some benefit from their hospitalization, but this represented only 5 per cent of the initial receptions; a somewhat inefficient process.

The reason for the inefficiency is gleaned from the differences between those recommended for treatment and those not. Bowden found that those recommended for treatment were acutely ill. The men not recommended for treatment had more extensive criminal histories, were more likely to be regarded as psychopathic, and more often had a history of excessive drinking. In other words the recidivist, heavy-drinking, personality-disordered individuals were being recognized as mentally abnormal by the courts but were not getting into psychiatric treatment. There are two main reasons for this. Firstly, psychiatric services do not really provide facilities for the chronically disruptive and personality-disordered. Secondly, borderline cases are unlikely to be accepted by the health-care system if they are first directed into the penal system. A patient remanded into a hospital or into an out-patient clinic is more likely to be accepted by those services. Doctors tend to refer patients to the services with which they are familiar. Prison doctors are familiar with prison facilities and unfamiliar with NHS facilities.

If courts are really concerned to introduce mentally abnormal offenders to the psychiatric services they will have to collect many more reports from those services. It has always been possible for courts to remand accused people on bail to hospital or clinics in order to obtain reports. There has however been a double-sided reluctance to undertake this work. Courts are concerned about 'security' and NHS clinics are not keen to have troublesome patients. From 1 October, 1984, the Mental Health Act has made it possible for courts to use a new remand to hospital order (see Chapter 7). This should encourage a further trend away from relying on prisons for psychiatric assessments, but it will not happen to any great extent unless there are changes of attitude in NHS staff and in magistrates and judges.

ETHICAL QUESTIONS

Very few branches of medicine are subjected to the constant ethical criticism which besets the PMS. As Smith (1983a) remarks, 'the idea that prison doctors drug prisoners, close their eyes to brutality, identify with prison governors rather than prisoners, and think of prisoners as prisoners first and patients second is deeply rooted – among both the public and doctors,' and to support his view he quotes a particularly aggressive and offensive leading article from a recent *World Medicine* entitled 'Perverted Medicine', which said that 'the practice of medicine in prisons is being perverted for reasons of political expediency.'

The PMS was set up to improve the health of prisoners. There is no evidence to suggest that it has deviated from that underlying objective. It is true that detailed health-care policies for prisoners have either never been formulated or never been made public but health-care policies are not often clearly formulated in any field of medical activity. We have to deduce what the policies are by noting, for example, the various attempts that have been made to improve the mental health of prisoners, either by setting up better psychiatric services within the prisons or by campaigning to have more mentally abnormal prisoners redirected to NHS hospital care.

Nevertheless the environment itself has its own effect. Prisons are depressing, overcrowded, demoralized places. Few inmates seem happy to be there, perhaps some institutionalized and inadequate prisoners have made it their home, but the majority of prisoners want out. The work of prison staff goes unnoticed and unsung until something goes wrong. Resources are often hard to come by. Dirty, smelly conditions and the constant urging, by a vociferous minority, for prison staff to be tough on men in their care tend to lower staff self-esteem. Prison doctors are not immune from these pressures and if they have infrequent contact with the outside world may come to accept, after a number of years, conditions which they would not have accepted when they first joined the service. At the very least they become what is called 'realistic' and strive only for minimal improvements for their patients when major ones are required.

A subtle but important issue for the prison doctor is the management structure in which he works. The ordinary prison doctor is responsible to his senior at the local level. In matters of 'security' (which could be interpreted widely) the prison governor is senior to everybody at the local level. In matters of 'health' (which again can be interpreted widely) the senior medical officer takes precedence over the discipline staff. This pattern is repeated right up to the prison directorate but it should be noted that in matters of finance and general prison policy the final authority must be non-medical, indeed political (i.e. ministerial). Clearly such a system can create conflict in the overlapping areas of health and security, especially in determining financial priorities between them. Such tensions arise in any health system, but they are particularly difficult for the doctor working for the Home Office as the primary aim of the parent organization is not the health of inmates but law and order in the community.

It is further argued that this problem of being employed by an organization whose primary aim is not health care creates difficulties even at the doctor/patient relationship level. Bowden (1976) has argued that 'a doctor cannot serve two masters.' His thesis is that the dual allegiance of the prison medical officer to the state and to those individuals who are under his care results in activities which largely favour the former. The activities of the doctor which support the state are making reports on behalf of the Director of Public Prosecutions, deciding fitness to undergo disciplinary procedures, and advising what kind of prison a man should be kept in and what kind of work he can manage. Bowden reminds us that the Declaration of Geneva exhorts a doctor to make the health of his prisoner his first consideration, to preserve confidences entrusted to him, and to abstain from collaborating in any form of medical service in which the doctor does not have professional independence. He goes on to argue that 'to the prisoner the doctor is sometimes seen as merely a facilitator of the process of punishment and his experience will perhaps colour his attitude to the medical profession and the way in which he is able to use it.' As a remedy Bowden proposes two levels of medical practice within prisons. A group of doctors employed by the National Health Service to provide a personal health service for prisoners, who would be governed by a system of medical ethics. Another group would concentrate on the administrative aspect of health care and would be employed by the Home Office as civil servants.

All this is an interesting approach to the inevitable conflict of interest outlined above, but it neglects some important points. First, for a doctor medical ethical obligations should always override other responsibilities; thus a factory doctor who finds unacceptable poisons in the working environment must first tell his employers but if they take no action he must tell the workers. Second, there are overriding citizen's obligations on a doctor wherever he practises, e.g. he must always inform the appropriate authorities if he knows one of his patients is endangering other people, such as an actively epileptic lorry driver, or an uncontrolled and uncooperative child rapist. If a dangerous patient tells his doctor of his escape plans the doctor must take preventive actions no matter who is his employer. What an individual doctor will actually do in these difficult and conflicting circumstances will depend on his personal judgement and on his courage. The other point neglected by Bowden in his argument is that already the majority of doctors working in prisons are employed by the NHS and this makes little difference to the fundamental issues he discusses. If the recent court decision (*Freeman* v. *Home Office*) that prison doctors are also prison officers becomes generally accepted then it will exacerbate the inherent difficulties.

Sometimes it is argued that psychiatrists should be careful not to write reports relating to impending punishment as that would be unethical. The argument is that it is colluding with a harsh punishment, such as solitary confinement, to certify some as fit and others as unfit for it. On the other hand others argue that to fail to certify a manifestly ill prisoner as sick and quite unsuitable for the punishment proposed would be worse. This issue can only be resolved in terms of prevailing attitudes and particular punishments. It could be argued that on balance medical integrity is better preserved by trying to excuse sick men and women from such a punishment than by refusing to examine the offenders. This kind of justification is used by psychiatrists every day when they provide evidence to courts about fitness to plead and the effects of imprisonment.

Prison doctors thus work in an especially sensitive arena; an arena for which medical students are not trained, indeed for which nobody seems to be formally trained, and for which there is no explicit medical model. In such circumstances it is easy for critics to have a field day. However, it does *not* logically follow that prison doctors are more likely to act unethically than other doctors (indeed their sensitive environment may make them less likely to do so), and it does *not* logically follow that transferring the PMS to the NHS would solve all the ethical problems; many of them are inherent in all forms of medical practice.

NUMBERS OF PRISONERS

It is almost a truism to say that there are too many prisoners in Britain and that a great number of the problems of prisons flow from this undisputed fact. The crisis high-water mark of 40,000 set by Mr Roy Jenkins when he was Home Secretary has long since been surpassed, the average daily population of 1982 being about 43,700, and it is still rising. This is a very high proportion of our population, the highest in Western Europe and only exceeded in the Western world by the USA and Canada. It is created partly by the large number of individuals on remand (approximately 7,400) and the increasing use of very long sentences.

Clearly this situation is remediable. Governments could implement the recommendations of the Advisory Council on the Penal System and thus sharply reduce the average length of sentences given (although retaining very long sentences in exceptional cases) (Advisory Council on the Penal System 1978). Courts could voluntarily co-operate with the Advisory Council by limiting their sentencing and by reserving the remand in custody arrangements for a few cases only. Governments could provide alternative medical facilities for the provision of psychiatric reports to courts. However, none of these very obvious things happens.

A sub-issue within the numbers problem is the so-called psychopath. This is not the place to get into a semantic discussion about the nature of psychopathy; the term is used here simply because others, especially the Butler Committee, have used it. It seems to refer to chronically neurotic individuals who are frequently aggressive but rarely psychotic. They may constitute between 20 and 30 per cent of the sentenced population (see p. 129). They are people who are rejected wherever they present, the NHS gets rid of them if it can and the prison system gets landed with a large number of them. Grendon, Barlinnie, and units of this kind are developed partly in response to the need to manage such people. The Butler Committee (Home Office and DHSS 1975) was in no doubt that there should be special units developed within the prisons 'for the training and treatment of dangerous anti-social psychopaths on a voluntary basis'. They further believed that such units should be the basis of a scientific study of treatment funded by the Medical Research Council. Again this seems unlikely to happen.

The role of psychiatry in prison

There seem to be four basic jobs for the psychiatrist in a prison: (1) to provide psychiatric reports in a number of different circumstances; (2) to provide general psychiatric treatment; (3) to provide psychotherapy and psychotherapeutic regimes; and (4) to influence the general milieu of prisons.

The provision of psychiatric reports seems straightforward. The bulk of such reports are requested by courts, which ask in effect, does this man have a psychiatric disorder, if so should he be punished, have you advice about his management? There is no obvious reason why the questions should be addressed to prison doctors. The fact that most psychiatric reports to court are provided by prison doctors seems an historical accident. Justice, the strain on prisoners, and the quality of reports would all be improved by a shift away from prisons to the NHS for this service. HM Government has weakly acknowledged this by the inclusion in the new Mental Health Act of possible provisions for remand to hospitals. If the NHS is to undertake a lot of court work, it will need a substantial increase in funds and staff.

Other psychiatric reports are required within prisons which cannot legitimately be provided by the NHS, although the work can be carried out by visiting psychiatrists as well as by prison doctors. These reports include those sent to the Parole Board, those given to governors who are dealing with breaches of discipline, and recommendations for courses of treatment (e.g. at Grendon Prison). The second role for the psychiatrists in prison is the provision of treatment. In England the prison doctor will struggle, often unsuccessfully, to get the sick psychiatric patients into the NHS; where he fails (often because of a complicating personality problem, drug-abuse or alcoholism), or where the disorder is of a lesser degree and the patient consents, it seems reasonable for the psychiatrist to provide treatment in prison. This might be anything from ECT to psychotropic drugs, from anticonvulsants to supportive counselling. Compulsory treatment is, however, not permitted within the prisons.

It seems likely that for the foreseeable future prisons are to be the main repositories for individuals with personality disorder who break the law. It is also clear that prison psychiatry has developed to respond to this group. Individual psychotherapy is provided in many prisons and group psychotherapy has developed in some establishments. Most importantly Grendon prison has shown the advantages in developing therapeutic communities within secure conditions.

The first three roles for prison psychiatry seem then to be fairly largely within the mainstream of medicine. The fourth role is more debatable and esoteric. Grendon Prison, as our research has shown, improves neurotic disorder and changes attitudes, but it does more than that. It provides a humane system of management for some otherwise unmanageable prisoners. It is debatable whether all unmanageable prisoners are 'sick' or in any way medically disordered; some are simply reacting to authority in a quasi-political fashion. The more that unmanageability is political the less likely it is to respond to a therapeutic community (e.g. the IRA prisoners creating their dirty protest) but in some cases it is difficult to determine how much is political and how much is neurotic; therapeutic communities may be helpful in cases where there is a suspicion of a political element. Let us take an example. The Scottish prison service had a group of long-term (mostly lifer) prisoners who were proving unmanageable because of persistent violence. The Grendon model was copied and a special wing in Barlinnie prison, Glasgow, was set up. Some highly dangerous, severely violent men were managed there and showed a good deal of personal growth. One prisoner, Jimmy Boyle, made himself famous by his sculpture and his writings. Was Jimmy Boyle mentally disordered or was he simply reacting to stress? Perhaps he was reacting against a life sentence he regarded as unjust, perhaps the conditions he found himself in (including the cages at Peterhead) were too much for him, perhaps he has an impulsive and volatile personality (see his book to make an assessment – Boyle 1977). Whatever the explanation, the special unit transformed him.

Psychiatry should not be hesitant about going beyond a concern with the mentally ill *provided* (and note the italics) it has something scientific to say which is testable and refutable. Psychiatry has been rightly ridiculed in the past for dabbling in politics, warfare, the arts, and all sorts of human activities with no basis at all. However, medicine does have things to say about non-pathological matters in some biosocial circumstances. Who would doubt the value and pertinence of medicine in the phenomena of pregnancy and childbirth? The science of physical hygiene is partly medical, partly social, but it is largely responsible for our high standard of health today. In prisons doctors can use their knowledge of group psychotherapy, therapeutic communities, and the consequences of stress to give advice about better management. This surely is as much a role for the prison doctor as is giving advice about correct feeding, hygiene, ventilation, and the like. Indeed ultimately such a preventive role could be developed into the most important psychiatric role of all within the prisons.

The Scottish Prison Medical Service

One last matter we should briefly consider before turning to remedies is the position of the doctor in the Scottish prison system, especially because it was regarded as a model system by the May Committee. Scotland has the advantage of a small population with approximately 5 million inhabitants. Of these 5 million, about 5,000 are locked away in prisons, a high ratio by European standards and higher even than in England and Wales, but even so a small problem when compared with the 43,000 south of the border.

It is sometimes said that the Scottish prisoners are serviced entirely by part-time medical officers. Although that is largely true it is significant to note that the largest prison (Barlinnie) in the urban area (Glasgow) has three full-time medical officers. So even Scotland, which traditionally relies on the NHS and general practitioners, uses full-time staff for a large prison. In addition Scotland has fifteen consultant psychiatrists providing fifty sessions a week to the prisons, but it is important to note that Scotland has twice as many psychiatrists per 100,000 population as does England and Wales.

In this climate of part-time and NHS practice it is interesting to note the same defensive postures adopted in this year's annual report (Scottish Home and Health Department 1983): 'All Prison Medical Officers have the same ethical standards as their colleagues practising outside prisons ... most Scottish Prison Medical Staff are also employed in the NHS and it is unthinkable that they would change, in any way, their working practices when they enter penal establishments,' and 'all medicines used in penal establishments are very carefully documented.'

Remedies

Some ideas to improve the services provided to mentally abnormal people in prison have already emerged. The total number of people in prison should be reduced and followed by a selective reduction in the number of mentally abnormal people, by ensuring that more mentally ill prisoners are transferred to the NHS and that the NHS develops better services for the provision of reports to courts. The decision must be taken as to whether offenders with severe personality disorders should be treated within prisons or mental hospitals. Whatever service is selected it should then be provided with the necessary resources. Even if the decision is a compromise to split the burden between the NHS and the PMS, extra resources are required.

It is clear, nevertheless, that these ideas will not be enough in themselves. Two other more radical and controversial ideas are therefore proposed. Firstly, the development of academic prison medicine; secondly, the creation of a Special Health Authority for prisons.

Neither the proposal for joint NHS/Home Office appointments nor the proposal suggesting the abolition of the PMS has found much favour within the Home Office. The first suggestion threatened to devalue the status and role of the prison doctor and the second to get rid of him altogether. Perhaps it is not surprising that the PMS did not greet these ideas enthusiastically. What needs to be done is to face the fact that prison medicine is different, is here to stay, and needs to increase its responsibilities and status. The proposals suggested here aim to achieve this.

ACADEMIC DEVELOPMENTS

No branch of medicine can flourish, perhaps even survive, without an academic centre. A discipline has to accumulate knowledge and make discoveries; it has to undertake research, unless it is to stand still and be left behind. A discipline has to be taught to the next generation. At present, prison medicine has very little educational and no research role. The lack of these two features is a serious handicap and a bad omen for the future of the PMS.

An obvious need for prison medicine is a university chair in a medical school. This is clearly a long way off. Therefore the immediate aim should be to develop close connections between the PMS and one or two university departments. Obvious centres where this could be done are Wormwood Scrubs and Hammersmith Hospital, Brixton Prison and the Institute of Psychiatry, Birmingham Prison and Birmingham medical school, Oxford Prison and Oxford University, Parkhurst Prison and Southampton University, and so on; there are plenty of examples. Such linkages would provide prison doctors with membership of an academic department and academic doctors with an opportunity to carry out research and teaching within the prisons. As an adjunct to this it would be essential to introduce a few training grades into the PMS, rather like those in general practice, so that a very real educational framework for the skills of prison medicine could be established, both for those planning on a full-time career and for those who simply require a small amount of knowledge of the system. There are developments in this direction now that a number of senior registrars in forensic psychiatry are undertaking prison work, but such developments should be expanded. There should be opportunities for undergraduates and psychiatric trainees to learn from prison doctors. The PMS might be advised to have one or two prisons which undertake complex work and are training centres, especially for future prison doctors.

The question of research within prisons is particularly important. In the 1960s and 1970s it seemed as if prison medical research was going to be welcomed and encouraged, and the Institute of Psychiatry undertook a great deal. However, the 1980s have brought difficulties. The very idea of doing 'research' (a sinister word to some people) on prisoners became questionable: spectres of American prisoners being bribed to become drug addicts were allowed to cloud the appropriateness of simple questionnaire enquiries. It is sometimes argued that prisoners have to be protected against the degradations of researchers who might upset them by talking to them; after all everything that a prisoner does is under duress! Some fear that prison doctors might be confronted with a man who says, 'I don't want to talk to you, I only want to talk to a research doctor,' thus losing him the opportunity for treatment. Others suspect that data collected for research purposes will be used in court against an individual, and so on. The negativity towards research created by such unfounded anxieties creates a much greater ethical concern, that of leaving significant medical problems unresearched and denying prisoners possible improvements. It is essential, if prison medicine is to develop, that research is actively encouraged, indeed canvassed. Genuine health ethics place research in a central position.

A PRISON HEALTH AUTHORITY

The Royal College of Psychiatrists' suggestion that the PMS should be completely amalgamated with the NHS is unrealistic. All kinds of institutions employ their own doctors: armed forces, factories, even the Scottish prisons. The more isolated the institution the more likely it is to employ its own doctors. More fundamentally, however, NHS staff, by and large, have no desire to service the prisons. Acceptance of the PMS as an independent service with its own directorate, but with a reorganized line of responsibility, seems a much more realistic remedy.

Without much difficulty there could be a Special Health Authority for prisons set up under the National Health Service Act which would give ultimate responsibility for the medical care of prisoners to the Secretary of State for Health and Social Services (he has it for most other citizens). In practice, however, the responsibility would be devolved to a multi-disciplinary health authority which could, let us say, comprise doctors (including psychiatrists), academics, judges, policemen, lay people, and of course members of the Home Office. Home Office officials could even be in the majority if they felt threatened by the development. Such an authority would ensure greater autonomy for the director of the PMS and his colleagues; it would ensure a budget which is separate both from the Home Office budget and from the rest of the NHS; it would compel the health ministers to plan for mentally abnormal offenders as a whole rather than discounting those in prison; it would make the introduction of training and research programmes much easier; it would answer the criticism that prison doctors work for a body whose primary aim is security. Above all it would create a much broader interest in the health problems of prisoners.

No doubt some will point out that such an authority would foster the development of a parallel service for mentally abnormal offenders rather than an integrated one, a development personally deprecated some time ago (Gunn 1977a). This is true and is the price that would have to be paid for an improvement in the services for the prisons. Trends are moving towards a parallel service anyway and it may be that they simply have to be accepted.

In-service developments

As a final comment it should be said that it is not only outsiders who have tried to provide solutions for the PMS. Three recent developments are worthy of special note. Firstly the director of the PMS has recently been appointed from outside the PMS. Admittedly Dr Kilgour has previously worked as a senior civil service doctor, but the fact that he is an outsider to the prison service is of great significance. Secondly there has been a change of policy about nursing within prisons. Until recently the nursing services to women's prisons were largely provided by women with nursing qualifications, whereas nursing services to male prisoners were provided by discipline officers who had undergone a brief hospital officers' course. As a result very few qualified male nurses worked within the prisons. Now it is proposed to recruit male nurses directly to the prison hospital system and give them a shortened course in discipline and security work. Thirdly and perhaps most significantly, the prison doctors have established their own association (the Prison Medical Association). This aims to look after the specialized interests of prison doctors and it began with a conference on prison medicine. Its chairman hopes that it will spearhead new developments in the acquisition and dissemination of knowledge about prison medicine. These new developments are already improving morale within the PMS. Improved staff morale will probably mean improved health care for prisoners.

References

Advisory Council on the Penal System (1978) *Sentences of Imprisonment: A Review of Maximum Penalties*. Cmnd 7948. London: HMSO.

Baly, W. (1852) in *Report of the Directors of Convict Prisons for 1851*. London: HMSO.

Bowden, P. (1976) Medical Practice: Defendants and Prisoners. *Journal of Medical Ethics* 2: 163–72.

—— (1978a) Men Remanded into Custody for Medical Reports: The Selection for Treatment. *British Journal of Psychiatry* 133: 320–31.

—— (1978b) Men Remanded into Custody for Medical Reports: The

Outcome of the Treatment Recommendation. *British Journal of Psychiatry* 133: 332–38.

Boyle, J. (1977) *A Sense of Freedom*. London: Pan.

Commissioners of Prisons (1921) *Report for 1919–20*. London: HMSO.

—— (1951) *Report for 1950*. London: HMSO.

—— (1958) *Report for 1957*. London: HMSO.

Dubler, N. N. (1980) Commentary on D. L. Bazelon, *The Law, the Psychiatrist, and the Patient. Man and Medicine* 5: 78–92.

East, W. N. (1949) *Society and the Criminal*. London: HMSO.

East, W. N. and Hubert, W. H. de B. (1939) *The Psychological Treatment of Crime*. London: HMSO.

Gunn, J. (1977a) Management of the Mentally Abnormal Offender: Integrated or Parallel. *Proceedings of Royal Society of Medicine* 70: 877–84.

—— (1977b) *Epileptics in Prison*. London: Academic Press.

—— (1981) Review of the Report of the Work of the Prison Department 1979. *Bulletin of the Royal College of Psychiatrists* 5: 31.

Gunn, J. and Robertson, G. (1982) An Evaluation of Grendon Prison. In J. Gunn and D. Farrington (eds) *Abnormal Offenders, Delinquency and the Criminal Justice System*. Chichester: Wiley.

Gunn, J., Robertson, G., Dell, S., and Way, C. (1978) *Psychiatric Aspects of Imprisonment*. London: Academic Press.

Guze, S. B. (1976) *Criminality and Psychiatric Disorders*. New York: Oxford University Press.

Hamblin-Smith, M. (1922) *The Psychology of the Criminal*. London: Methuen.

—— (1934) *Prisons and a Changing Civilisation*. London: John Lane.

Hansard (1982) House of Commons, 1 June, col. 625.

Home Office (1895) *Report from the Departmental Committee on Prisons*. Cmnd 7702. London: HMSO.

—— (1932) *Report of the Departmental Committee on Persistent Offenders*. Cmnd 4090. London: HMSO.

—— (1964) *Report of the Working Party on the Organisation of the Prison Medical Service*. London: HMSO.

—— (1980) *Report on the Work of the Prison Department 1979*. Cmnd 7965. London: HMSO.

—— (1982) *Report on the Work of the Prison Department 1981*. Cmnd 8543. London: HMSO.

Home Office and DHSS (1974) *Interim Report of the Committee on Mentally Abnormal Offenders*. Cmnd 5698. London: HMSO.

—— (1975) *Report of the Committee on Mentally Abnormal Offenders*. Cmnd 6244. London: HMSO.

Home Office, Scottish Office, and Northern Ireland Office (1979) *Report of the Committee of Inquiry into the United Kingdom Prison Services*. Cmnd 7673. London: HMSO.

Ignatieff, M. (1978) *A Just Measure of Pain: The Penitentiary in the Industrial Revolution*. New York: Pantheon.

James, J. F., Gregory, D., Jones, R. K., and Rundell, O. H. (1980) Psychiatric

Morbidity in Prisons. *Hospital and Community Psychiatry* 31: 674–77.

Orr, J. (1978) The Imprisonment of Mentally Abnormal Offenders. *British Journal of Psychiatry* 133: 194–99.

Robertson, G. and Gibbens, T. C. N. (1980) Transfers from Prisons to Local Psychiatric Hospitals under Section 72 of the 1959 Mental Health Act. *British Medical Journal* 1: 1263–266.

Roth, L. H. (1980) Correctional Psychiatry. In J. W. Curran, A. L. McGarry, and C. S. Petty (eds) *Modern Legal Medicine, Psychiatry, and Forensic Science*. Philadelphia: F. A. Davis.

Roth, L. H. and Ervin, F. R. (1971) Psychiatric Care of Federal Prisoners. *American Journal of Psychiatry* 128: 424–30.

Royal College of Psychiatrists (1979) The College's Evidence to the Prison Services Inquiry. *Bulletin of the Royal College of Psychiatrists* 3: 81–4.

Scottish Home and Health Department (1983) *Prisons in Scotland, Report for 1982*. Cmnd 8980. Edinburgh: HMSO.

Smith, R. (1983a) The State of the Prisons: Disorder, Disillusion and Disrepute. *British Medical Journal* 287: 1521–523.

—— (1983b) History of the Prison Medical Services. *British Medical Journal* 287: 1786–788.

Taylor, P. J. and Gunn, J. (1984) Violence and Psychosis: 1 – Risk of Violence among Psychotic Men. *British Medical Journal* 288: 1945–949.

Whitman, S., Hermann, B. P., and Gordon, A. C. (1984) Psychopathology in Epilepsy: How Great Is the Risk? *Biological Psychiatry* 19: 213–35.

Zusman, J. and Simon, J. (1983) Differences in Repeated Psychiatric Examinations of Literature of Litigants to a Lawsuit. *American Journal of Psychiatry* 140: 1300–304.

CASES

Freeman v. *Home Office* [1983] 3 All E.R. 589. upheld on appeal [1984] 1 All E.R. 1036.

5 The development of regional secure units

Robert Bluglass

The need for security was an essential element in the care of mentally disordered patients until recent times. (As to the history, see further Chapter 1.) In the eighteenth and early nineteenth centuries 'insanity' was a vague and ill-defined concept limited to major and acute mental disorder. The total population of England at the beginning of this period consisted of less than six million inhabitants, mainly living in small rural communities, and the mentally disordered were accommodated in private madhouses, workhouses, or existed as 'single lunatics' in isolation and frequently in restraint. The criminally insane were, until 1800, broadly indistinguishable from others convicted of crime and were to be found in gaols and Bridewells.

In 1744 Bethlem was the only public hospital in England devoted to the care of the insane, although further pioneering institutions, such as the York Retreat, subsequently emerged primarily as a result of local concern for the socially deprived in their midst. In 1807 a select committee was established by the House of Commons to 'enquire into the State of Criminal and Pauper Lunatics in England, and the Laws relating thereto'. It consisted of members of both political parties, prison and other social reformers (such as Wilberforce – associated with the abolition of slavery), together with lawyers and magistrates, but it did not have a medical member. The main concern of the committee was with confinement and as yet the medical profession had little interest in, or knowledge of, mental disorder. The following year Parliament enacted the County Asylums Act 1808 which implemented the committee's recommendations for the provision of county asylums and allowed a major improvement in the conditions of care for many individuals (Jones 1955).

The Act of 1808 provided for patients to be admitted to a county asylum who were too 'dangerous to be at large' under the Vagrancy Act 1744, or as criminal lunatics under the Act of 1800. An Amending Act of 1815 dealt with the question of admission and discharge of patients and, for the first time, introduced a need for a medical certificate; a recognition of rising standards, the developing knowledge of mental disease, and the influence of the medical profession from this date.

By 1815 three counties had established asylums and there were nine in operation by 1827 – Nottingham, Bedford, and Thorpe (1811), Lancaster (1816), Stafford (1818), Bodmin (1820), Lincoln (1820), and Gloucester (1823). The staff of the average asylum was so small that mechanical restraint was the principal method of maintaining order and there were high statutory penalties if a patient escaped, equivalent to at least one month's wages with a maximum of £10 (a keeper's total wages for five months). These institutions were often built in the countryside, on the edge of towns adjacent to the local prison (e.g. Stafford and Birmingham) which at the time provided the basic model for the development of methods of administration, control, and treatment in hospitals. However, the establishment of the country asylums provided an impetus to seek improved methods of humane care, and commencing at Lincoln and Hanwell mechanical restraint was gradually discarded, soon to be virtually abolished. Patients were only admitted as a result of certification but the introduction of an inspectorate, the lunacy commissioners, monitored standards of care.

By 1930 the county asylum was still the main source of psychiatric care, but new approaches to treatment had started to emerge based upon general hospitals with psychiatric out-patient clinics and observation wards. The Mental Treatment Act of 1930 introduced two new categories of patient, 'voluntary' and 'temporary', resulting in due course in the gradual reduction in the proportion of patients detained in hospital by certificate. Treatment now expanded to include drug therapy, psychological methods, education, occupation, and training, but most doors were still locked.

Criminal insanity was not recognized before 1800 and with some few exceptions the insane who committed crimes were treated as fully responsible for their actions. After James Hadfield's attempt on the life of George III and the recognition of 'partial insanity', the Criminal Lunatics Act of 1800 listed the circumstances in which a person might be detained as a criminal lunatic 'during His Majesty's Pleasure'. At this time no special accommodation was available to receive such individuals other than prisons, but eventually, as the county asylum system began to develop, counties which had an asylum were able to offer this more appropriate alternative. Others were sent to Bethlem or local gaols or Bridewells where they were kept in confinement in similar conditions to other responsible prisoners and without any specific treatment for their condition.

The Criminal Lunatics Acts of 1838 and 1840 provided more positive powers to send insane prisoners to asylums. The commissioners reported in 1844 that 139 criminal lunatics were confined in county and private asylums, 85 in Bethlem, and 33 in gaols. They observed that although the county asylums were not designed to accommodate major and dangerous offenders they increasingly did so. Lancaster Asylum, for instance, contained seven murderers, and most asylums had at least one patient who had committed arson. The commissioners were concerned that asylum conditions were often unsuitable for individuals who did not justify a separate ward and were sometimes dangerous to other patients. They concluded that 'it is highly desirable that arrangements be made for the separate care and custody of criminal lunatics.' There was a need for the construction of a special institution combining medical facilities with the security against escape to be found in a prison. Broadmoor Hospital was founded in 1863 to meet this need and was followed later by other similar hospitals.

The introduction of voluntary patients into the 'mental hospitals' (replacing 'asylum' in 1930) and the development of the special hospitals were the first steps towards the reduction of security for psychiatric patients. The proportion of patients who were severely abnormal and dangerous became progressively and proportionally smaller as the boundaries of abnormality extended to include the recognition of an increasingly wide range of psychiatric conditions. The increasing influence of psychotherapeutic methods of treatment and the development of psychopharmacology reduced still further the need for custody and control.

The Royal Commission on the Law Relating to Mental Illness and Mental Deficiency (1954–57) effected the most significant shift of this movement into the modern age by establishing the right of mentally ill patients to be cared for informally insofar as this was possible, limiting compulsory procedures to more clearly defined criteria, and desegregating the mental hospitals from the rest of the health-care system. The result was the Mental Health Act of 1959, a highly regarded and liberal reform of the legislation which coincided with the developing 'open door' policy for the psychiatric hospitals. The 'open door' philosophy was pioneered by Dr George Bell, the physician superintendent of Dingleton Hospital, Melrose, Scotland, who won the trust and co-operation of his staff and the support of a tolerant local population to the extent that a policy of open access and free movement of patients within the hospital and to the outside world was effectively established. It was a major advance in the care of patients; the most significant of its kind since Connolly led the humane reform movement and discarded methods of mechanical restraint. It was all the more admirable since Bell's achievements antedated the advent of tranquillizers which facilitated this new approach in the 1950s and beyond.

The 1959 Act, together with the open-door policy, widened the opportunities to develop methods of treatment in a more relaxed and less restrictive atmosphere. In many hospitals this was accompanied by an injection of money to upgrade the structure of the old Victorian buildings and there was a considerable improvement in the level of staffing. Previously many large mental hospitals were served by a physician superintendent and one or two assistant psychiatrists. Now they had seven or eight consultants and junior doctors with nursing staff rather than 'attendants', who previously had a mainly custodial role.

It was clear at that time, however, that these changes in approach to psychiatric care would bring new problems and new difficulties in management. In July, 1959 the then Minister of Health, Mr Enoch Powell, appointed a working party to consider the provision of security in psychiatric hospitals and the future task of the special hospitals. The working party reported in July, 1961 (Ministry of Health 1961) welcoming the open-door movement but concluding that some National Health Service hospitals should continue to provide secure accommodation for those patients who required it. Regional hospital boards should provide a variety of units of different types, including some designated secure units, so that transfer between them could be made without difficulty according to the patients' needs. The report also recommended that special diagnostic treatment and assessment centres should be set up with funding from the Ministry of Health. These recommendations were all accepted by the government but by 1975 it was observed that 'not a single unit has materialised'. The majority of psychiatric hospitals claimed to have implemented a totally open-door policy (although careful enquiry would reveal that a ward door was often quietly locked) and that the hospital regime would be undermined by providing special arrangements for a relatively small group of patients at the expense of the rest. The notion of the hospital as a 'therapeutic community' (Jones 1952) based upon the social organization of the institution to which all staff members made an important contribution was increasingly seen as incompatible with the security requirements of a relatively small group of disturbed or anti-social individuals. Whereas in the eighteenth and nineteenth centuries little distinction was drawn between prisons and hospitals (indeed, Bethlem was originally under the same administration as Bridewells), as hospitals became more therapeutic in character and purpose so the custodial or prison aspects were discarded, leading eventually to new problems of management. Scott (1965) quoted Dr Kidd (1961) as saying that 'the new freedom must not be lost for the sake of a few psychopaths ... for they derive no benefit, cause tension, upset other patients and waste the time of hard-pressed medical and nursing staff.'

The 'open-door policy' and the concept of the hospital as a 'therapeutic community' followed by the notion of 'community care' were attractive models for psychiatrists who were enthusiastic to rid themselves of their Victorian heritage. (See Chapter 2.) There was little support for the main recommendations contained in the 1961 report. Its authors (who included Dr Peter Scott and Sir Denis Hill, who was himself to join the Butler Committee of 1973) clearly recognized the likely consequences of the new movement. They observed:

(1) security precautions cannot be dispensed with for all psychiatric patients;
(2) security precautions are a necessary part of treatment for the sake of the patient as well as the public;
(3) the maximum security provided by special hospitals should not be used if suitable facilities can be made available locally;
(4) patients should be treated near their homes, insofar as this is possible, to maintain links with the local community.

The committee went on accurately to predict that in the absence of satisfactory security arrangements at NHS psychiatric hospitals the courts might well hesitate to make orders sending patients to these hospitals as they were now able to do under the Mental Health Act 1959.

During the following decade and beyond there were few, if any, initiatives to halt the trend. NHS hospitals became more openly reluctant to accept offenders or 'difficult' patients. The number of hospital orders made by the courts fell year by year from a peak of 1,259 in 1966 to 924 in 1972. According to the interim report of the Butler Committee (1974) there existed a 'yawning gap' between the overcrowded but secure special hospitals at one end of the range of available facilities and the NHS hospitals at the other which (now) provided no security. There were various reasons for this situation. The Royal Commission on the Law Relating to Mental Illness and Mental Deficiency 1954–57 had said in paragraph 519 of its report that dangerous patients should be specially accommodated in a few hospitals having special facilities for their treatment and custody, leaving other hospitals free to dispense with restrictive measures to the greatest possible extent; but such accommodation had not been provided. The development of treatment in 'open' conditions had made NHS hospitals increasingly reluctant to accept offenders. Custodial requirements cannot be reconciled with an open-door therapeutic policy and when offender patients abscond much time and trouble are involved in effecting their return. The nursing staff dislike the custodial role and their numbers were insufficient to deal with dangerous patients. They saw it as the proper function of the prisons and special hospitals to cope with these people. There was also concern that offenders may harm or pilfer from non-offender patients. Even when offender patients had been accepted by NHS hospitals it was sometimes found that they could not be contained satisfactorily and had to be transferred to special hospitals, which were placed in an invidious position. They were bound to accept dangerous patients from open hospitals but found it increasingly difficult to transfer patients to the psychiatric hospitals when they were no longer dangerous.

Two consequences followed from all this: one was that many patients in special hospitals did not need to be there for reasons of security; and the other was that the special hospitals had to refuse admission to cases that they could appropriately accept if they had room. In turn these problems rebounded on the courts, which now found increasing difficulty in finding the appropriate placement for mentally disordered offenders, and for the prisons, which often, reluctantly, had inappropriately to accept them.

Bowden (1975) surveyed one regional health authority area and noted that there had been a reduction of nearly 40 per cent in the number of closed beds during the previous five years. He observed that it was paradoxical that at a time when open-door psychiatry reflected a concern with individual liberty more people were incarcerated within hospitals because of staff shortages rather than as a result of direct management policy. The 'illusory freedom' was therefore selective, with the result that some patients were in fact detained outside the mental hospitals.

But which individuals are best cared for in hospitals and who would be better managed in prison? Scott (1970) in a key paper discussed the persistent dilemmas faced by those who struggle to find solutions: prison or hospital? punishment or treatment?

The appropriate environment to cope with many mentally abnormal offenders is often an arbitrary decision. Penrose showed in several papers many years ago (e.g. Penrose 1943) that the use of prisons and mental hospitals varies inversely according to prevailing policies. When prison accommodation is overstretched or reduced, the demand on mental health services increases; and vice versa. Scott implied that to attempt to clear the prisons of mentally abnormal people by placing them in hospitals where experience showed they were unwelcome was likely to be less successful than encouraging a radical improvement of the treatment facilities in prisons, utilizing and enhancing the high staff/patient ratio and potential expertise. In order that morale might be heightened and prisons and hospitals might be brought closer together, Scott even proposed that carefully selected and controlled voluntary admission to prison might be introduced.

Most experienced forensic psychiatrists are likely to agree that there is no clear dividing line between the 'mad' and 'bad'. The mentally disordered are not necessarily always totally lacking in responsibility and insight into the significance of their own behaviour, and offenders frequently have difficulty in coping with their impulses, mood swings, or aggressive tendencies. However, despite Penrose's and Scott's clear-sighted and rational observations, the system remains firmly established: the mentally disordered should be in hospitals; others, who justify it, should be in prison. Prisons are supported by limited 'general practitioner'-based medical services but are not designed to cope with severely disordered offenders. Hospitals may need to provide varying levels of security, but aim to avoid the trappings and appearance of prisons. They are for treatment, not punishment.

The Committee on Mentally Abnormal Offenders was established at a time when all these problems had virtually reached a point of crisis. A solution had to be found urgently to relieve the special hospitals of serious overcrowding, to relieve the prisons of mentally abnormal individuals who should not be there, and to provide an alternative to the open-door mental hospitals which now provided little or no security and a low tolerance of anti-social behaviour. The answer, provided in an interim report (Butler Committee 1974) in order that the seriousness of the situation might be emphasized, was to establish regional security units in the National Health Service 'as a matter of urgency'.

The Butler Committee advocated a secure unit in each of the fourteen regional health authority areas. The units were foreseen as centres for the development of forensic psychiatry services. They would fulfil a need for non-offender patients (as advocated in a parallel report from the Department of Health and Social Security, the Glancy Report (DHSS 1974)) while advancing the general cause of the open-door policy in psychiatric hospitals by enabling the most difficult cases to be treated in more appropriate conditions. But bearing in mind the main concern of the Butler Committee, the units were seen as crucial to the greater flexibility in placement needed for mentally abnormal offenders and to the relief of prisons and special hospitals. It was considered right that offenders and non-offenders should be treated together, sharing facilities, and without any distinction being made between them. The centres would provide a focus for multi-disciplinary professional activity and would offer improved assessment of offenders for the courts. They would have an essential role in training and research and should therefore be closely associated with the universities. Further, the Butler Report advocated that the units should be located accessibly in towns, closely integrated with the forensic psychiatry services assisting the courts, and providing out-patient services. The units should be therapeutically orientated and have the use of workshops and adequate recreational areas. Various kinds of work should be available and all should be as interesting and relevant to normal industrial conditions as possible, bearing in mind eventual opportunities in the outside industrial world. Educational facilities should also be available, especially for the not insignificant number of illiterates or near-illiterates. Besides relieving the general psychiatric hospitals and special hospitals, they would receive patients on transfer from prison and admit offenders directly committed by the courts. It should be their purpose to satisfy the needs of the regional areas in which they are placed with the advantage of being reasonably near to the patient's home and family; but they should not be precluded from accepting cases from other regional areas if this would be helpful in particular circumstances. The Butler Committee considered that the term 'medium-secure unit' for units of this kind was misleading and difficult to define. The units should not be as secure as the special hospitals but must be adequately secure for the safe containment of the people they would be intended to accommodate. These should not include aggressive psychopaths or any patients who would present an immediate danger to the public if at large. The necessary degree of security should be achieved partly by a high ratio of patients to staff, partly by the regime, and partly by the design and physical characteristics of the buildings.

The Butler Report attempted to estimate the number of secure places required to relieve all the institutions under pressure and concluded that an initial target of 2,000 secure places 'is by no means generous' to provide for all those concerned. They should be sited near centres of population, near to general hospital facilities, and might range in size from 50 to 100 beds but might in some cases be considerably larger, probably about 200 beds where sharing of facilities with adjacent hospitals is not possible.

The report recognized a risk that when the new accommodation had been provided it might gradually be diverted from its intended purpose by the accumulation of more or less permanent residents who are not acceptable elsewhere or fit for discharge. This trend must be resisted by minimizing the length of stay in each case and by establishing regular reviews of cases who were needing to stay a considerable time. There was a need for a high staff/patient ratio (one nurse to one patient must be regarded as the very minimum) and nursing should be of a high quality with a high proportion of specially trained staff. Staff of special hospitals and regional units should be interchanged – at least on a temporary basis. All junior psychiatrists should spend a period of work in a unit. There should be a permanent social work staff and social work trainees should gain experience in the unit. Psychiatric hospitals and general hospital psychiatric units should be made aware of the important part that they will be expected to play in the rehabilitation of patients who no longer require secure conditions.

Finally, the interim report of the Butler Committee proposed (and this they regarded as of the 'greatest importance') that the provision of the regional secure units should be financed by a direct allocation of central government funds to the regional health authorities and all help should be given to ensure that the units would become available in the shortest possible time.

In July, 1974 the then Secretary of State for Social Services, Mrs Barbara Castle, announced the government's acceptance of the Butler Committee's proposals for the establishment of regional secure units and the endorsement of the department's own report with respect to non-offender patients. It was decided that 1,000 secure places should be provided in the first instance and that they should be provided as soon as possible. Meanwhile interim security arrangements should be made in NHS psychiatric hospitals until the new units were established. The government also undertook to provide the capital costs of the units (Government Circular 1974: HSC(IS)61).

The initial response to Mrs Castle's urgent request to health authorities was luke-warm, although one or two of the five authorities with forensic psychiatrists in post made some effort to assess the local need for facilities of the kind envisaged. In October, 1975 the Butler Committee produced its final report (Butler Committee 1975) and declared that it was disturbed to learn that little progress had been made in establishing units or even in providing temporary arrangements. The committee recognized the difficulty in finding sufficient suitable staff, but noted that financial recognition (a 'lead payment') for nurses who will work in the units had been negotiated. They were, however, concerned that in some parts of the country there had been indications of unwillingness either to formulate plans at all or to give the proposals the priority which had been thought necessary. The committee recognized that regional health authorities would be obliged to meet future running costs from revenue, which would add an additional burden and might discourage progress. It was consequently now recommended that the cost of running the units should also be met from central government funds.

There was a swift response to this further proposal and in January, 1976 the government announced the provision of a special revenue allocation to be provided annually until secure units are fully established, to be given to regional health authorities according to the size of the population served, and to be based upon the initial need of twenty beds per million. The financial allocation was initially (1976) £5 million. It was to be used to support interim arrangements until the secure units were built and would represent approximately two-thirds of the estimated revenue required.

Progress in implementing the national secure-unit policy was not retarded by financial considerations in the early years. In most regions there was very little commitment to the proposals, which concerned a relatively small group of patients, for whom there was limited sympathy and minimal knowledge, but who appeared to be attracting considerable financial support when other patients, who often seemed to planners and health authority members to be more deserving, were beginning to feel the first effects of economic restraints.

In particular the impetus to introduce the new units required a local enthusiast or 'product champion' (Stocking 1983) with a sound knowledge of the problems of mentally abnormal offenders and difficult-to-place patients who could 'sell' the policy to others. In some regions (e.g. Mersey) an adminstrator took the lead, in others it was the incumbent forensic psychiatrist; in others, once a forensic psychiatrist had been appointed he took the initiative to press for secure-unit planning, sometimes with speedy results. But enthusiasm and leadership were often not enough and the slow progress to produce results has been the consequence of many different factors.

Because the secure-unit programme was a relatively new concept in Britain, each region has had to start from the beginning, each defining its own solution to meet local needs, restraints, and difficulties. The Butler Report, the Glancy Report, and the DHSS Guidelines (DHSS 1975) established the general principles, but each project team found it necessary to evolve its own concept of a secure unit before moving forward to planning considerations. For many it was necessary to seek inspiration overseas where a variety of units of varying types had been established during the previous two or three decades. Useful experience was to be found in Sweden (the National Forensic Clinic, Uppsala), Denmark (Herstedvester Treatment Centre and Horsens Prison), Netherlands (Van der Hoevenkliniek, Utrecht, and the Pompekliniek, Nijmingen), the regional forensic units in Canada, and others. During this early stage of reflection and consultation it became evident that the Butler Report concept of the secure unit as one arm of a comprehensive forensic psychiatry service was of crucial importance. The unit should not be planned in isolation but should be one part of an evolving service integrated into the existing mental health services. The Royal College of Psychiatrists, with the encouragement and support of the DHSS, took the Butler proposals one stage further in considering the role of security at every level of psychiatric care (Royal College of Psychiatrists 1980). In essence this report envisaged a range of different types of secure unit depending upon local needs, difficulties, and existing resources. They should be part of a forensic psychiatry service complementing and supporting local general psychiatry facilities. A variety of levels of security were required, from the maximum facilities of the secure hospitals at one end of the spectrum, to the open-door hospital at the other. Between these were envisaged larger secure units with less security than special hospitals, smaller units (like the interim units), and a small secure provision in each psychiatric hospital for the management of shorter-term acute behavioural disturbances. All of them should be well staffed and the basis of security, as Butler suggested, should be a high level of staffing and nursing supervision.

Once the concept was established there were often protracted difficulties in finding an appropriate site. There was often opposition from local medical, nursing, and other staff. Local residents were sometimes well organized and vocal in their objections. Several regions had to submit to non-statutory public planning inquiries (e.g. South-Western Regional Health Authority) and occasionally a local group successfully persuaded an authority to abandon initial plans and seek a site elsewhere (e.g. South-West Thames Regional Health Authority). The DHSS Capricode Planning Procedure is itself a slow and laborious matter requiring evidence of wide local consultation and approval of operational and building planning by the DHSS at each stage. Project teams sometimes became unacceptably large and unwieldy as every professional group claimed an interest in influencing the final building, and the wisdom of keeping the representative unions well informed was learned at an early stage. During the earlier years they frequently presented obstacles (particularly when interim units were developing), claiming for instance that other resources would suffer if scarce funds were diverted to secure units or that the units would tend to attract staff away from existing facilities.

The reasons for slow progress were not appreciated by critics such as Members of Parliament, who were given little or no explanation by the DHSS. At the same time interim secure units were equally slow to get off the ground with the result that in the earlier years the specially allocated funds had to be used for other purposes. This was in fact an acceptable accounting manoeuvre on the part of health authorities, but it appeared that the funds were being misused and that psychiatry was not benefiting from them. They were in fact subsequently used only to improve the care of psychiatric patients and as the programme moved forward this became a decreasing cause of criticism.

Meanwhile, the interim arrangements requested by Mrs Barbara Castle were slowly becoming established. Originally envisaged as temporary security within a ward or wards of a psychiatric hospital, they were planned as small secure units in most instances, each with its own range of professional staff, psychiatrist, psychologist, social worker, occupational therapist and additional nurses. Adaptations were made to provide room for group therapy, workshops, recreation, and other facilities. These units sometimes involved protracted planning procedures and local consultation. Sometimes they were expensive, but they provided important experience towards planning the more ambitious permanent units in due course. The first interim unit, Rainford Ward, opened at Rainhill Hospital, Mersey Region, in August, 1976 (Higgins 1979) to be followed by Prestwich Hospital, Manchester, and the Lyndhurst Unit, Knowle Hospital, Fareham, in 1977 (Faulk 1979a). By 1984 600 places were available in 'interim facilities' in England and Wales (see *Table 5.1*).

Eight years' experience of the interim units, the worsening economic climate, new policies for the mental health services, and the development of forensic psychiatry generally have to some extent influenced a change in approach to the secure-unit concept and a change in the attitudes of those who were previously so resistant to it. (As to the current operation of the units, see Chapter 6.) Small units of fifteen to twenty-five beds are now often regarded as successful models for the care of this difficult group of patients (Higgins 1981) and there are doubts about the wisdom of planning a secure unit of more than fifty beds. A small, domestic unit is seen to allow better control and supervision, with fewer administrative problems, than a large building coping with a region, and in a small unit staffing requirements are easier to meet. However, the arguments in favour of bigger units remain valid, and complex planning procedures cannot easily be interrupted, but the case for continuing the life of the smaller units in some regions is also strong. Indeed, they are now often seen as a valuable addition to local services, providing an important base for additional experience for medical and nursing staff in training.

The regional secure unit programme

All regional health authorities now have plans for permanent secure accommodation of some kind and seven regions have a unit in operation. (As to the operation of regional secure units, see Chapter 6.) However, it is a common experience that most regions have difficulty in opening beds to patients once the places are completed. There are two major problems. The first is a difficulty in recruiting sufficient nursing staff. The second is an increasing difficulty on the

Table 5.1 Interim and other secure facilities: summary at October 1983

region	interim facilities			other secure facilities	
	current facilities likely to cease when permanent unit becomes available	current facilities which are likely to continue when permanent unit becomes available	total interim places in operation	e.g. a ward which is lockable, or beds under close supervision	places planned in addition
Northern	—	—	—	391	12
Yorkshire	18	—	18	77	8
Trent	—	—	—	7	—
East Anglia	—	—	—	49	—
North-West Thames	61	15	77	—	—
North-East Thames	—	—	—	24	—
South-East Thames	27	—	27	—	—
South-West Thames	—	—	—	196	—
Wessex	14	—	14	33	—
Oxford	—	—	—	22	14
South-West	—	58	58	—	—
West Midlands	27	26	53	18	—
Mersey	—	—	—	40	—
North Western	44	—	44	54	—
Total	191	99	291	911	34

Source: DHSS.

part of regional health authorities in finding the revenue shortfall to meet the cost of running units, only part of which is provided by central government. *Table 5.2* summarizes the current provision of permanent regional secure units and plans for additional units. It will be seen that current plans will provide 708 places by the end of the 1980s, of which 20 are mental handicap beds (Borocourt Hospital, Oxford) and 20 are adolescent beds (Prestwich Hospital, Manchester). The two largest units are planned for West Midlands (100) and North West Region (88). Oxford has no plans for the mentally ill at the present time. South-East Thames has a complex multi-site programme with a central assessment unit at Bethlem and four peripheral units based at mental hospitals in the region. On 7 March, 1984 (*Hansard* March 1984) in the four purpose-built units so far opened, eighty-five beds were available to patients.

Current stage of development in the regions[1]

NORTHERN REGION

The first regional secure unit (RSU) was opened by Sir George Young at Middlesbrough in November, 1980. One of the first consultants in forensic psychiatry had been appointed at Durham in 1967 (the late Dr David Westbury) but local politics prevented his involvement in the RSU development, which was largely promoted by the consultants at the adjacent St Luke's Hospital. As a result the design of the unit has sometimes been criticized and the siting of the unit in one corner of the region may limit its role as a regional facility. Problems in the recruitment of nursing staff have so far prevented all the beds being utilized. There are now two consultants in the region.

YORKSHIRE REGION

A consultant appointment was made in Yorkshire in 1967 and a planning team was established in 1975, but the consultant's resignation in 1977 delayed progress until a successor was appointed in 1978. A forty-eight-bedded unit has been completed at Fieldhead Hospital, Wakefield (a mental handicap hospital). An interim unit (twenty-four beds) opened at Stanley Royd Hospital, Wakefield in January, 1983 and comprises eighteen forensic beds and six special-care beds. The permanent unit will be part of a forensic psychiatry service. Nursing recruitment is regarded as less of a

Table 5.2   *Current provision of permanent regional secure units: regional summary, March, 1984*[1]

regional health authority	*site of RSU*	*beds*	*progress*
Northern	St Luke's Hospital, Middlesbrough (opened November, 1980)	30	20 beds operational
Yorkshire	Fieldhead Hospital, Wakefield (mental handicap) (completed November, 1983)	48	to admit first patients mid-1984
Trent	Towers Hospital, Leicester	60	12 beds opened July, 1983
East Anglia	St Andrew's Hospital, Norwich (completed September, 1983)	36	to admit first patients May, 1984; gradual bringing into full use
North-West Thames	St Bernard's Hospital, Ealing (2 further units also under consideration)	40	tenders under consideration; building expected to start in 1984
North-East Thames	Runwell Hospital	30 10	Operational; RHA considering proposals for two further units (further 32 beds)

Region	Scheme	Beds	Status
South-East Thames	multi-site scheme		
	assessment unit – Bethlem Hospital	30	under construction;
	area unit – Canehill Hospital, Coulsden.	15	all units due for completion towards
	Bexley Hospital, Bexley	15	end of 1984 or early 1985.
	Oakwood Hospital, Maidstone	15	
	Hellingly Hospital, Hailsham	15	
South-West Thames	Netherne Hospital, Coulsdon	25	planning
Wessex	Knowle Hospital, Fareham	31	conversion started October, 1983; due for completion October, 1984
Oxford	Borocourt Hospital (mental handicap)	20	RHA reassessing policy for the mentally ill in the light of their strategic shift towards community-based services
South-Western	Langdon Hospital, Dawlish	30	first patients admitted June, 1983
	Glenside Hospital, Bristol	30	advanced planning stage
West Midlands	Rubery Hospital, Birmingham	100	plans approved; building late 1984/ early 1985.
Mersey	Rainhill Hospital, Prescot	50	opened August, 1983; 2/3 beds functioning
North-Western	Prestwich Hospital, Manchester	20	adolescent beds; opening 1984
	Prestwich Hospital, Manchester	88	adult beds; under construction, opening end of 1984/early 1985

Note: 1 Since preparing this chapter the Welsh Office has circulated proposals for four secure units in Wales providing a total of sixty beds.
Source: Hansard (1984) vol. 1302, cols 618–19 and DHSS.

problem than in some regions as additional nurses have been trained in anticipation of the completion of the new unit. There are now three consultants in the region.

TRENT REGION

A regional forensic psychiatrist was appointed in 1978 and, prior to this, planning was led by the University Department of Psychiatry at Leicester. The Trent unit is therefore sited in the south of the region at Towers Hospital, Leicester, and a unit to serve the Nottingham and Sheffield populations in the north of the region is also under discussion. The sixty-bedded RSU was completed in January, 1982 but severe nursing-recruitment difficulties have allowed only fifteen beds to be occupied. There were similar problems at the fifteen-bed interim unit at the Towers Hospital which also opened in January, 1982. A second consultant post has been advertised.

EAST ANGLIA

This region was one of the last to commence planning. There were considerable difficulties in finding an appropriate site and eventually a project team began work in late 1980 to plan a thirty-six-bed RSU for St Andrew's Hospital, Norwich. This was completed in record time in November, 1983. A consultant forensic psychiatrist was appointed in 1979. Nursing recruitment has been difficult and may delay opening all the beds.

NORTH-WEST THAMES REGION

This region also began planning at a late stage. A permanent unit is planned for St Bernard's Hospital, Ealing (forty beds) and two satellite units are contemplated. A fourteen-bed interim secure unit opened at St Bernard's Hospital in the summer of 1983. A consultant has been appointed.

NORTH-EAST THAMES REGION

There have been considerable difficulties in this region. A consultant was appointed in 1977 but with area, not regional, responsibilities and his expertise was little utilized in planning. A working party had been established in 1975 and eventually a unit was proposed to be sited at Friern Hospital, Barnet, but with a later decision to close this hospital (taken in 1982) the plans for the unit were dropped. The philosophy in the region has been to provide small sub-regional units and one of these at Runwell Hospital (ten beds) is operational. Further plans for the region are under consideration.

SOUTH-EAST THAMES REGION

This region has developed a unique model: a thirty-bed RSU at the Bethlem Hospital without a catchment area of its own and four fifteen-bed area secure units at Bexley, Cane Hill, Hellingley, and Oakwood Hospitals, each with a sub-regional catchment population. A regional forensic psychiatrist was appointed in 1977. Others have been appointed since. Planning commenced in 1975. An interim unit was established at Bethlem as a temporary measure.

SOUTH-WEST THAMES REGION

There were many problems in finding an appropriate site. An initial plan for a unit at the Royal Earlswood Hospital was abandoned after strong local protests. Eventually agreement was reached for a twenty-five bed unit at Netherne Hospital, Coulsdon, which is in the planning stage. No interim unit has been established in this region but a consultant has been appointed.

WESSEX REGION

A consultant forensic psychiatrist was appointed in 1971 and discussed the possibility of a secure unit before the Butler Committee was established. A fourteen-bed interim unit was opened at Knowle Hospital, Fareham in 1977 (see Faulk 1979b). This gave valuable experience in planning a single RSU for the region, to be sited on the edge of Knowle Hospital campus, and due to be completed in October 1984 (thirty-one beds). A second consultant has been appointed.

OXFORD REGION

This region has not yet appointed a consultant and planning has involved local consultants. There has been uncertainty about the need for a secure unit for the mentally ill following a regional survey. A twenty-bed purpose-built unit is now planned for Borocourt Hospital (mental handicap) and the region has been considering a RSU for mentally ill patients at Milton Keynes or elsewhere.

SOUTH-WESTERN REGION

Discussions began in 1972, planning commenced in 1975, and a thirty-bed sub-regional unit was completed in July, 1982 and opened on 17 June, 1983 (the Butler Clinic, Langdon Hospital, Dawlish). A forensic consultant was appointed in November, 1981 and required alterations to the original design. A consultant has also been appointed for the Bristol area of the region and a thirty-bed unit is under consideration at Glenside Hospital to provide for the north-eastern part of the region.

WEST MIDLANDS REGION

One of the first consultant appointments was made in this region in 1967 and a regional forensic psychiatric service has developed since that date. The consultant made initial proposals for a fifty-bed unit in 1969 and after the Butler Report a project team was established in 1975. Approval has been given for a 100-bed purpose-built unit on a site at Rubery Hill Hospital to commence building late 1984. Two interim units are in operation. There are four consultants in post.

MERSEY REGION

This region had the first interim unit in 1976. A fifty-bed purpose-built unit (the Peter Scott Clinic) opened in August, 1983 at Rainhill Hospital. This is part of a forensic service which includes an out-patient base in Liverpool. Three consultants in post (see Higgins 1979).

NORTH-WESTERN REGION

This region has been running three interim units and following several changes of plan a twenty-bed purpose-built unit for adolescents was completed at Prestwich Hospital in February 1983 and became operational in March, 1984. An eighty-eight bed adapted unit at Prestwich Hospital is due for completion in November, 1984.

Discussion

There can now be no doubt that the secure-unit policy proposed in 1975 is at last moving steadily forward despite the many difficulties that have impeded progress during the past ten years. It remains to be seen whether or not this very expensive and elaborate programme will provide the solutions intended by the Butler Committee by relieving the pressures on special hospitals and prisons. Dr Peter Scott had doubts. He believed that the available finances should be used to improve the range of therapeutic facilities in prisons. He considered that the secure-unit programme was wrong in principle and will fail to fill the gap in caring for 'embarrassing patients': those who are dangerous and those who are unrewarding, dependent, chronic, and ungrateful. He predicted that the new units will eventually become increasingly selective, be useful for teaching and for rehabilitating special hospital patients, but they will eventually tend to reject some whom other institutions will continue to feel they should take (Scott 1975). Will some new form of institution eventually be created to 'relieve' the regional secure units? Scott, percipient as he always was, gave us a warning that we should not forget.

It is too early to say to what extent the units will fulfil their intended functions. It is unlikely that they will reduce the demand upon the special hospitals significantly. Indeed they may well create new problems. The existence of a secure unit in a region tends to reduce the tolerance of general psychiatric hospitals still further, yet the success of the RSUs requires the co-operation and support of the local hospitals to care for the long-stay patients and those who are no longer dangerous. Equally, there is over-optimism about the likely effect on the prison population. There will certainly be some help for the seriously mentally ill who will be removed from prison hospitals, but it is unlikely that the large numbers of inadequate, dull, neurotic, and personality-disordered offenders will be accommodated in the secure units. Prisons will always have a proportion of mentally unstable individuals. However, it is with the development of regional forensic services, working co-operatively with local consultants, special hospital colleagues, and prison medical officers as part of a unified system that the new units are likely to have the most success. They must rely upon continued goodwill and close working relationships, without which the free flow of patients into and out of the units could come to a standstill. There is a need for equal co-operation from local social service authorities to provide social workers in sufficient numbers and of a high quality. They must also provide community accommodation and support.

Perhaps the greatest danger is financial. The first signs of ambivalence are already being demonstrated by some regional health authorities who are finding difficulties in meeting the revenue consequences of the units. Other medical specialities will always be strong competitors for limited resources and it requires a firm commitment on the part of regional health authorities and central government to ensure the continued support that the units require. The regional health authorities will also have to be continually reminded of the need to support the community services, out-patient clinics, and community nurses as part of the general mental health provision for which they are responsible. As Butler indicated, the universities too have an important task to encourage the development of new techniques, improved training, and, importantly, research. The existing academic centres will require a further development and others could justifiably be added, particularly in the north.

Note

1 I have been greatly assisted by Dr Peter Snowden in preparing this summary and by his reviews (Snowden 1983 and 1984).

References

Bowden, P. (1975) Liberty and Psychiatry. *British Medical Journal* 4: 94–6.

Butler Committee (1974) *Interim Report of the Committee on Mentally Abnormal Offenders*. Cmnd 5698. London: HMSO.

—— (1975) *Report of the Committee on Mentally Abnormal Offenders*. Cmnd 6244. London: HMSO.

DHSS (1975) *Regional Secure Units: Design Guidelines*. London: DHSS.

Faulk, M. (1979a) The Lyndhurst Unit at Knowle Hospital. *Bulletin of the Royal College of Psychiatrists* 44–6.

—— (1979b) Mentally Disordered Offenders in an Interim Regional Medium Secure Unit. *Criminal Law Review* 686–95.

Hansard (1984) House of Commons, vol. 1302, cols 618–19.

Higgins, J. (1979) Rainford Ward, Rainhill Hospital. *Bulletin of the Royal College of Psychiatrists* 43–4.

—— (1981) Four Years' Experience of an Interim Secure Unit. *British Medical Journal* 282: 889–93.

Jones, K. (1955) *Lunacy, Law and Conscience*. London: Routledge & Kegan Paul.

Jones, M. (1952) *Social Psychiatry*. London: Tavistock Publications.

Kidd, M. B. (1961) *Lancet* ii. Letter, 18 August.

Ministry of Health (1961) *Special Hospitals: Report of a Working Party.* London: HMSO.

Penrose, L. S. (1943) Psychiatry and Genetics. *American Journal of Mental Deficiency* 47: 462.

Report on Security in NHS Hospitals (1973) London: DHSS.

Royal College of Psychiatrists (1980) *Secure Facilities for Psychiatric Patients: A Comprehensive Policy.* London: Royal College of Psychiatrists.

Royal Commission on the Law Relating to Mental Illness and Mental Deficiency 1954–57 (1957) *Report.* Cmnd 169. London: HMSO.

Scott, P. D. (1965) Provisions for the Treatment of Psychopathy. In H. Freeman (ed.) *Psychiatric Hospital Care.* 286–90. London: Balliere, Tindall & Cassell.

—— (1970) Punishment or Treatment: Prison or Hospital. *British Medical Journal* 2: 167–69.

—— (1975) *Has Psychiatry Failed in the Treatment of Offenders?* Fifth Denis Carroll Memorial Lecture. London: ISTD.

Snowden, P. R. (1983) The Regional Secure Units Programme: A Personal Appraisal. *Bulletin of the Royal College of Psychiatrists* 7: 8. August 1983.

—— (1984) *British Journal of Psychiatry* (in press).

Stocking, B. (1983) Personal communication.

6 Current practice in regional interim secure units

I. H. Treasaden

In July, 1974 the Butler Committee on mentally abnormal offenders was so convinced of the urgent need to establish regional security units that it published its recommendations in an interim report (Home Office and DHSS 1974) recommending their provision in the National Health Service as 'a matter of urgency' to fill the 'yawning gap' between the service provided by the overcrowded special hospitals and the NHS hospitals providing little or no security. An initial target of 2,000 secure places was regarded as 'by no means generous' to ease all the areas under increasing strain and pressure.

Many difficulties in establishing both interim and full regional secure units have arisen (Royal College of Psychiatrists 1980). There are now a variety of regimes in existence, some providing locked-door security, others using open-door policy with high staff/patient ratios. Other regions in England are in an advanced stage of planning a regional secure unit (Snowden 1983). (As to the development of regional secure units, see Chapter 5.) However, should the secure units eventually be widely established, how far they will help is debatable. The units will be highly selective, taking those who require medium security between that provided by special hospitals and that of NHS psychiatric hospitals. The patients are to be disruptive rather than dangerous (Bluglass 1978). Aggressive psychopaths and the severely mentally handicapped are excluded. The patients are to be short-stay, less than eighteen months, with a prospect of responding to secure psychiatric treatment within that period (DHSS 1974a; Home Office and DHSS 1975).

Not all psychiatrists were in favour of the proposed security units. For example, the distinguished forensic psychiatrist, the late Dr Peter Scott (1974) opposed the units because they would make little impact on the problem of the dangerous offender. He mentioned several criticisms: (1) security is immensely expensive, materially and in staff; (2) skilled nurses would be extremely hard to find; (3) the units would select only the 'nicer' band of the psychiatric spectrum (short-term and requiring only intermediate degrees of security); (4) the units would not relieve the overcrowding in the special hospitals; and (5) the units would not help long-term dangerous prisoners who are so difficult to help in prison. Scott's own proposal was that energy and resources should be spent on improving psychiatric facilities within the prisons. This was also the approach suggested by MIND (Gostin 1978).

Resistance to the need to provide for this large group of patients has influenced plans to provide relatively large purpose-built secure units to complement the services provided by district psychiatric hospitals. However, more recently the success of interim units established at Rainhill Hospital opened in 1976 and Knowle Hospital opened in 1977 and to a lesser extent at Prestwich Hospital opened in 1976 (where union pressure initially severely restricted its functioning) has led others to reconsider their policies and similar units are beginning to appear in other parts of the country.

Experience in these well-established interim units suggests that small units with fifteen to twenty beds can apparently cope with patients referred from within their regions and on transfer from special hospitals. These patients show, or have shown, a serious level of behavioural disorder, usually arising from mental illness, and are likely to require up to one to two years' treatment in conditions of security greater than those prevailing in NHS psychiatric hospitals but less than those in special hospitals. The patients are accommodated near their homes and close to their catchment-area hospitals.

Small units have been established by conversion of existing accommodation in one hospital to provide for the need of one or more other hospitals within the geographical area. Physical security may be less than that required for a larger regional secure unit. However, existing experience suggests that with good staffing it may sometimes be minimal (Faulk 1979; Higgins 1979). The government gave the go-ahead in 1979 to the expensive South-East Thames regional scheme based on the idea that inter-linked medium-security programmes need to be developed in all parts of the region, depending on high nursing ratios rather than physical structures. The proposal is linked with the postgraduate Institute of Psychiatry at the Maudsley Hospital, which should aid staff recruitment of a high quality (Knesper 1978), a critically important issue in the debate about secure units. The South-East Thames Region is attempting to integrate forensic facilities into the existing psychiatric service by encircling a central assessment unit at the Bethlem Royal Hospital by a chain of small secure units in each of the local mental hospitals. This approach may encourage other psychiatrists to care for mentally ill offenders within existing hospitals and prevent the tendency for forensic psychiatry to develop as a service separated from the main stream of psychiatric practice (Gunn 1977).

Different interim units evolve their own policy but all rely, to some extent, on a milieu-therapy regime. Full pre-admission staff discussions are essential and as a general rule patients are not admitted without the agreement of the staff most closely involved in their care and at most risk from their behaviour. In those interim secure units which have been established, emergency admissions are neither welcomed nor encouraged.

Table 6.1 summarizes the number of beds, staffing and security, ward policy, and facilities of the interim secure unit at Knowle Hospital, Fareham, Hampshire (the Lyndhurst Unit) (Treasaden and Shepherd 1983), on Rainford Ward, Rainhill Hospital, Liverpool (Higgins 1981), on Elton Ward, Prestwich Hospital, Manchester (Reid, Lea, and Wallace 1982), and the Bethlem Royal Hospital, Beckenham, Kent (Gudjonsson and MacKeith 1983). All these units have a high staff ratio, low numbers of patients, orientation towards treatment rather than custody, a system of parole for patients, and access to secure rooms for emergency use.

Security

All four interim secure units are housed in converted wards in established NHS mental illness hospitals close to population centres as recommended in the DHSS Guidelines (DHSS 1975). The conversions have provided single bedrooms which are lockable at Rainhill Hospital. The Rainhill, Prestwich, and Bethlem Royal interim secure units are permanently locked, each with one secure room. The Lyndhurst Unit has two secure rooms, is locked at night but for the initial three years it was possible for the most part to run this unit perfectly safely as an 'open ward' with most patients on controlled parole, though subsequently the ward has had to be locked to avoid patients slipping unobserved from the ward. The security of the units depends on having a high staff/patient ratio and on the relationships formed by the patients with the staff of the unit, as well as on the physical security of each unit.

The non-physical aspects of security depend upon the skills and attitudes of the staff and the considered selection of patients to avoid admitting those who should properly be treated in special hospitals. Careful observation of patients and effective channels of communication serve to forestall violent situations. Patients are assisted by trying to reduce their feelings of tension and frustration, by giving them considerably more individual attention than is possible on an ordinary ward. Interaction with in-patients is governed by individuals rather than by house rules. There is an effort to avoid undue restriction that breeds its own reaction, and to detect (and intervene at the start of) worrying behaviour from patients who are not persistently dangerous, but who have long periods of relative stability. Different areas within the unit (e.g. the secure rooms) provide varying degrees of security. It is wasteful of resources to provide the same level of security for all patients. Some individuals in the acute stages of a florid illness require intense supervision by 'specialing'. Other patients undergoing essentially rehabilitative treatment require much less intensive supervision and observation. In the last resort, a disruptive patient can be confined in a secure room. In practice this is generally enough but if the patient continues to be too dangerous in the unit, a transfer request to a special hospital is made.

The provision of security in these units is one of the more contentious issues. The Butler Committee thought the term 'medium-secure unit' misleading, as it would be difficult to define what medium security means, and ambiguity of intention would create uncertainties and difficulties for the staff. The Glancy Report stated that the units need not be as secure as the special hospitals, but must be adequately secure for the safe containment of the people they would be intended to accommodate (DHSS 1974a). This indeed appears to be the situation pertaining in the existing interim secure units. As the department stated (DHSS 1975), these units did not have the function of trying to contain the determined absconder or the type of patient who if he escaped would present an immediate and grave threat to the public; nor were they to be expected to take account of the possibility of outside 'rescue attempts'.

Table 6.1   *Comparisons of four interim secure units*

	Knowle	Rainhill	Prestwich	Bethlem Royal
period data collected	Jan. 1977 to Dec. 1980	1976–80	Sept. 1976 to Feb. 1981	Oct. 1980 to Dec. 1981
number of beds	14 (5–9 day-patients on ward also)	14	14	15
minimum staff to patient ratio	1.5:1	1.5:1	1:1	2.3:1
security	3 exits including fire-escapes; only locked at times in first 3 years	permanently doubly locked	permanently doubly locked; check system	permanently doubly locked

	2.7 million Wessex RHA	1 million Mersey RHA	4.1 million North-Western RHA	3.6 million South-East Thames RHA
catchment-area population	2.7 million Wessex RHA	1 million Mersey RHA	4.1 million North-Western RHA	3.6 million South-East Thames RHA
ward policy	little structure; policy of non-confrontation; milieu therapy	a behavioural therapeutic community approach	a highly structured behavioural approach	milieu therapy assessment and treatment to enable return to ordinary psychiatric unit or area clinic, rather than rehabilitation
facilities, occupational therapy, etc.	little on ward; patients participate fully within hospital facilities	little on ward; patients use hospital sports facilities	all facilities and therapy on ward	nearly all facilities on ward

Sources: Knowle – Treasaden and Shepherd 1983; Rainhill – Higgins 1981; Prestwich – Reid, Lea, and Wallace 1982; Bethlem Royal – Gudjonsson and MacKeith 1983.

Staffing

The Knowle, Rainhill, and Bethlem Royal Hospital interim secure units have nursing staff ratios as can be seen from *Table 6.1* above that recommended by the DHSS of 1:1 with 1:4.5 at any one time. The Prestwich interim secure unit has a nursing staff ratio of 1:1 in keeping with the DHSS Guidelines. The Lyndhurst Unit has a rotating three-weekly three-shift system which covers nights. The Rainhill Unit has twelve-hour shifts whilst the Bethlem Royal Hospital has some permanent night staff. The high nursing staff ratio allows nursing staff to visit patients in the community for assessment and follow-up. There is an appropriately mixed-sex nursing staff which reduces tension and creates a warm therapeutic environment more closely mirroring social situations in the community. Nursing staff are employed permanently and exclusively on such units and receive a pay lead (DHSS 1975).

Multi-disciplinary staffing and decision-making have been found to be essential (Higgins 1979; Faulk 1979), which is in keeping with DHSS advice (DHSS 1975). Prior to the acceptance of patients for admission full multi-disciplinary pre-admission staff discussions are held.

Ward policies

All four units to some extent aim to cope with their patients with a milieu-therapy regime. Conventional physical treatments, psychological treatments, and recreational activities as would take place in an ordinary psychiatric ward play a similar role in these units. As the average length of stay is greater than for the general psychiatric admission, considerable time is devoted to genuine rehabilitation programmes.

Table 6.2 shows the number of patients, their sex and age, the total number of admissions and readmissions and the mean length of stay in each of the four interim secure units. In terms of the admission rate and average length of stay, the Knowle and Bethlem Royal interim secure units have outperformed the units at Rainhill and Prestwich Hospital. However, thirty-two of the eighty-seven subjects admitted to the Lyndhurst Unit (37 per cent) during its first four years' work were subsequently readmitted within that period.

Length of stay

A point of central concern is the length of time patients should stay in secure units. While not advocating an absolute limit on length of stay

Table 6.2 *Ward policies in four interim secure units*

	Knowle	Rainbill	Prestwich	Bethlem Royal
total no. of first admissions	87 in 4 years	35 in 4 years	48 in 4 years 5 months	23 in 14 months
sex	73 men (84%) 14 women (16%) (no women in first year)	21 men (60%) 14 women (40%)	all male	16 men (70%) 7 women (30%)
total no. of admissions	142 in 4 years	39 in 4 years	48 in 4 years 5 months	23 in 14 months
no. of readmissions	55	4	—	—
mean age on first admission (range in years)	32 (17–55)	30 (17–56)	30.4 (18–64)	34.5 (18–79)
mean length of admission in months (range)	for first admission 5.7 (1 day to 22 months) for all admissions 4.1 months	8 (2 weeks to 3 years 2 months)	12 (5 days to 35 months)	7 (1–13 months)

that would be of general applicability, the Glancy Report stated: 'If no progress is being made after, say, eighteen months, consideration should be given to an alternative placement such as return to prison, admission to a Special Hospital, or return to an ordinary psychiatric hospital' (DHSS 1974a). The Butler Interim Report drew attention to the risk of the accumulation of more or less permanent residents who are not acceptable elsewhere or fit for discharge. The report urged that every effort should be made to prevent the use of the units as permanent accommodation for difficult long-stay patients (Home Office and DHSS 1974).

As can be seen from *Table 6.*2 the mean lengths of stay of patients in the interim secure units are well within the maximum of eighteen months recommended in the Glancy Report, though for isolated patients difficulties have been experienced in all units in their transfer to ordinary NHS mental illness hospitals though in the opinion of the units concerned these patients were fit for such a move. The one-day first admission of a patient to the Lyndhurst Unit was due to an informal patient taking his own discharge.

The Glancy Report assessed the number of female beds required as 15 per cent for a regional secure unit. The subsequent experience in the interim secure units who admitted female patients suggests that in fact the proportion may be greater (40 per cent at Rainhill, 30 per cent at the Bethlem Royal, and 25 per cent at the Lyndhurst Unit for the three years where females were admitted there).

Source of admissions to the interim secure units

One fear arising from the Glancy Report was that regional secure units might mainly accommodate patients currently in local hospitals (Gostin 1978), given that there were ample numbers of 'troublesome' patients in local hospitals to fill the secure beds and that the existence of a regional secure unit might lower the tolerance of ordinary psychiatric hospitals where the demand for secure beds may continuously increase to meet the available supply. The Glancy Report stated: 'this demand would not necessarily be one which could or should be met.' Thus the fear was that special hospitals and prisons may not receive the relief the Butler Committee originally envisaged.

However, as can be seen from *Table 6.3*, which shows the source of referral for first admissions to the respective four interim secure units being considered, these fears have proved unfounded. Indeed it is those referrals originating from courts, remand centres, and

Table 6.3 Source of referral of first admissions to four interim secure units

	Knowle	Rainhill	Prestwich	Bethlem Royal
NHS hospital	23 (26%)	9 (26%)	7 (15%)	7 (30%)
special hospital	15 (17%)	7 (20%)	10 (21%)	7 (30%)
courts remand centres	38 (44%)	12 (34%) ⎱ 15 (43%)	17 (35%) ⎱ 30 (62%)	8 (35%)
prisons		3 (9%) ⎰	13 (27%) ⎰	
probation	8 (9%) ⎱ 11 (13%)		1 (2%)	
other community agencies, out-patients, day-patients	3 (4%) ⎰	4 (11%)		1 (4%)

prisons that are the main single source of referral to these units, with the number of admissions from special hospitals being approximately equal to the number from NHS ordinary psychiatric hospitals. For the Lyndhurst Unit significantly more admissions originated from NHS mental illness hospitals in the first two years of its functioning in 1977 and 1978 than in the years 1979 and 1980. This reflected a significant increase in admissions from special hospitals from the number in the earlier years.

Legal status

The Glancy Report stated that regional secure units could admit formal and informal (if the patient were willing and in need of a secure psychiatric setting) patients; the criteria for admission should not depend on legal or offender status but on behaviour and need for security (DHSS 1974a). As a matter of policy, in view of the units being permanently locked, no patients have been admitted on an informal basis to the Rainhill and Bethlem Royal Hospital interim secure units (for comparison among the four units, see *Table 6.4*). The high number of informal patients, twenty-nine out of eighty-seven (33 per cent), admitted to the Knowle Unit reflected the high number, sixteen out of thirty subjects (52 per cent), who were admitted informally to the Knowle Unit in 1977, a number significantly greater than in later years. Some informal admissions to the Knowle Unit prevented unprofitable police and legal action and long periods of remand in prison. By 1980, however, only one of the sixteen subjects (6 per cent) admitted for the first time in that year was of informal status.

Psychiatric diagnosis

Table 6.5 shows the primary and secondary psychiatric diagnoses of those subjects admitted to the four interim secure units under consideration. All units have predominantly admitted those with a primary diagnosis of functional psychosis, the majority of whom have a diagnosis of some type of schizophrenia. The number of subjects with a primary psychiatric diagnosis of personality disorder reflects the admission of those with a legal diagnosis of psychopathy from special hospitals as a graded move towards discharge to the community or to an NHS open ward as well as those admitted in a crisis with superimposed neurotic depression.

Table 6.4 *Legal status at first admission of subjects admitted to four interim secure units*

	Knowle	Rainhill	Prestwich	Bethlem Royal
informal	29 (33%)	—	3 (6%)	—
condition of probation	6 (7%)	—	1 (2%)	—
condition of bail	—	3 (3%)	3 (6%)	—
under MHA 1959				
s. 25	1 (1%)	1 (3%)	3 (6%)	—
s. 26	10 (11%)	13 (37%)	5 (10%)	8 (35%)
s. 60	14 (16%)	4 (11%)	6 (12%)	5 (22%)
s. 60 with restriction order s. 65	22 (25%)	5 (14%)	21 (44%)	7 (30%)
s. 72	3 (3%)	2 (6%)	4 (8%)	1 (4%)
s. 73	1 (1%)	4 (11%)	3 (6%)	—
s. 72 with restriction order s. 74	1 (1%)	—	—	—
Criminal Procedure Insanity Act, 1964 (unfit to plead)	—	3 (9%)	—	2 (9%)

Table 6.5 Psychiatric diagnoses of subjects admitted to four interim secure units

	Knowle	Rainhill	Prestwich	Bethlem Royal
1° psychiatric diagnoses				
psychoses				
organic psychosis	1 (1%)	2 (6%)	—	—
schizophrenias	42 (48%) (60%)	24 (68%) (80%)	27 (56%) (62%)	13 (57%) (74%)
paranoid psychosis	1 (1%)	—	—	1 (4%)
	$\underline{52}$ $(\underline{60\%})$	$\underline{28}$ $(\underline{80\%})$	$\underline{30}$ $(\underline{62\%})$	$\underline{17}$ $(\underline{74\%})$
manic–depressive psychosis	8 (9%)	2 (6%)	3 (6%)	3 (13%)
personality disorders				
neurosis + personality disorder	8 (9%)	4 (11%)	1 (2%)	—
personality disorder (including psychopathy)	24 (28%)	3 (9%)	17 (35%)	6 (26%)
	$\underline{35}$ $(\underline{40\%})$	$\underline{7}$ $(\underline{20\%})$	$\underline{18}$ $(\underline{37\%})$	$\underline{6}$ $(\underline{26\%})$
sexual deviance	3 (3%)	—	—	—

2° psychiatric diagnoses				
personality disorder (including psychopathy)	32 (37%)	7 (20%)	—	6 (26%)
alcohol-abuse	5 (6%)	—	6 (12%)	1 (4%)
borderline mental handicap	14 (16%)	—	—	—
mild mental handicap	3 (3%)	3 (9%)	5 (10%)	2 (9%)

The Butler Committee (Home Office and DHSS 1975) reviewed much of the hopeful work undertaken, both at home and on the continent, with psychopathic patients, but concluded that these treatment programmes had had little long-term effect. It was therefore recommended that in future the care of the aggressive psychopath should remain the responsibility of the prison service and that the inadequate psychopath should be supervised in the community by the probation and social services. The Butler and Glancy Committees both made it abundantly clear that interim and regional medium-secure units should concentrate on the mentally ill and not accept those with a psychopathic disorder, except where there is very good reason to do so, i.e. a good 'prospect of benefiting from' treatment.

By contrast some writers have urged that it is the highly dangerous offender who presents the greatest case of need (*BMJ* 1973; Scott 1974). The Glancy Report stated that secure-unit accommodation may be required for patients who present severely disruptive behaviour and who may be mentally ill or mildly mentally handicapped and also suffering from mental illness or from psychopathic or severe personality disorder. The Glancy Report indicated however that the proposed units were not intended for very severely mentally handicapped patients who are destructive, highly disruptive, and overactive. (These were excluded because they are unlikely to abscond, if properly supervised; they are vulnerable to manipulation by more intelligent patients; and their needs are very different from those patients whom the authors envisage going into secure units.)

This view is endorsed by the Royal College of Psychiatrists (1980) who considered that such severely mentally handicapped patients should as in the past remain in the care of mental handicap hospitals, some of which should be provided with special intensive care units for the care of this difficult group. In keeping with the above the interim secure units have not admitted the severely mentally handicapped. Indeed they have also tended to avoid admitting those with any degree of mental handicap.

Behaviour problems leading to admission to the interim secure units

The criteria for admission of patients to interim and regional secure units should be seen, according to the Royal College of Psychiatrists (1980), in behavioural terms, rather than rigidly depending on psychiatric diagnosis or legal classification. Such patients would be those identified as creating continual difficulty in management and with a potential to respond to the secure treatment facilities offered by the unit, an essential element in determining suitability for admission.

The Glancy Report admitted that 'there is a very real difficulty in defining those who should be admitted to the secure unit' – not the 'elderly wanderer', 'the severely mentally handicapped' or 'the patient difficult only in an acute phase of illness' (DHSS 1974a).

Table 6.6 shows the main behaviour problems leading to first admission to the Knowle, Rainhill, and the Bethlem Royal interim secure units, the exact behaviour not being specified by the Prestwich Unit. Personal violence predominates. Five of the nine subjects admitted to the Rainhill Unit who had committed homicide were female, having killed their children, and may not necessarily represent, in view of the low risk of repetition of such family killings, a high security risk.

However, patients' behaviour problems are multiple and the mean number of behaviour problems for each first Lyndhurst Unit admission was 5.1 (range 1 to 16). The commonest behaviour problems within six months of first Lyndhurst admission were (1) refusing treatment (53 per cent); (2) threats of violence (37 per cent); and (3) violence involving moderate harm (34 per cent). These three behaviour problems combined were the commonest combination of behaviour problems leading to first Lyndhurst admission. However, those subjects with a diagnosis of personality disorder had a third-equal commonest behaviour problem of minor offences (34 per cent). Subjects admitted from special hospitals often had a past history of serious violence but had not exhibited such behaviour for some time before transfer to the Knowle and other units.

Comparison of past criminal, institutional, and employment histories of subjects admitted to the interim secure units at Prestwich Hospital and the Lyndhurst Unit at Knowle Hospital is shown in *Tables 6.7* and *6.8*. *Table 6.7* shows that subjects admitted to the Lyndhurst Unit were less likely to have a past history of convictions involving actual personal violence but more likely to have a history of all other types of convictions.

Actual discharge location from first interim secure unit admissions

Most patients admitted to the interim secure units at Rainhill, Prestwich, and Bethlem Royal Hospitals have been discharged to

Table 6.6 *Main behaviour problems leading to first interim secure unit admission to three interim secure units*

	Knowle	Rainhill	Bethlem Royal
personal violence			
serious harm, e.g. GBH, murder/att. murder	8 (9%)	10 (29%)	8 (35%)
moderate harm, e.g. ABH, wounding, assault	30 (34%)	11 (31%)	10 (43%)
threats of violence	20 (23%)	4 (11%)	1 (4%)
	58 (67%)	25 (71%)	19 (82%)
sexual			
rape/att. rape	1 (1%)	—	—
moderate harm, e.g. indecent assault	2 (2%)	1 (3%)	2 (9%)
threats of sexual harm with past history of indecent assault	6 (7%)	—	—
	9 (10%)		
other			
fire-raising/arson	12 (14%)	5 (14%)	2 (9%)
actual destructive behaviour	2 (2%)	—	—
minor offences	—	2 (6%)	—
harm to self (life-endangering)	6 (7%)	1 (3%)	—

Table 6.7   *Comparison of past criminal histories of subjects admitted to the Lyndhurst and Prestwich interim secure units*

	Lyndhurst (N = 87) (73 men, 14 women)	Prestwich (N = 48) (48 men)
convictions pre-admission		
none	8 (9%)	5 (10%)
1	5 (6%)	9 (19%)
2–6	30 (34%)	18 (37%)
more than 6	44 (51%)	16 (33%)
types of convictions		
personal violence		
involving serious harm, e.g. murder, attempted murder, GBH	11 (13%)	8 (17%)
involving moderate harm, e.g. ABH, wounding, assault	28 (32%)	23 (48%)
involving threats of violence	16 (18%)	4 (8%)
sexual	23 (26%)	8 (17%)
acquisitive		
burglary	36 (41%)	—
robbery	5 (6%)	—
theft	52 (60%)	23 (48%)
fraud and forgery	10 (11%)	4 (8%)
other		
arson	15 (17%)	6 (12%)
other criminal damage	32 (37%)	7 (15%)
other offences	33 (38%)	12 (25%)

NHS open psychiatric hospitals, while most of the patients admitted to the Lyndhurst Interim Secure Unit at Knowle Hospital (77 per cent) were discharged to the community in spite of having comparable behaviour problems pre-admission and shorter first admissions. Associated with this policy at the Lyndhurst Unit as already stated was a higher readmission rate. The actual discharge locations are shown in *Table 6.9*.

Follow-up

The account so far has been largely a descriptive one of how four interim secure units work and how their current practice is in

Table 6.8   *Comparison of past institutional and employment histories of subjects admitted to the Lyndhurst and Prestwich interim secure units*

	Lyndhurst (N = 87)	Prestwich (N = 48)
institutional history		
none	—	8 (17%)
institutional history before age 16 years	34 (39%)	13 (27%)
total over 5 years in length	33 (38%)	10 (21%)
employment record pre-admission in regular employment	3 (3%) (2 full-time 1 part-time)	10 (21%)
interrupted employment	15 (17%)	8 (17%)
usually unemployed	56 (64%)	29 (60%)
never worked	13 (15%)	—
student	—	1 (2%)

Table 6.9   *Actual location of subjects at discharge from first admission to three interim secure units*

	Knowle	Rainhill	Bethlem Royal
	(N = 86)	(N = 25)	(N = 13)
community	66 (77%)	8 (32%)	2 (15%)
NHS psychiatric hospital	16 (19%)	11 (44%)	10 (77%)
special hospital	1 (1%)	1 (4%)	—
another ISU	—	—	1 (8%)
prison	3 (3%)	5 (20%)	—

keeping with that recommended by the Butler and Glancy Reports. These descriptions do not attempt to evaluate the therapeutic effectiveness of the units. To do this it is necessary to follow up those discharged, charting their post-discharge histories and comparing their pre- and post-admission histories in terms of clinical, behavioural, social, and forensic measures.

Such a follow-up was not described for the Rainhill and Bethlem Royal Hospital interim secure units. However, the description of the functioning of the Prestwich Unit included the location of subjects at a mean twenty-two months post-discharge (range 1–47 months). The differing lengths of time since discharge for the subjects makes it difficult to interpret the results but *Table 6.10* shows a comparison with sixty subjects followed up from the Lyndhurst Unit at two years post-discharge when the majority of subjects continued to remain in the community as at discharge (Treasaden and Shepherd 1983). Of the eighty-seven subjects admitted to the Lyndhurst Unit from 1977 to 1980, sixty (69 per cent) were followed up for two years and seventy-five (86 per cent) for one year post-discharge from their first Lyndhurst admission. Only twelve subjects (14 per cent) had no follow-up (Treasaden and Shepherd 1983), due to not having been in the community for one year by the end of the study.

The proportion of all admissions, including readmissions, where the clinical outcome was improved, increased during successive years since the Lyndhurst Unit opened in 1977, reflecting the experience of the unit leading to better selection of subjects likely to benefit from admission to the secure unit.

Table 6.10 *Location at follow-up of subjects discharged from the Lyndhurst and Prestwich interim secure units*

	Lyndhurst	Prestwich
	At 2 years post-discharge (N = 60)	at mean 22 months post-discharge (range 1–47 months) (N = 39)
community		
home	29 (48%) ⎤	14 (36%) ⎤
hostel	3 (5%) ⎥ 36	5 (13%) ⎥ 20
group home	— ⎥ (60%)	1 (3%) ⎥ (51%)
no fixed abode	4 (7%) ⎦	— ⎦
hospital		
NHS mental illness	9 (15%) ⎤	4 (10%) ⎤
special hospital	4 (7%) ⎥ (15	7 (18%) ⎥
interim secure unit	2 (3%) ⎦ (25%)	⎥ 13
general medical	—	1 ⎥ (3%)
epileptic hospital	—	⎦
prison	9 (15%)	1 (3%)
not known/dead	—	
employed at follow-up	16 (27%)	6 (15%)

The number of subjects exhibiting behaviour problems involving personal violence, sexual behavioural problems, actual destructive behaviour, harm to self (life-endangering), and refusing treatment was significantly less common *during admission* than in the six months pre-admission, showing that the Lyndhurst Unit could manage these patients admitted more successfully than had been achieved in their pre-admission locations.

The number of subjects exhibiting behavioural problems prior to first Lyndhurst admission compared with at *discharge* were significantly reduced for behaviour problems involving personal violence of all types, sexual behavioural problems, actual destructive behaviour, fire-raising, minor offences, alcohol- and drug-related problems, nuisance non-criminal behaviour, harm to self (both life-endangering and not life-endangering), and refusing treatment, although it can be argued that for some at least of these behaviour problems (e.g. sexual, alcohol, and drug-related problems) the opportunities to exhibit these behaviours were not present within the Lyndhurst Unit.

Behaviour problems involving personal violence, sexual behavioural problems, harm to self (not life-endangering), and refusing treatment were all exhibited significantly less in the one year post-discharge than in the six months pre-admission by those subjects who completed one year's follow-up. These behavioural problems were those that had often precipitated first Lyndhurst admission. No significant differences, however, were found for the other behavioural problems, including those that had been significantly reduced at discharge compared to pre-admission. This reflects the falling off of the effect of admission to the Lyndhurst Unit on behavioural problems of subjects post-discharge.

For those who completed the second year's follow-up the number of subjects exhibiting the serious behaviour problems of personal violence, refusing treatment, and harm to self (not life-endangering) remained significantly reduced compared to pre-admission, though the number exhibiting sexual behavioural problems was no longer significantly reduced. The trend for actual destructive behaviour and fire-raising to be reduced post-discharge compared to pre-admission reached significance in the second year of follow-up.

Compared to pre-admission, subjects were less likely to be compulsorily detained in hospital at discharge from their first admission to the Lyndhurst Unit or during the one and two years' follow-up periods. There was also a significant reduction in the number of subjects who were in-patients in a special hospital during the two years post-discharge compared to the two years pre-admission. However, this reflects in part the number of subjects admitted to the Lyndhurst Unit from special hospitals as a graded step towards either an NHS open hospital or discharge to the community. The outcome of psychiatric-hospital admissions of all types were significantly improved for those subjects admitted in the two years post-discharge compared to two years prior to first Lyndhurst Unit admission. A significant reduction in the number of subjects with convictions of personal violence involving moderate harm was found in the one year post-discharge compared to the one year prior to first Lyndhurst Unit admission and with convictions involving criminal damage in the two years post-discharge compared to the two years pre-admission. Subjects who had been convicted of the serious offences of GBH, attempted rape, and arson did not similarly re-offend in the two years post-discharge.

Compared to their pre-admission actual location, subjects were significantly more likely to be discharged home and more likely to be discharged to the community in general. They were also significantly less likely to be discharged to a special hospital and less likely to be discharged to a prison compared to pre-admission actual location, though this largely reflects the source of referral; in particular, in the case of special hospitals, admission to an interim secure unit was merely a graded step back into the community. Compared to pre-admission actual location subjects were still significantly more likely to be at home in the one year post-discharge and more likely to be in the community as well as less likely to be in prison. By two years, however, compared to pre-admission location, subjects were only significantly less likely to be in prison.

There was a significant increase in those in either full-time or part-time employment in the one year post-discharge and in the second year post-discharge compared to pre-admission.

Subjects were significantly more likely to be in receipt of social services care on discharge and during the first year post-discharge compared to pre-admission. By the second year post-discharge, however, there was no significant increase in social services care compared to pre-admission. This fall off in contact in the second year post-discharge mirrors that with contact with members of their family and other behavioural measures during the second year of follow-up and presumably reflects the fact that by this time the effect of admission to the Lyndhurst Unit itself has been counteracted by other environmental factors.

Subjects were more likely to spend more time in the community in the two years post-discharge than in the two years pre-admission. It appears that the Lyndhurst Unit not only discharged more subjects directly to the community compared to other interim secure units but is able to sustain them there by virtue of taking the responsibility of continuing their out-patient and day-patient psychiatric care.

Lyndhurst out-patient care at discharge or Lyndhurst follow-up of any kind during the two years post-discharge also reduced the time in hospital in the two years post-discharge spent by subjects compared to the two years pre-admission.

Subjects were more likely to have less convictions in the two years post-discharge compared to the two years pre-admission, or to continue to have no convictions in either the two years pre- or post-admission. Twenty-three subjects (39 per cent) had fewer convictions, fifteen subjects (25 per cent) no convictions in two years pre- or post-admission, two subjects (3 per cent) had an equal number of convictions in each period, and nineteen subjects (32 per cent) had more convictions in the two years post-discharge.

Subjects were significantly more likely to have more convictions in the two years post-discharge compared to the two years pre-admission, the greater the number of previous sentencing episodes or convictions or prison sentences.

Of the sixty subjects who completed two years' follow-up, only two (3 per cent) did not improve on at least one of the three measures of increased time in the community, reduction of time in hospital, and reduction of number of convictions in the two years post-discharge compared to the two years pre-admission. However, only six (10 per cent) improved on all three of these measures.

Will the regional secure units meet the unmet need for secure psychiatric care?

The four interim secure units described have a current practice in keeping with the recommendations of the Butler and Glancy Reports. A two year post-discharge follow-up study of sixty subjects admitted to the Lyndhurst Unit at Knowle Hospital (Treasaden and Shepherd 1983) indicates that such units can be therapeutically effective in terms of a number of behavioural, clinical, social, and forensic measures. However, these studies do not themselves answer the question of whether interim or full regional secure units will indeed meet the need for secure provision as described in the Interim Butler Report (1974), which describes the units as 'crucial to the greater flexibility in placement needed for mentally abnormal offenders and to the early relief of the prison and special hospitals'.

The estimation of numbers in need of such a medium-secure provision has proved exceeding difficult and unsatisfactory. The Butler Committee, acknowledging the difficulty in estimating numbers, judged that the total number of secure places required was about 2,000; this figure being made up of 1,000 mentioned in the Glancy Report, together with a hidden demand from the prisons and special hospitals amounting to about 900 places.

The Oxford University Department of Psychiatry reported (Gath and Orly 1976) the results of a survey carried out in the Oxford Region (population 2,074,000) in 1975 (which came too late to influence the recommendations of the Butler and Glancy Reports). The six-month survey collected information, from case notes and discussions with referring agents, on 193 possible patients referred for the study by prisons, NHS mental illness and handicap hospitals, special hospitals, and social and the probation services. Forty-one individuals were already in suitable care; 125 required further facilities, which were not currently available. Only twenty-six were considered to need a security unit for the mentally ill, and thirty-seven a secure training unit for the mentally handicapped. The remainder could be placed in various other possible ways, and generally without secure conditions. A principal finding not expected was that there were, in fact, more mentally handicapped or borderline mentally handicapped offenders than mentally ill offenders misplaced in prisons or the community. The authors recommended that two sorts of units were likely to be needed, one for the mentally ill, as recommended by the DHSS and a second separate unit for the mentally handicapped group not properly accounted for in the DHSS recommendations to the regional health authorities. These findings were confirmed by a replication study (Gath 1978).

As part of the evaluation of the Lyndhurst Interim Secure Unit (Treasaden and Shepherd 1983) a survey of the total unmet need for secure psychiatric care in the Wessex Region was carried out, using a modification of the method adopted in the Oxford study by Gath and Orly (1976). The Wessex Region is the catchment area of the Lyndhurst Unit at Knowle Hospital, Fareham, Hampshire. All psychiatric hospitals, including those for the mentally handicapped within the region, special hospitals, community physicians, the Prison Medical Service, probation and social services dealing with subjects from the Wessex Region, were asked to name individuals in their care on our census date of 30 June, 1980, in need of additional secure psychiatric facilities, including medium-secure units.

A total of 228 notifications was received of 210 subjects felt to be in need of additional secure psychiatric facilities on the prevalence study census day of 30 June, 1980. Seventeen subjects were notified by two care agencies and one by three. Twenty-nine subjects (14 per cent) were notified by mental illness hospitals, seventy-six (36 per cent) by mental handicap hospitals, fifty-four (26 per cent) by special hospitals, eighteen (9 per cent) from Broadmoor, twenty-seven (13 per cent) from Rampton, and nine (4 per cent) from Moss Side), eleven (5 per cent) from prison (two (1 per cent) were on remand), thirteen (6 per cent) by area social services, twenty-seven (13 per cent) by hospital social services, seventeen (8 per cent) by probation services, and one by a community physician. The subjects comprised 131 males (62 per cent) and 79 females (38 per cent). Fifty per cent of those notified by mental handicap hospitals were women, a proportion significantly greater than for other sources of notification. One hundred and twenty-nine subjects (61 per cent) had a mental handicap diagnosis. Twenty-eight subjects (18 per cent) were of borderline mental handicap and thirty-nine subjects (19 per cent) of mild mental handicap. However, fifty-two subjects (25 per cent) were of moderate, severe, or profound mental handicap and therefore not suitable for a regional secure unit provision (DHSS 1974a). The mean length of hospital stay was ten years, five months (SD = nine years, three months). All 54 subjects notified by the special hospitals were compulsorily detained on the census day, compared to only 23 of the remaining 156 subjects (15 per cent).

Subjects were notified due to a combination of behaviour problems and a lack of suitable psychiatric facilities, including lack of staff, in which they could be managed. The mean number of behaviour problems exhibited by subjects notified was 4.7.

The most frequent behaviour problems exhibited in the six months pre-census-date by those notified were personal violence involving moderate harm (54 per cent), threats of violence (32 per cent), nuisance non-criminal behaviour (32 per cent), actual destructive behaviour (28 per cent), and refusing treatment (25 per cent). One hundred and ninety-five subjects (93 per cent) had shown personal violence at some stage in the past and eighty-four subjects (40 per cent) within two years of the census date. Eighty-two subjects (39 per cent) had exhibited sexual behaviour problems in the past and fifty-six subjects (27 per cent) within two years of the census date.

Repeated personal violence involving moderate harm and harm to self (not life-endangering) were significantly associated with notification by a mental handicap hospital. Sixty-seven of the mental handicap notifications (88 per cent) had exhibited personal violence involving moderate harm while twenty-one subjects (28 per cent) had shown the behaviour problem of harm to self (not life-endangering). The commonest behaviour problem exhibited by mental illness hospital notifications (59 per cent of subjects) was isolated personal violence involving moderate harm. The commonest behaviour problems shown by special hospital notifications were threats or risk of violence (in twenty-four out of fifty-four subjects (44 per cent)) and nuisance non-criminal behaviour (in thirty-five out of fifty-four subjects (65 per cent)). Alcohol- and drug-abuse were significantly more common in those notified by the probation service. It was the commonest problem (43 per cent) of those so notified. The commonest behaviour problem exhibited by both area and hospital social services notifications was nuisance non-criminal behaviour, which was shown in twenty-one of the forty subjects (54 per cent), while refusing treatment was the commonest behaviour problem of those notified by penal establishments (in seven out of eleven subjects (64 per cent)).

One hundred and six of these subjects (50 per cent) had had at least one conviction (mean = 9.9 convictions). Sixty-four per cent of those notified by mental illness hospitals, 18 per cent of those notified by mental handicap hospitals, 77 per cent of those notified by special hospitals, 50 per cent of those notified by area social services, 13 per cent of those notified by hospital social services, and all those notified by penal establishments and the probation services had a past history of convictions. Thirty-six of those notified (17 per cent) had convictions in the two years pre-census-day.

Different notifying agents gave different reasons why the subjects they notified were not manageable in ordinary psychiatric hospitals. The reasons given were usually multiple but always included the characteristics of the subjects notified. Mental Illness and Mental Handicap Hospitals were significantly more likely to give insufficient nursing staff as a reason for the subjects they notified not being suitable for their hospitals. Special hospitals gave the lack of security in ordinary psychiatric hospitals and their staff's refusal to accept ex-special-hospital patients significantly more often as the reason why those they notified were not suitable for ordinary hospitals.

Penal establishments were significantly more likely to cite a disputed psychiatric diagnosis or amenability to treatment together with the lack of security as a reason why those they notified were not acceptable in ordinary psychiatric hospitals. A disputed psychiatric diagnosis or amenability to treatment was also given as a reason significantly more often by the probation service and area social services. Area social services were also more likely to give staff refusal as a reason. Hospital social services were significantly more likely to cite the characteristics alone of those they notified as making them unsuitable for ordinary psychiatric hospitals.

In the opinion of their notifying agents eighty-two of those notified (39 per cent) were considered to be best placed in a regional secure unit but only thirty-eight of them (46 per cent) for periods of less than eighteen months, the length of stay suggested by the Glancy Report.

In the light of the considerable detailed information obtained from the case notes of the 210 subjects notified and the views of their notifying agents, each subject was allocated by the research workers to one of ten categories/treatment facilities including regional secure units.

The survey suggested that the Lyndhurst Interim Secure Unit had made a significant contribution to the group who were of normal intelligence, described in the Glancy Report as suitable for a regional secure unit. Only ten suitable cases in this group were identified on our census date as requiring a *regional secure unit for the mentally disordered of normal intelligence*. We also identified a further thirteen subjects on our census date of similar characteristics and treatment prospects but of borderline or mild mental handicap whom we felt would best be placed in a *regional secure training unit for the mentally handicapped*. The Lyndhurst Unit has tried to avoid admitting individuals with mild mental handicap, though they are a group which the Glancy and Butler Reports felt were suitable for a regional secure unit. This, therefore, represents one area of unmet need for secure psychiatric care within the region. The plan to double the size of the Lyndhurst Unit will, therefore, probably meet the unmet need we identified for regional secure provision both for those of normal intelligence and for those of borderline or mild mental handicap. This is in spite of the fact that the Lyndhurst Unit had only fourteen beds for a catchment area of 2.7 million, approximately five beds per million population, and on its expansion it will have approximately ten beds per million population. This compares with the Butler Report recommendation of forty beds per million and the Glancy Report's twenty beds per million.

However, an area of great need in the Wessex Region was for an *intensive nursing care service for the moderate to profoundly mentally handicapped*. Forty-four such cases were identified in our survey as requiring intensive nursing care with a requisite high number of nurses with the required skills, rather than physical security, though they might be managed more readily within a secure perimeter. This group was excluded from regional secure units by the Glancy Report and includes those who are aggressive and destructive in hospital and who require long-term care.

Of the forty-nine subjects allocated to the category of NHS mental illness hospital, thirty cases were chronically mentally ill long-stay patients who would be suitably placed in this facility if extra staff and/or facilities, such as secure rooms and lockable wards, were available in their own hospital as were available in other better-provided NHS hospitals within the region. This, therefore, represents another area of great need for secure psychiatric facilities within the Wessex Region. Regional secure units will do little to improve the resources for the management and care of such patients (Gostin 1978).

The remainder of notifications were placed into the remaining six categories. Included among those not considered suitable for psychiatric hospital placement were a sizeable group of those with personality disorder, with or without borderline or mild mental retardation, who are often referred for treatment by courts and the social services but for whom psychiatry has little to offer. The disposal of notified subjects by research criteria are shown in *Table 6.11*.

Conclusion

The Lyndhurst Interim Secure Unit has made a significant contribution to those in Wessex who meet the characteristics of the Glancy Report, require regional secure provision, and are of normal intelligence. In terms of the number of admissions to the unit during its first four years work (1977–80), the average length of stay of patients, and the discharge rate to the community, the unit has out-performed other interim secure units in England.

A sustained improvement in behaviour measures, including those of personal violence, refusing treatment, harm to self (not life-endangering), actual destructive behaviour, and fire-raising, was

Table 6.11   *Disposal of notified subjects by research criteria*

	no. of patients
RSU for the mentally disordered of normal intelligence	10
regional secure training unit for the mentally handicapped	13
special hospital	32
mental illness hospital (includes 30 chronic long-stay patients)	49
mental handicap hospital	15
intensive care unit for the moderate to profoundly mentally handicapped	44
sheltered accommodation	10
community support	23
penal establishment	7
law to take course	7
total	210

maintained two years after discharge from first Lyndhurst Unit admission by those who completed that length of follow-up. Compared to pre-admission, the improvement in other behavioural and social measures, including contact with members of the family and social services, was significantly improved during the first year post-discharge from the Lyndhurst Unit but not during the second year of follow-up, reflecting that by this time the effect of admission to the Lyndhurst Unit itself had been counteracted by other factors. Spending more time in the community and less time in hospital in the two years post-discharge, compared to the two years pre-admission, was significantly associated with the Lyndhurst Unit taking the responsibility for continuing their out-patient or day-patient psychiatric care, a policy out of keeping with most other established interim secure units.

In spite of the fact that the Lyndhurst Unit had fourteen beds for a catchment area of 2.7 million (approximately five beds per million) it had largely met the region's need for regional secure provision for those of normal intelligence, as evidenced by the prevalence study of unmet need for secure psychiatric facilities within the region, which identified only ten suitable cases of whom eight were admitted to the unit during the following year. The Butler Report's recommendation for forty regional secure unit places per million population and the Glancy Report's recommendation of twenty places per million would therefore appear to be excessive for the Wessex Region, and probably nationally, assuming the Wessex Region is not atypical.

The unmet need we identified for a similar regional secure provision of the size of the current Lyndhurst Interim Secure Unit for those of mild mental handicap would be likely to be met by the region's proposals for a full regional secure unit double the size of the current fourteen-bedded interim unit. However, there is an area of great need for an intensive nursing care service for the moderate to profound mentally handicapped and for improved staff and facilities, such as secure rooms and lockable wards, for the chronic mentally ill in the region's NHS mental illness hospitals. From the evidence provided by the type of subject notified as in need of regional secure unit provision in the prevalence study, there remains a need for an improvement in the understanding of the functions of a regional secure unit, especially in terms of admission criteria, including both the prospect of a subject admitted responding to secure psychiatric treatment within eighteen months and the exclusion of aggressive psychopaths and the severely mentally handicapped.

There is also a real problem in the placement of mentally disordered subjects who require hospital treatment in conditions of more security than ordinary NHS psychiatric hospitals, for a longer duration than the recommended maximum eighteen months of admission to an interim/regional secure unit, yet are also excluded from admission to the special hospitals as they do not represent an immediate grave danger to the public if they were to abscond from hospital. Indeed the limited facilities and size of both interim and regional secure units compared to the special hospitals makes prolonged admission of over eighteen months to the units unacceptable in terms of meaningful psychiatric rehabilitation and the quality of life for those so admitted.

It is as yet unclear how far changes introduced in the Mental Health Act 1983, such as orders to remand subjects to hospital for a report and for treatment (ss 35 and 36) and interim hospital orders (s. 38), will affect the practice of and demand for places in regional secure units in the future. Also problems are already evident in recruiting adequate numbers of staff, especially nursing staff, to interim and regional secure units, and a number of regions, starved of cash for all medical services, are attempting to reduce their share of revenue allocation, in addition to that provided centrally by the DHSS, putting the security and whole philosophy of the units at risk. Not to finance adequately regional secure units, even if this means continued financial discrimination in their favour at the expense of other medical services, would be to risk the repetition of circumstances that have led to inquiries into psychiatric hospitals over recent years, including that into Rampton Hospital in 1980.

References

Bluglass, R. (1978) Regional Secure Units and Interim Security for Psychiatric Patients. *British Medical Journal* 1: 489–93.

BMJ (1973) Editorial: Dangerous patients. *British Medical Journal* 1: 247.

DHSS (1974a) Revised Report of the Working Party on Security in N.H.S. Psychiatric Hospitals (The Glancy Report). London: DHSS.

—— (1974b) Health Service Circular. Security in N.H.S. Hospitals for the Mentally Ill and the Mentally Handicapped (HSC(15)61). London.

—— (1975) *Regional Secure Unit: Design Guidelines*. London: DHSS.

—— (1980) *Report of the Review of Rampton Hospital* (The Boynton Report). London: HMSO.

Faulk, M. (1979) The Lyndhurst Unit at Knowle Hospital, Fareham. *Bulletin of the Royal College of Psychiatrists* 3(3): 44–6.

Gath, D. (1978) *Secure Psychiatric Facilities in the Oxford Region*. Oxford: Oxford Regional Health Authority.

Gath, D. and Orly, J. (1976) *Survey of the Need for Secure Psychiatric Facilities in the Oxford Region*. Oxford: Oxford Regional Health Authority.

Gostin, L. O. (1978) *A Human Condition*. Vol. 2: *The Law Relating to Mentally Abnormal Offenders*. London: MIND.

Gudjonsson, G. H. and MacKeith, J. A. C. (1983) A Regional Interim Secure Unit at the Bethlem Royal Hospital: The First Fourteen Months. *Medicine, Science and The Law* 23(3): 209–19.

Gunn, J. (1977) Management of the Mentally Abnormal Offender: Integrated or Parallel. *Proceedings of the Royal Society of Medicine* 70: 877–80.

Higgins, J. (1979) Rainford Ward, Rainhill Hospital, Merseyside. *Bulletin of the Royal College of Psychiatrists* 3(3): 44–6.

—— (1981) Four Years' Experience of an Interim Secure Unit. *British Medical Journal* 282: 889–93.

Home Office and DHSS (1974) *Interim Report of the Committee on Mentally Abnormal Offenders*. Cmnd 5698. London: HMSO.

—— (1975) *Report of the Committee on Mentally Abnormal Offenders* (The Butler Report). Cmnd 6244. London: HMSO.

Knesper, D. J. (1978) Psychiatric Manpower for State Mental Hospitals – A Continuing Dilemma. *Archives of General Psychiatry* 35: 19.

Ministry of Health (1961) *Special Hospitals: Report of a Working Party*. London: HMSO.

Reid, A., Lea, J., and Wallace, D. (1982) Rehabilitation on Elton Ward, an Interim Secure Unit: A Description of the Unit After Four and a Half Years. *Nursing Times* 78: 20–32.

Royal College of Psychiatrists (1980) *Secure Facilities for Psychiatric Patients – A Comprehensive Policy.* London: Royal College of Psychiatrists.

Scott, P. D. (1974) Solutions to the Problems of the Dangerous Offender. *British Medical Journal* 4: 640–41.

Snowden, P. R. (1983) The Regional Secure Units Programme: A Personal Appraisal. *Bulletin of the Royal College of Psychiatrists* 7(8): 38–40.

Treasaden, I. H. and Shepherd, D. (1983) Evaluation of the Lyndhurst Interim Secure Unit, Knowle Hospital. Unpublished DHSS-funded study.

Part III The Law

7 Mentally disordered offenders and the sentencing process[1]

Andrew Ashworth and Larry Gostin

In the Mental Health (Amendment) Act 1982 Parliament made several changes to the powers of the courts when dealing with mentally disordered offenders, and the provisions have now been consolidated in the Mental Health Act 1983.[2] The aim of this article is to assess the implications of the new legislation for the practices and policies of the courts when dealing with mentally disordered offenders. After outlining the amended definition of mental disorder, we examine in turn each of the orders specifically provided for mentally disordered offenders, and conclude by considering how courts might choose the most appropriate measure in a particular case.

Mental disorder

The foundation upon which mental health legislation is based is the statutory definition of mental disorder and the four specific categories of mental disorder. A court cannot make a hospital or a guardianship order unless the offender is suffering from one of the specific disorders, and a patient (even if subject to a restriction order) must be discharged once he is no longer suffering from mental disorder (*Kynaston* v. *Secretary of State for the Home Department and Secretary of State for Social Services*).[3]

Mental disorder is a generic term defined in the Mental Health Act 1983 as 'mental illness, arrested or incomplete development of mind, psychopathic disorder and any other disorder or disability of mind' (s. 1(2)). The Act stipulates that a person may not be classified as mentally disordered 'by reason only of promiscuity or other immoral conduct, sexual deviancy or dependency on alcohol or drugs' (s. 1(3)). Before any order can be made under Part III the person must be suffering from one of the specific forms of mental disorder – mental illness, severe mental impairment, mental impairment, and psychopathic disorder. It is helpful to divide the four categories into major disorders (mental illness and severe mental impairment) and minor disorders (mental impairment and psychopathic disorder); there are certain orders (e.g. remand to hospital for treatment (s. 36) or removal to hospital for unsentenced prisoners (s. 48)) which can be made only in respect of those suffering from one of the major forms of mental disorder.

Mental illness is the only specific category of mental disorder which is not defined in the Act. Several attempts to define the term have been made, notably by the Butler Committee (1975: paras 1.13, 18.35, app. 10) and by the DHSS (1976: app. II), but these were thought to be overly restrictive and were not adopted in the Act. In the absence of any statutory definition of mental illness much will depend upon medical opinion, which should be well founded upon behavioural evidence and adequate clinical assessment. Article 5(1)(e) of the European Convention of Human Rights (which allows detention of persons of unsound mind) is relevant only to the extent that it places discernible limitations on the kind of mental disorder that can justify confinement under international standards. The European Court in *Winterwerp* said 'unsoundness of mind' would not include persons only because their 'views or behaviour deviate from the norms prevailing in a particular society'. Any classification must be based upon objective medical expertise. (See also Gostin 1982.) Lord Justice Lawton's view that mental illness is what the ordinary sensible person would term 'mad' is surely unacceptable; 'mental illness' was envisaged as a serious form of mental disorder and it could not be dependent upon any common person's misinformed view of behaviour which is perhaps only eccentric or anti-social (*W. v. L.*; see also Hoggett 1983: 179).

Severe mental impairment is defined as 'a state of arrested or incomplete development of mind which includes severe impairment of intelligence and social functioning and is associated with aggressive or seriously irresponsible conduct'. The term *mental impairment* is defined in exactly the same way, except that it encompasses 'significant' (as opposed to 'severe') impairment of intelligence and social functioning (s. 1(2)). The legal difference between 'severe' and 'significant' is by no means clear, reflecting only a subtle difference in emphasis. Despite the difficulty in distinguishing between the two classifications, there are real differences in the consequences of adopting one rather than the other; mental impairment, for example, is a minor disorder requiring a showing of treatability while severe mental impairment is a major disorder which has no such requirement.

The term subnormality, which was used in the 1959 Act, has been completely replaced by mental impairment in the 1983 Act. The difference between the two terms is of interest. First, 'susceptibility to treatment' was part of the definition of subnormality in the 1959 Act. This concept is not in the *definition* of mental impairment; instead, an explicit 'treatability' requirement has been placed in the *criteria* for making a hospital order. Second, a person cannot be classified as suffering from mental impairment unless there is an association with abnormally aggressive or seriously irresponsible conduct.

'Mental handicap' remains within the scope of the Act, because the general definition of mental disorder includes those who are suffering from 'arrested or incomplete development of mind'. The effect of the new terminology is that mentally handicapped people can no longer be subject to long-term compulsory admission or to an order under Part III of the Act unless their conduct is associated with abnormally aggressive or seriously irresponsible conduct. However, they will continue to be included within the Mental Health Act and other legislation which employs the definition of mental disorder – for example, they can be compulsorily admitted for up to twenty-eight days' assessment (s. 2) or for up to seventy-two hours for emergency assessment (s. 4). They may also be subject to the jurisdiction of the Court of Protection.

Careful examination shows that the definition of 'mental impairment' in the Act constitutes an amalgamation of the previous definitions in the 1959 Act of subnormality and psychopathic disorder; there is a stigma which could arise in future from a confusion between these two conditions. As the definition of mental impairment suggests a rather static unremediable condition which has a connection with undesirable conduct, the term brings with it the danger of prejudice, alienation, and rejection.

Psychopathic disorder means 'a persistent disorder or disability of mind (whether or not including significant impairment of intelligence) which results in abnormally aggressive or severely irresponsible conduct' (s. 1(2)). The statutory definition can be distinguished from mental impairment only in that the Act expressly provides that the conduct must be 'persistent', and it must 'result from' rather than be 'associated with' the condition; the latter criterion suggests that causality between the condition and the conduct must be stronger in the case of psychopathic disorder. The three disorders actually defined in the Act are remarkably similar in their scope in that they all refer to 'abnormally aggressive or seriously irresponsible conduct' and can also include 'impairment of intelligence'. They appear to be tautological in that they infer a disease from anti-social behaviour, while purporting to explain the behaviour by a disease (see Wootton 1960).

There is no guidance as to what behaviour is 'abnormally aggressive or seriously irresponsible', or whether the behaviour must be likely to be repeated. The Act suggests only that the classification of severe mental impairment, mental impairment, or psychopathic disorder must be based upon evidence of *conduct* which significantly deviates from social norms; further, the conduct must be currently connected in some way with a person's mental condition. These are rather vague standards upon which to decide whether a person should be confined in a mental hospital as they fall short of insisting that the conduct should be dangerous (see Walker and McCabe 1973: 218–20).

Arguably, the requirement to show a connection with 'abnormally aggressive or seriously irresponsible behaviour' would not affect a court's sentencing powers because in any case where the person has committed an offence there is aggressive or irresponsible conduct. However, the definitions suggest some current association with such behaviour. In many cases the mentally disordered person commits an offence from quite normal motives such as hunger, jealousy, anger, or greed. It may be difficult to demonstrate that there is any particular relationship between the person's mental condition and a pattern of behaviour. Further, the question could be asked whether an isolated offence, without additional medical or social evidence, gives grounds by itself for showing a connection with aggressive or irresponsible behaviour. Courts should require doctors who give evidence to address themselves fully to the question of whether the offender meets the criterion for mental impairmant or psychopathic disorder under the Act.

Hospital orders

CRITERIA

The Crown Court can make a hospital order in any case where a person is convicted of an offence punishable with imprisonment unless the sentence is fixed by law; the magistrates' court can make an order if the person is convicted of an offence[4] punishable on summary conviction with imprisonment. The court must first be satisfied, on written or oral evidence of two doctors (one of whom is approved under s. 12), that the offender is suffering from one of the four specific forms of mental disorder of a nature or degree which makes it appropriate for him to be detained for medical treatment. In the case of the minor disorders (mental impairment and psychopathic disorder) the person must satisfy the 'treatability criterion'. The court must also be of the opinion, having regard to all the circumstances, that a hospital order is the *most* suitable method of disposing of the case. This suggests, *inter alia*, that if the same objective of providing treatment for the patient can be achieved by a non-custodial order, this should be preferred to a hospital order if there is no significant risk to the public.

The 'treatability' criterion

The Act introduces a 'treatability' test which must be applied by the court before making a hospital order in respect of an offender suffering from psychopathic disorder or mental impairment. In such cases, medical treatment must be 'likely to alleviate or prevent a deterioration of his condition'. It is conceivable that the introduction of an explicit treatability criterion may limit the powers of the court to make a hospital order. The court must find it is *likely* that treatment will effect some change in the offender's mental condition – in the sense either that the condition can be cured or remedied or that it can be prevented from becoming worse. This would preclude purely custodial confinement even with a humane intention (e.g. for asylum or protection against exploitation). The wide definition of 'medical treatment' must be referred to: it 'includes nursing, and also includes care, habilation, and rehabilitation under medical supervision'. It is suggested that if the patient is simply going to receive medical treatment (e.g. nursing care) this does not necessarily mean he is 'treatable'. The treatment (whether medical treatment, nursing care or otherwise) must be shown to be able to effect a change in the patient's symptomology or condition in the way contemplated by the statute. (But see construction suggested by DHSS 1983: para. 19.)

The new treatability test is more likely to affect sentencing practice than the concept of 'requires or is susceptible to treatment' under the 1959 Act. 'Requires' suggested that the person could benefit from, for example, nursing care, but there did not have to be any 'cure' (in the sense of perceivably altered behaviour or affect) or prevention of deterioration of the person's condition.

The result of the 'treatability' test is that these people and others may well be sent to prison or youth custody. For those who are considered treatable, prison is not merely inappropriate but cruel (May Committee 1979: para. 3.36). On the other hand, it seems wrong that those who are *not* considered treatable should be subject to a hospital order – principally because it is illogical and unjust that their release should depend on treatment criteria when they are considered untreatable, and also because they are occupying scarce specialist facilities. But since they do fall within the statutory definition of 'mental disorder', and this applies particularly to those suffering from 'psychopathic disorder', the prisons should provide some special facilities for them. While the Health Service bears the responsibility for ensuring that sufficient hospital places are available for mentally disordered offenders who are considered treatable, the prison department has a duty to deal sympathetically and constructively with those who cannot benefit from treatment who are committed to its establishments (cf. Ashworth and Shapland 1980).

There is no 'treatability' test to apply before making a hospital order in respect of an offender suffering from mental illness or severe mental impairment. However, such a patient will be discharged at the end of a period of detention (e.g. after six months from the making of the order) unless the responsible medical officer states that the offender's condition is treatable or that, if discharged, he is unlikely to be able to care for himself, to obtain the care he needs, or to guard against serious exploitation (s. 20(4)). This 'viability' criterion at the time of renewal brings its own conceptual difficulties. Since the health and social services have a duty to provide after-care for patients discharged from hospital orders (s. 117), do not such patients have a right to the care they need? Further, if a patient is untreatable and there is no expectation of future therapeutic benefit in hospital, should possible exploitation in the community be a sufficient justification for prolonged detention in hospital under Part III of the Act?

Consent of the receiving hospital

Before making a hospital order the court must be satisfied, on the evidence of the doctor who would be in charge of the treatment of the patient or of another representative of the managers, that arrangements have been made for the person's admission to hospital (s. 37(4)). The hospital managers have the powers to make a bed available in a hospital. The managers are the Secretary of State for Social Services in relation to the special hospitals; the district health authority in relation to local NHS hospitals; and the person(s) registered in relation to a mental nursing home (s. 45(1)).

Judges have expressed considerable frustration at the difficulties of finding a hospital bed for mentally disordered offenders (e.g. Scarman LJ in *McFarlane* and McCullough J in *Gordon*). Section 39 was designed to provide courts with every possible assistance to overcome these difficulties, but ultimate discretion still rests with the managers to refuse admission to hospital. Section 39 allows a court which is minded to make a hospital order or an interim hospital order to request the regional health authority (or, in Wales, the Secretary of State for Wales) to furnish information about hospitals where arrangements could be made for admission of the offender. The RHA cannot avoid responsibility, because the court is empowered to request information from *any* appropriate RHA and the information to be given could relate to *any* region.

In *Harding* Lawton LJ said that 'anyone who obstructed the execution of [a hospital] order or procured others to obstruction might be guilty of contempt of court'. However the making of satisfactory arrangements for the offender's admission to hospital is a *condition precedent* to making a hospital order. Thus, failure of the managers to make a bed available could not obstruct the execution of the order. It is, however, conceivable that, once the managers make arrangements for admission and a hospital order is duly made, the unlawful obstruction of that order could be contempt.

HOSPITAL ORDER WITHOUT RECORDING A CONVICTION

The magistrates' court has the power to make a hospital order without recording a conviction. The person must be suffering from a major form of mental disorder and the court must be satisfied that he did the act or made the omission charged (s. 37(3)). The question arises whether the magistrates' court must conduct a 'trial' before making a hospital order without recording a conviction; if the court does not hear evidence it would not be possible for them to satisfy themselves that the person did the act or made the omission charged.

In *R.* v. *Lincoln (Kesteven) Justices, ex parte O'Connor* (see Wasik 1983), the defendant (an informal psychiatric patient) could not consent to a summary trial as required by the Magistrates' Court Act 1980 (see ss 18–20). The magistrates considered that they were not empowered to proceed to a trial and that they were bound to commit him to the Crown Court for the determination of the issue of fitness to plead. Lord Lane CJ held that the magistrates' court did have the power to make a hospital order without recording a conviction and that no trial was called for. The Divisional Court was acting under the humane supposition that it was preferable to make a hospital order; this would avoid the cumbersome procedure for committing the case for trial to the Crown Court and the spectre of a restriction order being made following a finding of disability. However humane such a course of action may be, the decision appears to be contrary both to the express language of the Mental Health Act, which requires the court to be satisfied that the defendant committed the act or omission charged, and to the clear language of the Magistrates' Court Act that no trial of an 'either-way' offence can proceed without the consent of the accused. The power of the magistrates' court under section 37(3) was not intended to be a substitute for a finding of unfitness. The harsh consequences for the accused (i.e. a restriction order) could be dealt with by giving the magistrates power to hear the question of disability and, generally, by giving the courts sentencing discretion following such a finding.

Where a magistrates' court makes a hospital order without recording a conviction the person has the same right of appeal against the order as if it were made on his conviction (s. 45(1)). On appeal, the Crown Court can pass any sentence which the magistrates' court could have made if it had heard the whole case and convicted (Courts Act 1971, s. 9(2)).

EFFECT OF A HOSPITAL ORDER

Once a court makes a hospital order the offender is beyond the reach of the court and (unless a restriction order is made) the Home Secretary. The patient is admitted to the hospital as if under an application for treatment under section 3. This means that the patient can be detained for an initial period of six months, which can be renewed for a further period of six months, and then for periods of one year at a time. A hospital-order patient can be discharged at any time by the responsible medical officer, a mental health review tribunal, or the hospital managers (ss 23(2), 66). There are only two significant differences in effect between a hospital order and a civil admission for treatment: the nearest relative of a hospital-order patient cannot order his discharge under section 23 (Sched. 1, paras 2, 8); and the patient does not have the right to apply to a tribunal within six months following the hospital order being made (Sched. 1, paras 2, 9). The first occasion on which either the hospital-order patient or his nearest relative can apply to a tribunal is in the period between six and twelve months of the making of the order (33 66(1)(f), 69(1)).[5]

Guardianship orders

Guardianship orders under the Mental Health Act are seldom used.[6] This is unfortunate as they provide a useful alternative to detention in hospital by providing a means by which the offender can be made subject to some control, supervision, and support in the community. Such orders may be particularly helpful in meeting the needs of mentally impaired offenders who could benefit from occupation, training, and education in the community. In these cases a guardianship order could provide a less restrictive setting in which care and habilitation could take place.

CRITERIA AND PROCEDURES

The magistrates' court or the Crown Court has the power to place an offender under the guardianship of a local social services authority or a person approved by the authority (s. 37(1)). The criteria and procedures which govern the making of a guardianship order are almost identical to those for a hospital order. The major differences are that there is no 'treatability' test to apply in making a guardianship order; and a guardianship order can be made only if the offender is aged sixteen or older (s. 37(2)).

EFFECT

Some local authorities were reluctant to accept guardianship patients under the 1959 Act, partly because they carried wide powers over the patient (i.e. all those powers a father would exercise over a child). The guardianship order now confers on the guardian quite specific powers: to require the patient to reside in a specific place; to require the patient to attend for medical treatment, occupation, education, or training; and to require access to the patient to be given at the place where the patient is residing, to any registered doctor, approved social worker, or other specified person (s. 8(1)). It is to be noted that, although the guardianship patient can be made to attend for treatment, he cannot have treatment imposed without his consent under Part IV of the Act (s. 56). The duration of the order is the same as for a hospital order and the effect is the same as a guardianship order under Part II of the Act. Thus, the patient can be discharged from guardianship at any time by the social services authority, the responsible medical officer, or a tribunal (ss 23, 69). However, the nearest relative cannot discharge a patient subject to a guardianship order (s. 40(4), Sched. 1, paras 2, 8); but the nearest relative does have the right to apply to a tribunal (s. 40(4), Sched. 1, Pt 1, paras 2, 9).

Remands to hospital and interim hospital orders

The Mental Health Act 1983 adopts proposals originally put forward by the Butler Committee for remand to hospital for a medical report; remand to hospital for treatment; and an interim hospital order for the purpose of determining whether a hospital order would be suitable. The object of these provisions is to provide an opportunity for a person who has been brought before a court to be examined or treated in hospital before the court takes a final decision in his case. Because the provisions have resource implications they were not implemented with the rest of the Act (s. 149); they were brought into force on 1 October, 1984.

REMANDS TO HOSPITAL

A Crown Court already has power to remand a defendant for medical reports to be obtained. The Court may remand in custody or on bail with a condition of residence in hospital. However, facilities for psychiatric assessment and treatment in prison are restricted. Further, bail may be inappropriate because the accused is dangerous or because he cannot be compelled to remain in hospital on bail. Magistrates' courts have similar powers and face the same difficulties. The Act now empowers courts to remand to hospital for report or treatment. Custodial remands or bail will continue where appropriate. The Act specifies that the remand is an alternative to a remand in custody; it should not be used where the granting of bail is appropriate. It should also be used in preference to a transfer to hospital of an unsentenced person under section 48; such transfers should be reserved for use in emergencies and are, in any case, within the power of the Home Secretary and not the court.

A remand for report can be made on the evidence of one doctor who is approved as having special experience in the diagnosis or treatment of mental disorder under section 12 (ss 35(3), 54(1)). The Court must find that there is 'reason to suspect' that the accused is suffering from one of the four forms of mental disorder and it would be impracticable for a report on his mental condition to be made if he were remanded on bail. A person remanded to hospital for report cannot be given treatment without his consent under Part IV of the Act (s. 56(1)(b)).

A remand for treatment can be made on the evidence of two doctors, one of whom must be approved under section 12 (ss 36(3), 54(1)). The Court must find that the accused is suffering from a *major* form of mental disorder of a nature or degree which makes it appropriate for him to be detained in hospital for medical treatment.

Remands to hospital for report or treatment can be made for a maximum of twenty-eight days, with further periods of twenty-eight days, and for not more than twelve weeks in all. The accused is entitled to commission an independent medical report at his own expense and to apply for termination of the order.

INTERIM HOSPITAL ORDERS

An interim hospital order can be made on the evidence of two doctors, one of whom must be approved under section 12 (ss 38(1), 54(1)). The Court must be satisfied that the offender is suffering from one of the four forms of mental disorder and there is reason to suppose that the disorder is such that it may be appropriate for a hospital order to be made. The order is for a maximum of twelve weeks, renewable for twenty-eight days at a time but not for more than six months in all.

Restriction orders

By section 41 of the Mental Health Act 1983 a court is empowered to add to the therapeutic hospital order (s. 37) an order imposing special restrictions on the offender's discharge, not by way of punishment (*Haynes*) but as a measure for the protection of the public from serious harm. A restriction order may not be made unless at least one of the medical practitioners has given oral evidence to the court, a provision which enables a court to ascertain the doctor's view of the appropriateness of special restrictions. Many restricted patients are thought to require the security of a special hospital, admission to which requires the consent of the Secretary of State for Social Services.

Before it may impose a restriction order, the court must reach the conclusion that in this case special restrictions are 'necessary for the protection of the public *from serious harm*', the italicized words have been added by the new legislation. In deciding this question, the court must have regard to the nature of the offence, the antecedents of the offender, and the risk of his committing further offences if set at large. The purpose of restriction orders is essentially protective, and so the court's decision is predictive. This raises the question of *degree* of risk of serious harm which is required to justify making a restriction order. Clearly if the medical reports indicate a high risk that the offender will re-offend but the probable offences do not amount to 'serious harm', a restriction order should not be imposed. If the new legislative formula is to have any effect, it must exclude such cases. On the other hand, if there is little doubt from the present offence or previous offences that the offender is capable of causing serious harm, what degree of risk of further offending should the court require? The question becomes even more pointed when the offender has not yet committed a really serious offence but the medical reports argue that he may well do so, if not placed in secure conditions. There is ample evidence that the prediction of danger-ousness is fraught with uncertainty and mistakes, and, whilst it is not possible here to review the relevant literature (see Floud and Young 1981: app. C; *BJC* 1982), there is strong reason for stating that courts should require at least a probability and should question doctors painstakingly about the basis for their prediction in each case before imposing a restriction order.

Whilst the estimation of the degree of risk present in a particular case remains a fallible process, it ought to be possible to attach a more specific meaning to 'serious harm'. In the leading case of *Gardiner* Lord Parker CJ held that a restriction order ought to be imposed in 'the case of crimes of violence and of the more serious sexual offences': so long as the reference to violence does not extend to minor assaults, this ruling survives the 1983 Act. Other decisions in the last ten years must be re-examined. In *Toland* the Court of Appeal upheld a restriction order imposed on a young burglar who had twice absconded from local mental hospitals. 'It is true that the case is not in the same category as the case of a violent sexual offender to which Lord Parker referred. But this boy is certainly an anti-social person. He is a pest.' This reasoning would no longer justify a restriction order, for it does not lead to the conclusion that the offender presents a risk of *serious* harm. In a number of decisions the Court has stated that it is not necessarily wrong to impose a restriction order on conviction for modest offences such as obtaining by deception (*Smith*), damaging two window panes (*Eaton*), or stealing a purse (*Allison*). As a matter of statutory interpretation this remains correct, for the nature of the present offence is merely one matter to be considered in determining whether the offender presents a risk of serious harm. Yet in cases where the offence is not of a serious nature, the court can only reach the conclusion that the offender presents a risk of *serious* harm if it places reliance on his antecedents or on predictions contained in the medical reports. In the case of the schizophrenic fraudster, for example, the psychiatric report referred to the offender's 'desire to protect himself by carrying round a loaded air pistol and a sword stick' (*Smith*). Depending on the circumstances such behaviour might justify a prediction of 'serious harm'. But, even apart from the hazards of prediction, a court must surely satisfy itself of the factual basis of a statement about behaviour which has not been the subject of a charge and conviction.[7] Why was he charged with the deception offences and not with the offensive weapon and firearms offences?

The aim of the insertion of the words 'serious harm' into the 1983 Act was to narrow the types of offence from which public protection by means of a restriction order is justifiable. It is submitted that 'serious harm' should generally be confined to serious offences of violence and serious sexual offences, together with inchoate forms of those offences (including serious cases of possessing weapons), serious forms of arson, aggravated burglary, and burglary with intent to rape or injure. One way of being more precise about the seriousness of the harm required for a restriction order would be to adapt the judicial approach to life imprisonment[8] and to require that the predicted offence should be of a kind which might, in the case of an offender not suffering from mental disorder, warrant a sentence of about seven years' imprisonment. Some would suggest that the threshold for restriction orders should be lower than for life imprisonment – say, five years' imprisonment – but the narrow provisions for the discharge of restricted patients suggest that the restriction order is no less a deprivation of liberty and ought therefore to be confined to really serious cases.

The effect of the order depends on whether the court specifies a period for which the special restrictions should last or makes an order without limit of time. The courts have developed the principle that a determinate restriction order should only be made in the rare cases where doctors state with confidence that the offender will recover from the mental disorder within a specified period (*Gardiner*; *Haynes*). Although a higher proportion of restriction orders in recent years have been for fixed periods (3 per cent during 1976–78 compared with 10 per cent in 1982), the majority are without limit of time. There are grounds for arguing that special restrictions ought not to last longer than a period proportionate to the gravity of the offence for which they were imposed (Gostin 1977: 91–7) – at least, unless the case meets the criteria which would justify the imposition of life imprisonment on a person not suffering from a treatable mental disorder. It seems unlikely, however, that such an argument will succeed on existing legislative and judicial authority.

The effect of a restriction order without limit of time is now different from Lord Parker's description in *Gardiner*. The offender may be discharged conditionally or absolutely either by the Home Secretary *or*, and this is the change, by a mental health review tribunal. Although there are advantages for the offender, since he may make an application with legal representation directly to a tribunal with the power of discharge, it does not follow that he is more likely to be discharged or, correspondingly, that there will be reduction in public protection. Tribunals will be chaired by a circuit judge or recorder when considering restricted patients, and the criteria for discharge from a restriction order are narrower than those for imposing it initially. Thus the tribunal has a duty to discharge a restricted patient if the disorder is no longer 'of a nature or degree which makes it appropriate for him to be liable to be detained in a hospital for medical treatment' (perhaps illogically, it is not required at this stage that further treatment should have any effect); the tribunal also has a duty to discharge the patient if 'it is not necessary for the health and safety of the patient or the protection of other persons that he should receive such treatment' (it is not required at this stage that there be a danger of *serious* harm to others). That a patient can continue to be detained under a restriction order without requiring a showing of 'treatability' or of the probability of serious harm to others (even if suffering from a minor form of mental disorder) seems to us to be misconceived.

Psychiatric probation orders

The most frequently used of the orders specially for mentally disordered offenders is the probation order with a condition requiring submission to medical treatment. Probation orders may be from six months to three years. The court may add a condition requiring submission to medical treatment for the whole or part of the probation period if the offender consents, if the court receives evidence from a duly qualified medical practitioner, and if the court is satisfied that the offender's 'mental condition requires and is susceptible to treatment but is not such as to warrant his detention in pursuance of a hospital order' (Powers of Criminal Courts Act 1973, s. 3(1)). The term 'mental condition' suggests that this order may be made where the offender is not suffering from one of the four specific forms of mental disorder discussed above.[9] The treatment specified in the order may be as an in-patient in a local mental hospital, as an out-patient at such a place or elsewhere.

Whilst the psychiatric probation order may be appropriate in many cases where neither the mental disorder nor the offending is so serious as to call for a hospital order, decisions of the Court of Appeal show that it may also be used in cases which might otherwise warrant a substantial custodial sentence – e.g. for wounding with intent attracting a sentence of three years (*Hayes*) and for arson with intent to endanger life attracting three years (*Hoof*). Where the mental disorder is said to be treatable, a psychiatric probation order may well provide a greater degree of public protection than a prison sentence, since the treatment which the former can provide and the latter cannot may ameliorate the mental disorder and thus reduce the offending in the long term, as the Court of Appeal recognized in *Nicholls*. Although one small research project suggested that liaison between the supervising probation officer and the psychiatrist has sometimes been poor (Lewis 1980), a court may exercise some control by asking each of them to submit a report on the offender, say, every six months.

Policy in dealing with offenders suffering from mental disorder

In principle, the task of dealing with mentally disordered offenders should be approached on the basis that the law should facilitate treatment where it is possible and available, but that in general a person should not be deprived of his liberty unless that is essential and, if the court does so deprive him, he should not be deprived of his liberty for a period longer than is necessary. The court's approach is sometimes constricted by the unavailability of certain facilities. Local mental hospitals are rarely able to guarantee security, and sometimes refuse to admit certain kinds of patient. The four special hospitals are administered by the DHSS and, because of pressure on places, sometimes decline to accept a patient. Regional secure units were intended to fill the gap between the two, but only a limited number of units are in operation (see Chapter 5). These problems must be borne in mind in the following discussion.

First we consider cases in which the offender is said to be suffering from a form of mental disorder which is treatable, and where the facilities for treatment are available. In some cases an absolute or conditional discharge will be sufficient if the court is satisfied that the offender will undertake or continue a course of treatment. A fine or an ordinary probation order might be appropriate in other cases.[10] Where the court believes that a legal framework for medical treatment should be provided, the possibilities to be considered initially are the psychiatric probation order, the hospital order, and the guardianship order. As we have seen,[11] the psychiatric probation order is a flexible order which will often be appropriate when the consent of the offender and the co-operation of a probation officer and a psychiatrist are forthcoming. As the least intrusive upon the offender's liberty of the three orders, it should be considered first. Moreover, neither a hospital order nor a guardianship order should be chosen unless it is the 'most suitable' means of dealing with the offender, whereas a psychiatric probation order is intended for cases where the offender's mental condition does not warrant detention in pursuance of a hospital order. If the court forms the view, after reading the reports and considering the facts of the case, that a psychiatric probation order will not provide the treatment which this offender requires, it should consider a guardianship order. In a limited number of cases it is possible that neither a probation order nor a psychiatric probation order will be sufficiently wide to provide the necessary assistance for a mentally disordered person to manage in his own home or a hostel, and to ensure that he attends for medical treatment or occupational training and that there is no self-neglect. A guardianship order may also be appropriate in cases where the offender refuses to consent to a probation order and some degree of control is required to ensure that he receives treatment, care, habilitation, or training in the community. It would be preferable to a hospital order where there is no immediate risk to the public and where it is desirable that therapeutic objectives are met in a less restrictive community setting, and particularly for offenders who are mentally impaired.

Both the guardianship order and the hospital order are to be reserved for cases in which they are the 'most suitable' measure: this requires the court to consider and to discuss each alternative means of dealing with the offender, and to take account of the effects which flow from making a guardianship or hospital order. For example, a local hospital can rarely guarantee that an offender will be detained under secure conditions, and discharge will depend largely on the view of the responsible medical officer or the tribunal on his response to treatment. Of course a hospital order is for treatment and the court should not be concerned with the duration of an offender's stay in hospital in terms of 'time for crime'. On the other hand, a court may be concerned about whether the hospital is capable of ensuring the patient's detention until treatment has been completed. This concern with security has sometimes led courts to add a restriction order, but section 41 makes it clear that this is permissible only where it is necessary to protect the public from 'serious harm' – a requirement examined above.

This legal framework of orders for the mentally disordered might be thought to leave a gap – the offender with a criminal record who has committed an offence which, in an offender not suffering from mental disorder, would result in loss of liberty for one, two, or three years. If sent to a local hospital under a section 37 order he might well abscond and re-offend. The availability of a place in a regional secure unit might solve the problem by providing security until the termination of treatment, but in many cases neither a RSU place nor a special hospital place is available. If a place in a local hospital is available and the offender's condition is 'treatable', should the court make the hospital order in the knowledge that it does not guarantee security, or should it impose a custodial sentence simply in order to ensure that the public is protected from the offender for a given period? Since we are dealing here with an offender for whom a hospital order is available, the proper course is surely to make such an order. The amount of public protection provided by a prison sentence of, say, two years can be overestimated. 'Public protection' means the risk that any member of the public will fall victim to a certain kind of offence within a given period. Removing one offender from circulation for sixteen months (i.e. two years less remission) is likely to have an infinitesimal effect on that risk in the short term (see Ashworth 1983: 32), and if the offender can be placed in an environment where he will receive treatment (i.e. a hospital not a prison), there is at least the possibility of a longer-term amelioration of the mental condition and thus of the offender's behaviour. If he goes to prison, he will be released without treatment, and possibly in an even worse mental condition than before.[12]

Thus far we have been dealing with the offender who is stated by doctors to be mentally disordered, whose condition is said to be treatable, and for whom a hospital place is available. In the real world the three elements sometimes do not come together. For some, there is mental disorder but it is not regarded as treatable. For others, there is no hospital place even though the condition is said to be treatable. How could the courts deal with these cases?

There is considerable authority, as we shall see below, for the proposition that it is wrong to deal with a mentally disordered offender more severely than the seriousness of the offence would justify: proportionality ought to be maintained. For this reason it is important not to leave out of consideration the ordinary range of disposals such as absolute and conditional discharge, fine, and even the probation order. Some disposals might, however, be regarded as unsuitable for offenders suffering from mental disorder. A detention centre order should not be made upon a boy who is unsuitable by reason of his medical condition (Criminal Justice Act 1982, s. 4(J); Home Office 1983); mental disorder may be thought to render an offender unsuitable for a community service order (Young 1979: 132); and the 'sword of Damocles' reasoning behind the suspended sentence might be thought to presuppose a control over offending behaviour which a mentally disordered person may not possess.

In many cases each year, courts feel that they have no alternative but to impose a sentence of imprisonment or youth custody on a mentally disordered offender. Since it is widely agreed that prison is an inappropriate and sometimes damaging environment for many persons suffering from mental disorder, the justifications for these sentences must be scrutinized with great care. The most difficult cases are those in which the offender's disorder is said to be treatable, but there is simply no hospital place available. The courts have made vehement protests about this predicament (e.g. Scarman LJ in *McFarlane* and McCullough J in *Gordon*), and occasionally a hospital place has been found when the case has come before the Court of Appeal. Granted that these cases arise, how is the court to approach sentence? If in this hour of need the sentencer looks to the

Court of Appeal's decisions for guidance, he will find a hopelessly confused jumble of rulings. On the one hand there is the principle that the courts should not use the prisons in order to 'make up for the deficiency in the medical and social services', trenchantly stated by Lawton LJ in *Clarke*, followed by Bridge LJ in *Tolley* and by Shaw LJ in *Slater* (itself followed in *Thompson*), and reasserted by the Court in *Fisher*, with Shaw LJ presiding: 'the sentences to be imposed ... must of course be commensurate with the offence in question.' On the other hand, there is a line of decisions in which the Court of Appeal has accepted that the prison sentence is 'too long for the offence itself' but has nevertheless upheld it on grounds of public protection: *Arrowsmith, per* O'Connor J; *Scanlon, per* Waller LJ; *Walsh, per* Jupp J; and most brazenly by Skinner J in *Gouws*, with Lord Lane CJ presiding. The Court of Appeal has not taken the trouble to consider these rulings together and to explain, to sentencers and others, the reasons for taking different approaches and the factors which distinguish the cases.

In principle proportionality ought to be the guiding consideration unless there are clear and cogent grounds for departing from it. The only circumstances in which it is justifiable to depart from it in English law are where the conditions are met for an extended sentence, which is rarely applicable, and for life imprisonment, which must now be examined. Life imprisonment is the discretionary maximum sentence for several serious crimes. Release of lifers is in the hands of the Home Secretary, advised by the Parole Board, and the uncertainty and its deleterious psychological effects on lifers were prominent among the reasons given by the Advisory Council on the Penal System in 1978 for strongly criticizing the use of the life sentence (Advisory Council on the Penal System 1978: ch. 11). Recent decisions of the Court of Appeal circumscribe the use of life imprisonment more narrowly than decisions in the mid-1970s had done. The criteria were laid down in *Hodgson* (1967):

(1) 'where the offence or offences are in themselves grave enough to require a very long sentence': recent decisions suggest that the offence(s) must be such as to justify a sentence of at least seven years' imprisonment (*Gray*, and decisions cited therein). There are earlier cases which suggest that, as the evidence under condition (2) below becomes more compelling, so condition (1) becomes less important, but these cases (*Ashdown* and *Thornton*) might no longer be followed.

(2) 'where it appears from the nature of the offences or from the

defendant's history that he is a person of unstable character likely to commit such offences in the future': although this reference to 'unstable character' has never been held to require evidence of a mental disorder falling within the Mental Health Act definition, it has been stressed that there must be medical evidence of a 'marked degree' of mental disturbance (*Picker* and *Pither*),[13] and several life sentences have been quashed recently because of failure to meet this requirement (*Owen*; *Laycock*; *Bryant and Mead*).

(3) 'where if such offences are committed the consequences to others may be specially injurious, as in the case of sexual offences or crimes of violence': in a number of recent cases a life sentence has been quashed because the medical evidence did not suggest that the offences which the offender might commit presented a sufficiently great danger to people at large (*Headly*; *Blackburn*; *Mottershead*; *Spencer*).

All three conditions must be satisfied before life imprisonment is imposed, and a judge who is minded to impose this sentence must communicate his intention to counsel, so as to allow argument on the issue (*MacDougall*). Life imprisonment is potentially the most severe sentence known to English law: for the defendant it adds uncertainty and anxiety about release to lengthy deprivation of liberty, and in principle it ought to be reserved for the really serious cases.

Limitations on the use of the life sentence create further difficulties for sentencers who have to deal with moderately grave cases of mentally disordered offenders with a prognosis of 'dangerous' behaviour. Regrettably, the courts have recently breached the general principle that the sentence should not go beyond the upper limit set by reference to the seriousness of the latest offence. In *McCauliffe* and in *Gouws*, the Court upheld a sentence more severe than the facts of the offence merited. In both cases there were medical reports, and it appears that the courts were applying a modified form of the criteria for a life sentence so as to pass a disproportionate fixed sentence. It has been cogently argued that those who break the law have a general right not to be subjected to punishment out of proportion to the crime, and that this right ought only to be overridden in cases where the offender presents a vivid danger to the physical safety of other people (Bottoms and Brownsword 1982). There is ample evidence of a tendency to over-predict dangerous behaviour (Floud and Young 1981: app. C; see also Chapter 9), and it is wrong that an offender should be liable to have his sentence lengthened on the basis of predictions by 'experts'. If the life sentence is justifiable at all, then the justification is that the offender has committed such a serious offence on this occasion that he has already rendered himself liable to a substantial custodial sentence (i.e. at least seven or eight years). That is hard proof that the offender is *capable* of inflicting serious harm, but even then the imposition of a life sentence incorporates an element of prediction that he is *likely* to commit further such offences. Such predictions are no more reliable in the case of mentally disordered offenders than for other offenders (see e.g. National Institute of Mental Health 1978, and Levinson and Ramsay 1979). Moreover, the accuracy of predictions leading to life sentences cannot be tested since, as a Home Office study aptly points out, 'presumably no-one is prepared to risk testing the preventive effects of indeterminate sentences by releasing these people and seeing what happens' (Brody and Tarling 1980: 34).

The Court of Appeal should take an early opportunity to review the conflicting decisions and to give clear guidance to lower courts. In our view it should adopt the proportionality principle stated in *Fisher* (see also Shaw LJ in *Judge*, and now *Thompson*) recognizing the life sentence as the only significant exception to that principle. As the Home Office study concluded, 'predictions of future behaviour are rightly recognised as too fallible to enter into sentencing decisions' (Brody and Tarling 1980: 34).

Conclusions

In our judgement there are two assumptions which have led to confusion and inconsistency in the sentencing of mentally disordered offenders. First, since the special disposals are intended for therapeutic, not punitive, purposes, the use of ordinary sentencing principles such as proportionality is inapposite. Second, dangerous behaviour in a mentally disordered person is more probable and more predictable than in the case of an ordinary offender. We have sought to demonstrate that neither assumption should be used as a guiding principle by the sentencer. Any custodial order, even if the intention is to care for and treat the offender, involves a deprivation of liberty. The length of the deprivation should not be disproportionate to the gravity of the offence and the antecedents of the offender. There appears to us to be insufficient justification for extending the length of detention – e.g. by the imposition of a prison sentence longer than would otherwise be given for the offence or by the inappropriate use of a restriction order. Medical evidence suggesting that the offender is mentally disordered and could benefit from treatment should primarily be an indication for the court to ensure that the offender is placed in a setting where he will receive care and treatment. The entire range of therapeutic dispositions should be considered and, wherever possible, the least restrictive order and care setting should be chosen which is compatible with the patient's need for treatment and society's right to be protected.

Notes

1 This chapter was first published in the *Criminal Law Review* [1984] 195–212.
2 For a more detailed examination of the Mental Health Act 1983 and related legislation, see Gostin (1985).
3 For a commentary on *Kynaston*, see Gunn (1982). See also X v. *United Kingdom*.
4 A hospital or guardianship order can be made in certain circumstances by a magistrates' court without convicting the defendant (s. 37(3)). See further below pp. 217–18.
5 As to the right of patients to apply to tribunals, and the Rules of Procedure, see Gostin, Rassaby, and Buchan (1984).
6 In 1982, nine people were made the subject of guardianship orders (Home Office 1982: table S4.9).
7 This is a matter of general concern in sentencing (Ashworth 1983: 91–6).
8 See below, pp. 229–31.
9 See pp. 211–14.
10 In the case of Skelton a recorder took the unusual course of deferring sentence for six months, on the defendant's undertaking to reside in a particular mental hospital and receive treatment. This might be an unwise use of the power to defer, since a short probation order with a condition of mental treatment would surely have been preferable, but the Court of Appeal held that the recorder's use of the power was *unlawful*. This was surely wrong, and has been roundly criticized by Dr D. A. Thomas (1983) and Judge McLean (1983).
11 Above, p. 225.
12 Imprisonment 'might not just be wrong in the sense that it did not provide the best solution for her, but might positively cause harm, because imprisonment might lead to her deterioration' (McCullough J in *Gordon)* .
13 cf. *de Havilland*, suggesting that medical evidence is not essential.

References

Advisory Council on the Penal System (1978) *Sentences of Imprisonment: A Review of Maximum Penalties*. London: HMSO.

Ashworth, A. (1983) *Sentencing and Penal Policy*. London: Weidenfeld & Nicholson.

Ashworth, A. and Shapland, J. (1980) Psychopaths in the Criminal Process. *Criminal Law Review*: 628.

Bottoms, T. and Brownsword, R. (1982) The Dangerousness Debate after Flond. *British Journal of Criminology* 22: 229.

Brody, S. and Tarling, R. (1980) *Taking Offenders Out of Circulation*. Home Office Research Study No. 64. London: Home Office.

Butler Committee (1975) *Report of the Committee on Mentally Abnormal Offenders*. Cmnd 6244. London: HMSO.

DHSS (1976) *Review of the Mental Health Act 1959*. London: DHSS.

DHSS (1983) *The Mental Health Act 1983: Memorandum*. London: DHSS.

Floud, J. and Young, W. (1981) *Dangerousness and Criminal Justice*. London: Heinemann.

Gostin, L. (1977) *A Human Condition*. Vol. 2. London: MIND.

—— (1982) Human Rights, Judicial Review and the Mental Disordered Offender. *Criminal Law Review*: 779–93.

—— (1985) *Mental Health Services: Law and Practice*. London: Shaw.

Gostin, L., Rassaby, E., and Buchan, A. (1984) *Mental Health: Tribunal Procedure*. London: Oyez Longman.

Gunn, M. J. (1982) Commentary on *Kynaston. Journal of Social Welfare Law* :104.

Hoggett, B. (1983) The Mental Health Act 1983. *Public Law*: 172.

Home Office (1982) *Criminal Statistics in England and Wales: Supplementary Tables 1982*. Vol. 4. London: HMSO.

—— (1983) Circular No. 122/1983.

Lewis, P. (1980) *Psychiatric Probation Orders*. Cambridge: Institute of Criminology.

Levinson, R. and Ramsay, G. (1979) Dangerousness, Stress and Mental Health Evaluation. *Journal of Health and Social Behavior* 20: 178–87.

May Committee (1979) *Report of the Committee of Inquiry into United Kingdom Prison Services*. Cmnd 7673. London: HMSO.

McLean, J. (1983) Deferred Sentences. *Justice of the Peace* 147: 755–66.

National Institute of Mental Health (1978) *Dangerous Behaviour: A Problem in Law and Mental Health*. Washington: US Department of Health, Education, and Welfare.

Thomas, D. A. (1983) R. V. Skelton: Commentary. *Criminal Law Review*: 687.

Walker, N. and McCabe, S. (1973) *Crime and Insanity in England*. Vol. 2. Edinburgh: Edinburgh University Press.

Wasik, M. (1983) Hospital Orders Without Trial. *Justice of the Peace* 147: 211–13.

Wootton, B. (1960) Diminished Responsibility: A Layman's View. *Law Quarterly Review* 76: 224.

Young, W. (1979) *Community Service Orders*. London: Heinemann.

Cases

(D. A. Thomas, *Current Sentencing Practice*, 1984, is referred to as *CSP*.)

Kynaston v. *Secretary of State, the Home Department, and Secretary of State for Social Services*, 18 Feb., 1981.

R. v. *Allison* (1977) *CSP* F2.4(d).

—— v. *Arrowsmith* [1976] Crim. L.R. 636, *CSP* A7.5(a).

—— v. *Ashdown* (1973) *CSP* F3.2(e).

—— v. *Blackburn* (1979) 1 Cr. App. R. (S.) 205, *CSP* F3.2(b).

—— v. *Bryant and Mead* [1983] Crim. L.R. 691.

—— v. *Clarke* (1975) 61 Cr. App. R. 320, *CSP* A7.5(a).

—— v. *de Havilland* [1983] Crim. L.R. 489.

—— v. *Eaton* [1976] Crim. L.R. 390, *CSP* F2.4(d).

—— v. *Fisher* (1981) 3 Cr. App. R. (S.) 112, *CSP* A7.5(a).

—— v. *Gardiner* (1967) 51 Cr. App. R. 187, *CSP* F2.4(a).

—— v. *Gordon* (1981) 3 Cr. App. R. (S.) 352, *CSP* A7.3(a).

—— v. *Gouws* (1981) 3 Cr App. R. (S.) 325, *CSP* A7.3(a).

—— v. *Gray* [1983] Crim. L.R. 691.

—— v. *Harding, The Times*, 15 June, 1983.

—— v. *Hayes* (1974) *CSP* F1.2(a).

—— v. *Haynes* (1981); 3 Cr. App. R. (S.) 330, *CSP* F2.4(a).

—— v. *Headley* (1979) 1 Cr. App. R. (S.) 158, *CSP* F3.2(b).

—— v. *Hodgson* (1967) 52 Cr. App. R. 113.

—— v. *Hoof* (1980) 2 Cr. App. R. (S.) 299.

—— v. *Judge* (1980) *CSP* A7.5(a).

—— v. *Laycock* (1981) 3 Cr. App. R. (S.) 104, *CSP* F3.2(b).

—— v. *Lincoln (Kesteven) Justices, ex parte O'Connor* [1983] 1 W.L.R. 335, [1983] Crim. L.R. 621 (DC).

—— v. *McCauliffe* [1982] Crim. L.R. 316, *CSP* A7.3(a).

—— v. *MacDougall* [1983] Crim. L.R. 570, *CSP* F3.2(k).

—— v. *McFarlane* (1975) 61 Cr. App. R.

—— v. *Mottershead* (1979) 1 Cr. App. R. (S.) 45, *CSP* F3.2(b).

—— v. *Nicholls* (1981) *CSP* F1.2(b).

—— v. *Owen* (1980) 2 Cr. App. R. (S.) 45, *CSP* F3.2(b).

—— v. *Picker* (1970) 54 Crim. App. R. 330, *CSP* F3.2(a).

—— v. *Pither* (1979) 1 Crim. App. R. (S.) 209, *CSP* F3.2(a).

—— v. *Scanlon* (1979) 1 Crim. App. R. (S.) 60, *CSP* A7.5(a).

—— v. *Skelton* [1983] Crim. L.R. 686.

—— v. *Slater* (1979) 1 Cr. App. R. (S.) 349, *CSP* A7.3(a).

—— v. *Smith* (1976) *CSP* F2.4(b).

—— v. *Spencer* (1979) 1 Cr. App. R. (S.) 75, *CSP* F3.2(b).

—— v. *Thompson* [1983] Crim. L.R. 823.

—— v. *Thornton* (1974) *CSP* F3.2(e).

—— v. *Toland* (1973) *CSP* F2.4(c).

—— v. *Tolley* (1978) 68 Cr. App. R. 323, *CSP* A7.5(a).

—— v. *Walsh* (1981) 3 Cr. App. R. (S.) 359, *CSP* A7.5(a).

W. v. *L*. [1974] QB 711, 719 (CA).

Winterwerp v. *The Netherlands*, European Court of Human Rights, 24 Oct., 1979.

X v. *United Kingdom*, European Court of Human Rights, 5 Nov., 1981.

8 Legal aspects of secure provision

Brenda Hoggett

Introduction

The object of this chapter is to examine the legality of secure provision as applied to all categories of hospital in-patient. 'Secure provision' is taken to encompass all types of confinement or restraint, and thus many differing cases. In some, all patients within a particular hospital or unit will be subject to a degree of security, ranging from the simple device of locking the ward door at night to the maximum-security conditions of a special hospital. In others, restraint will be applied to individuals over and above that which is applied to other patients in the same hospital or unit. This again may range from a short period of therapeutic time out, as part of a programme of behaviour-modification, to the sort of prolonged solitary confinement revealed to the European Commission of Human Rights in the case of *A.* v. *United Kingdom*. The patient was suspected of causing a fire at Broadmoor and was confined in a bare cell-like room with very limited opportunities for exercise or association for some five weeks.

He alleged that this was a breach of Article 3 of the European Convention for the Protection of Human Rights and Fundamental Freedoms, which provides that: 'No one shall be subjected to torture or to inhuman or degrading treatment or punishment.' The Commission declared his complaint admissible in 1977 and embarked upon an investigation of the merits, but in 1980 the parties reached a friendly settlement after new guidelines were introduced for the use of seclusion at Broadmoor. We cannot know what facts the Commission might have found, or what conclusion the European Court of Human Rights might eventually have reached, but the case serves as a reminder of what *can* be meant when we talk of 'secure provision' and also of remedies other than those of the domestic law which are our prime concern.

Domestic law proceeds from the premise that, unless some lawful justification exists, the total restraint or confinement of any person amounts to a false imprisonment. A person may probably be imprisoned without being aware of it, for Atkin LJ stated in *Meering* v. *Grahame-White Aviation Co. Ltd* that 'a person can be imprisoned while he is asleep, while he is in a state of drunkenness, while he is unconscious and while he is a lunatic.' Although this is controversial (in the light of *Herring* v. *Boyle*) any other view would render some severely ill or handicapped patients without a remedy, were they to be confined outside the circumstances permitted by the common law or by the Mental Health Acts, and without the safeguards attached to the latter.

The major part of this chapter will therefore be devoted to considering in turn the various legal justifications which may be advanced for the imposition of confinement or restraint. These may be placed into two categories. In the first are those which apply, largely at common law, irrespective of the patient's status as 'informal' or 'detained' under the Mental Health Acts. In the second are those which result from the powers to detain and to treat patients under those Acts, and which for our purposes are restricted to detained patients. Each of these justifications contains its own limits, so that the nature and degree of the restraint which may be imposed should become clear in the course of discussion.

The patient's legal remedies, if any, will depend upon the way in which the law has been infringed. If the confinement itself is unlawful, the patient must at least be able to secure his release, if need be through the writ of habeas corpus. He may also be entitled to damages for the tort of false imprisonment, which is a species of trespass to the person, and the perpetrator may also be guilty of the crime of the same name.

Even if the confinement itself is lawful, the way in which it is carried out may amount to the trespass of assault or battery, for example where excessive force is used to prevent a crime. It was also argued by Her Majesty's Government, in resisting the application in *A.* v. *United Kingdom*, that there might be an action for the mental suffering caused by a breach of the duty of care owed by hospitals and individuals not to cause harm to their patients. It is always interesting to observe the efforts of the government to push back the boundaries of the common law in an effort to persuade the Commission that an applicant has not exhausted his local remedies, but in this case they failed to persuade the commission that such a claim stood a reasonable prospect of success. It would be otherwise if physical injury were caused, whether intentionally or carelessly, for then a claim in trespass or negligence would lie. But, save in the excessive force cases, the essence of the wrong done by unlawful confinement is the deprivation of liberty and not any physical harm. In the case of wilful neglect or ill-treatment of patients, of course, there might also be a prosecution under section 127 of the Mental Health Act 1983, should the Director of Public Prosecutions give his consent, as well as prosecutions for the ordinary assault offences.

However, save for the offence under section 127, section 139(1) of the 1983 Act provides that no civil or criminal proceedings may be brought against any individual in respect of any act purporting to be done in pursuance of the mental health legislation (even if it was not in fact authorized by that legislation) unless the act was done in bad faith or without reasonable care. Further, under section 139(2), the leave of the High Court must be sought for any civil action, and the consent of the Director of Public Prosecutions to any prosecution. An assault committed by a nurse on duty in purported exercise of his power to control patients was held to fall within this protection (*Pountney* v. *Griffiths*). There is, however, Crown Court authority for the view that acts in relation to informal patients do not purport to be done under the Mental Health Act and are not protected (*R.* v. *Runighian*).

The section no longer applies to actions against the Secretary of State or health authorities, but this raises the problem of distinguishing breaches of their own 'non-delegable' duties from their purely vicarious liability for the torts of their employees: for if the employee would have the substantive defence provided by section 139(1), it would appear that no purely vicarious liability can lie (see *ICI* v. *Shatwell*; but see also discussion in, for example, Winfield and Jolowicz 1984: 599–602). Indeed, the same argument might be raised to suggest that the procedural barrier in section 139(2) is not a breach of the right given by Article 6 of the European Convention to a fair hearing in determination of civil rights and liabilities, because section 139(1) means that no civil right exists. Section 139 may eventually be held contrary to the Convention, but until that time, all that follows, at least in relation to detained patients, must be read subject to the substantive and procedural protection which it provides for individual members of the hospital staff.

However, although that section may exonerate a person from intentional acts which he wrongly but reasonably believes he is entitled to commit, it does not relieve him of the duty to take reasonable care to conform his actions to the law. In what follows, considerable emphasis will be given to the limits of the legal justifications for the use of restraint. It is of course appreciated that there are many disturbed and dangerous patients for whom such measures are either permanently or temporarily essential. There is no warrant, however, for the assumption that all patients may be dealt with in the manner which is justified in relation to the most disturbed. The object is to match the measures used to the purposes and the patient for which they are employed.

Common law powers of restraint

The heading to this section is not entirely accurate, as the common law on one point has now been replaced by statute, but in essence we are dealing with the principles developed by the common law to meet various contingencies which may arise irrespective of whether the patient is liable to be detained under the Mental Health Act. They are of two quite different kinds, for one is founded on the patient's consent or voluntary submission, and the other is founded on the prevention of harm to the patient, to others, or to property.

CONSENT

Surprising though it may seem, a patient may well have agreed to a degree of confinement or restraint. A patient who enters hospital might agree to observe certain rules which are internally prescribed to enable a large and complex organization to function properly. An example might be that, for the protection of patients and property, hospital wards are locked at night and staff cannot always be made available to unlock them on demand. Rather different is the case of a patient who agrees to embark upon a programme of behaviour-modification which, in certain events, may involve brief periods of confinement or other deprivations of ordinary legal rights. In each case, the patient's agreement might afford the defence of *volenti non fit injuria* (i.e. that to which a man consents cannot be considered an injury). However, there are some practical difficulties particularly likely to be encountered in this context.

The first difficulty is that consent is only a defence if that which was done is that which was agreed. However honest and reasonable his mistake, a surgeon is still liable for amputating the wrong leg. Thus it is advisable to preclude argument about precisely what was agreed. Internal rules should be communicated and made clear to patients on admission; the full possibilities of any treatment plan which could result in deprivation of ordinary rights should be made clear when consent is sought. A general consent to 'behaviour-modification' would be no protection if this had not been done.

Explaining what it is proposed to do, however, is not the same as explaining all the arguments for and against doing it. Provided that the patient's consent is 'real', there will be no liability for assault or battery (or probably false imprisonment), even if he was not fully 'informed' as to the risks and benefits inherent in the procedure. The English courts have refused to accept the doctrine of 'informed consent' developed in the United States (*Canterbury* v. *Spence*; *Cobbs* v. *Grant*) and Canada (*Hopp* v. *Lepp*; *Reibl* v. *Hughes*). In *Chatterton* v. *Gerson*, the plaintiff was twice treated by intrathecal phenol solution injection for chronic and intractable pain following a hernia operation. She found that the second injection failed to relieve her pain but left her leg completely numb. She claimed that her consent to the injection had been vitiated by the defendant's failure to explain all the possible attendant risks. Rejecting that claim, Bristow J observed: 'In my judgment, once the patient is informed in broad terms of the nature of the procedure which is intended and gives her consent, that consent is real.' A similar approach was adopted by Hirst J in *Hills* v. *Potter*, where the plaintiff had elected to undergo an operation to alleviate a deformity of the neck and was left paralysed from the neck down. Similarly, in the recent Court of Appeal decision in *Sidaway* v. *Board of Governors of the Bethlem Royal Hospital and the Maudsley Hospital and Others*, where the facts were very similar to those in *Hills* v. *Potter*, Sir John Donaldson MR stated that a consent was not vitiated by a failure on the part of the doctor to give the patient sufficient information before the consent was given. It was only if the consent was obtained by fraud or misrepresentation that it could be said that an apparent consent was not a true consent.

This does not mean that a doctor is under no duty to explain matters to his patient, merely that any claim based upon a failure to give proper advice must be framed in negligence rather than in assault or battery. Negligence consists in the failure to take such steps as a reasonable doctor would take in all the circumstances of the case to avoid causing harm to the patient. In questions of diagnosis and treatment, a doctor is not negligent if he acts in accordance with a body of skilled and responsible medical opinion on the matter, even if there is an equally skilled and responsible body of opinion which thinks otherwise (*Bolam* v. *Friern Hospital Management Committee*, approved by the House of Lords in *Whitehouse* v. *Jordan*). In *Hills* v. *Potter*, Hirst J applied this same 'medical opinion' test to the matter of advice, and this was the Court of Appeal's view in *Sidaway* v. *Board of Governors of the Bethlem Royal Hospital and the Maudsley Hospital and Others*. The Master of the Rolls, however, appears to have been rather more prepared to allow the courts to challenge medical opinion, for 'the courts could not stand idly by if the profession, by an excess of paternalism, denied their patients a real choice. The law would not permit the medical profession to play God.' Hence he proposed to add the word 'rightly' to the medical test: 'The duty is fulfilled if the doctor acts in accordance with a practice rightly accepted as proper by a body of skilled and experienced medical men.' The point is shortly resolved by the House of Lords. But even if the plaintiff shows that he was not properly informed, he must also show that the doctor's breach of duty caused him harm. Where the treatment has been properly carried out, this means that he must show that he would not have agreed to have it had he known of the possible risks. The plaintiff in *Chatterton* v. *Gerson* was manifestly unable to show this, as had been the patient in *Bolam* v. *Friern Hospital Management Committee*, who agreed to ECT and was injured when it was given without a muscle relaxant, at a time when medical opinion was divided upon the advisability of using one. The chances of success in a claim based upon a failure to warn of the inherent risks in a medical procedure are therefore extremely slim.

These decisions may be criticized for devaluing the patient's claim to a full explanation so as to enable him to make a free and rational choice (see the discussion in Robertson 1981). Goldstein (1975), however, has pointed out that the concept of 'informed consent' can place more emphasis upon what the patient can understand than upon what he wants, and may therefore encourage the authorities to deprive some patients of the right to decide. This tendency was to some extent visible in the discussions preceding the Mental Health (Amendment) Act 1982. But if only a 'broad terms' explanation of what is proposed is required in order for the consent to be 'real', the corollary should be that the patient is capable of giving consent if he is capable of understanding such a 'broad terms' explanation. This low threshold of capacity may therefore serve to preserve the autonomy of a large number of mildly mentally handicapped people. As Glanville Williams (1983: 572) suggests: 'The consent of an impaired patient is easily obtained, but that fact does not rob the consent of its validity. Mentally ill persons should have the right both to give consent to therapeutic procedures and to withhold such consent, unless there are extremely good reasons against this.' Paradoxically, therefore, *Chatterton* v. *Gerson* could assist the rights of mental patients, provided that it can be concluded that the English courts would recognize a capacity to dissent as logically identical to a capacity to assent.

This is particularly important in the light of the finding of the joint working party on behaviour-modification (Royal College of Psychiatrists and others 1980) that mental handicap hospitals are quite extensively involved in such programmes. Some of the patients concerned, however, may even be below the low threshold of capacity indicated above. It is unfortunate that in its summary and recommendations the working party make what is no doubt a sensible practical recommendation, that the nearest relative be asked to agree, without repeating their earlier warning that 'in law, no one has the power to consent to treatment on behalf of any adult patient who is incapable of giving that consent' (1980: 17). Sometimes the treatment of incapable patients may be justified by a doctrine of implied consent or necessity (see Skegg 1974), for example where surgery is urgently needed after a road accident. However, this has never been extended beyond urgent necessity or to cases where the patient is known to object (save *possibly* in the case of suicide), and is most unlikely to apply to the measures of confinement or restraint under discussion here: justifications for their imposition without consent must therefore be sought in the later sections of this chapter.

One final aspect of the requirement that consent be 'real' is that consent induced by force or fraud is no consent. Thus 'it might perhaps be tentatively suggested that the plaintiff cannot give a real consent unless he has in fact the freedom to choose whether or not he should do so' (Clerk and Linsell 1982: 14–08). This statement is supported by the recent decision of the Court of Appeal in *Freeman* v. *Home Office*, in which a prisoner claimed that he had not in fact consented, and was incapable of giving a free consent, to the administration of drugs while he was serving a sentence of life imprisonment. The Court confirmed the trial judge's finding that the prisoner had in fact given a real consent. But they accepted his statement that 'where in a prison setting a doctor has power to influence a prisoner's situation and prospects the court must be alive to the risk that what might appear on the face of it to be a real consent was not in fact so.'

How far can this concept be applied to psychiatric patients? An informal patient who is told that he must agree to stay in hospital or continue with his treatment or else he will be obliged to do so under a compulsory 'section' clearly does not have the real freedom to choose. If the 'section' would not be justified in law or in fact, then his consent cannot be real and any restraint or confinement would be unlawful unless it could be justified on other grounds. But if the threat of a section is justified, it might be suggested that a claim that duress vitiated consent would not succeed (for in *Buckland* v. *Buckland* it was said that a man could not complain that he had been forced into marriage by the threat of imprisonment for unlawful carnal knowledge if he had in fact been guilty of the offence). Once a patient has been 'sectioned', of course, the Mental Health Act 1983 gives power to detain and to impose some treatments without consent (see further p. 256). However, those powers are limited, and in relation to some treatments the patient is better protected than he is under the common law (there is, for example, a doctrine of 'informed consent'). To use the threat of a section, therefore, in order to secure consent to something which would not be permitted under the section, must be unjustified.

The most important practical difficulty in the way of a defence of consent, however, is that (unlike a surgical operation) the patient clearly has the opportunity of changing his mind while the confinement is in progress. In principle, consent may be revoked at any time, and if the patient gives a clear indication that he wishes to be released, then he should be set at liberty unless some special justification for keeping him can be found. For example, in the case of *Symm* v. *Fraser*, the patient complained of restraints imposed by attendants allegedly sent to her home by her doctors, the defendants. Cockburn CJ directed the jury that: 'even assuming that a medical man, when called in by a patient, was intrusted with power and authority to do all that was necessary, there was positive evidence that the plaintiff had repeatedly desired that the attendants should be removed, and consequently if they were placed and continued there by the defendants the plea of leave and licence would not avail them.' Mrs Symm failed in her claim for other reasons, but the editor of the law report comments that a revocation of the previous licence would 'be nothing unless in a sound state of mind'. This suggested gloss does not accord with the principle in the law of agency that an authority to act is automatically revoked when the principal becomes insane (see, for example, *Yonge* v. *Toynbee*), although it is likely that if a previous consent were revoked while the patient remained both insane and dangerous, the common law power to detain (discussed shortly) would have been invoked.

However, there are two highly controversial false imprisonment cases which suggest that if a person has voluntarily entered a confined space upon clear terms as to how and when he is to get out, he cannot complain if he is only released in accordance with those terms (*Robinson* v. *Balmain New Ferry Co.* and *Herd* v. *Weardale Steel, Coal and Coke Co. Ltd*). In each of these cases, however, there was a contract between the confiners and the confined; in the first, the plaintiff was under an obligation to pay a penny on leaving the company's pier; in the second, the miner was not only under an obligation to work his shift but the contract also defined the time at which he was entitled to the services of the lift to get him out of the mine. Although each may be an example of *volenti*, they go no further than to suggest that there may be cases in which a person is contractually bound not to revoke his consent.

NHS services are not supplied under a contract with the patient (*Pfizer* v. *Ministry of Health*). By agreeing to enter hospital, a patient does not place himself under a contractual obligation to obey the hospital's rules, still less to see his treatment through to the bitter end. Even if he did, it is doubtful whether the law would now allow the hospital to lock him up in order to enforce such a duty (for how long could the Balmain New Ferry Company have kept Mr Robinson locked on their pier simply because he failed to pay them a penny?). The more likely analysis is that the hospital is entitled to decline to continue treating a patient who refuses to co-operate, so that the sanction is to let him go rather than to force him to stay. The *Weardale* case could, however, support the proposition that a patient who has agreed to enter hospital on terms that he will not seek discharge during the night is not entitled to call upon staff to let him out at three o'clock in the morning, but even that must be doubted where no special effort is required for them to do so.

It must be emphasized that, although hospitals undoubtedly have a duty to take reasonable care to protect their patients from harm (and that this includes dissuading an elderly and confused patient from wandering out), this duty does not extend to overriding the patient's clearly expressed wishes.

PREVENTION OF HARM

In *Pountney* v. *Griffiths*, Lord Edmund-Davies remarked that it had been conceded on behalf of the patient concerned 'that a hospital staff has powers of control over all mentally disordered patients, whether admitted voluntarily or compulsorily, though the nature and duration of the control varies with the category to which a patient belongs'. Glanville Williams (1983: 484) suggests that the authorities of a psychiatric hospital possess common law powers of discipline similar to those enjoyed by the master of a ship, which involve 'no more than restraining passengers or crew who are endangering the vessel or those aboard, or who are seriously disrupting life aboard'. Neither of these statements is supported by authority, and it may be that in the case of informal patients powers of control and discipline (apart from those agreed to by the patient) extend no further than the four situations in which it is clear that there is power on the part of any person to employ restraint for the purpose of preventing harm. There is a substantial degree of overlap between these four powers, but there are some points of difference, and each has been devised for slightly different reasons.

The first is the prevention of crime, now covered by section 3(1) of the Criminal Law Act 1967, which provides: 'A person may use such force as is reasonable in the circumstances in the prevention of crime, or in effecting or assisting in the lawful arrest of offenders or suspected offenders or of persons unlawfully at large.' The 1967 Act was primarily designed to abolish the ancient common law distinction between felonies and misdemeanours; it therefore replaced the earlier complex rules upon the lawfulness of force for these purposes with this deceptively simple 'reasonableness' formula (s. 3(2)). What this means will be discussed shortly, but it should also be noticed that section 3(1) applies only to the *prevention* of a crime which is actually in progress or about to be committed. It cannot justify retaliation or punishment. Nor, logically, can it apply where no crime is committed because the perpetrator is so insane as to fall within the M'Naghten Rules, rare though this will be even in a psychiatric hospital.

Apparently distinct from section 3(1) is the second principle, recently reiterated by Lord Diplock in *Albert* v. *Lavin*, that: 'every citizen in whose presence a breach of the peace is being, or reasonably appears to be about to be, committed has the right to take reasonable steps to make the person who is breaking or threatening to break the peace refrain from doing so; and those reasonable steps in appropriate cases will include detaining him against his will. At common law this is not only the right of every citizen, it is also his duty.' Once again, the breach must be in progress or imminently threatened; punishment or retaliation for one which is completed is not permitted. This common law power appears to have survived the

1967 Act, perhaps because a breach of the peace as such simply justifies the citizenry in the preventive steps outlined, and in bringing the transgressor before a justice of the peace, who may then bind him over to keep the peace or imprison him if he refuses to be so bound. Without more, this is not regarded as a conviction for crime. The preventive power might therefore exist even though the peace-breaker is insane within the M'Naghten Rules, although binding over is scarcely an appropriate remedy in such a case. (See the remarks of Lord Mansfield in *Brookshaw* v. *Hopkins*, quoted later, an inconclusive case which is concerned as much with breach of the peace as with the power to detain the insane.)

The standard textbooks give differing definitions of a breach of the peace, but in *R.* v. *Howell*, the Court of Appeal offered this: 'the word "disturbance" when used in isolation cannot constitute a breach of the peace ... there is a breach of the peace whenever harm is actually done or is likely to be done to a person in his presence to his property or a person is in fear of being so harmed through an assault, an affray, a riot, an unlawful assembly or other disturbance.' Violence, or its threat or apprehension, now appears essential; but although many breaches of the peace take place in public, they may be committed on private property.

Also distinct from section 3(1) is the concept of self- or private defence. Once again, there is overlap, because the right to defend oneself, one's property, or another person against attack almost invariably involves the prevention of a crime, but the objects are different. One is to assist in the preservation of law and order, the other is to enable individuals to escape being harmed by aggressors, and this includes aggressors who are not criminals because they are insane. Once again, retaliation or revenge is not permitted. The person attacked 'should demonstrate by his actions that he does not want to fight', before meeting force with force (*R.* v. *Julien*). Once again, the force used must be reasonable. It may be possible to rely on private defence when going to the rescue of a stranger under attack, but the language of the Court of Appeal in *R.* v. *Duffy* is more consistent with the defence of crime prevention, and in the Northern Irish case of *Devlin* v. *Armstrong* it was denied that private defence applied in respect of strangers.

The point could only be important where one patient was under attack from another who happened to be insane within the M'Naghten Rules (for hospital staff can clearly go to the defence of hospital property, as the game-keeper defends his master's birds), and it is inconceivable that the common law would not allow a defence in such cases. As Lord Mansfield said in *Brookshaw* v. *Hopkins*: 'God forbid, too, that a man should be punished for restraining the fury of a lunatic, when that is the case.' The fourth power is indeed a common law power to detain the insane (for a full discussion see Lanham 1974; cf. Carson 1982). As far back as the seventeenth century, Bacon's Abridgement stated that a private person might confine a person disordered in his mind who seems disposed to do mischief to himself or any other person (see, for example, *Scott* v. *Wakem*; *Symm* v. *Fraser*). This power has never been abrogated by the statutes prescribing commitment procedures. (Indeed, in *Re Shuttleworth*, Lord Denman CJ suggested that if the court had found the commitment process defective, it could still decline to discharge such a lunatic – and although this may be doubted in the context of a statute which prohibited licensed houses from receiving lunatics otherwise than upon such commitment, no such prohibition exists today for NHS hospitals.) The definition of insanity for this purpose may not lie in the M'Naghten Rules as such for they are addressed to the different question of ascribing guilt for a particular deed, but serious mental illness of the sort popularly thought of as 'madness' is probably required. As Lord Campbell CJ said in *Fletcher* v. *Fletcher*: 'By the common law of England no person can be imprisoned as a lunatic unless he is actually insane at the time ... It would place in jeopardy the liberty of many persons of eccentric habits, though in perfect possession of their faculties.' Further, mere insanity is not enough, for the person must also seem disposed to do mischief to himself or others (see, for example, *The Queen* v. *Pinder, ex parte Greenwood*). Clerk and Linsell (1982: 14–68) go so far as to suggest that the power is simply an example of the right to use force to prevent a deadly act of violence being done, but it certainly includes power to prevent harm to the patient himself as well as to others or to property.

All four powers may, it would seem, be summed up for our purposes in a general proposition that there is a right to restrain a patient who is doing, or is about to do, physical harm to himself, to other persons, or to property. It is also likely that all four powers are governed by a concept of 'reasonableness'. There is a clear statement in *R.* v. *McInnes* (at p. 302) that the Criminal Law Act concept of reasonable force applies equally to self- or private defence (and see Harlow 1974). If so, the other two powers are clearly analogous in principle and should be approached in the same way.

'Reasonableness' involves two separate propositions. One is that the force or restraint involved is no more than is in fact necessary to accomplish the purpose for which it is allowed. Nice calculation is not expected of people responding to an emergency, but neither is gross over-reaction to the danger presented, or the continuation of force once the need for it has gone. An example in the context of lawful arrest is *Allen* v. *Metropolitan Police Commissioner*, in which two young policemen over 6 feet tall put arm-locks upon a middle-aged man of 5 feet 2½ inches and summoned a van-load of reinforcements; four officers then carried him bodily to the van and put him 'not over-gently' on the van floor, knocking off his glasses and treading on them; they then 'restrained him with their feet' in the van. He suffered a grazed chin, tender abdomen, and a small piece of bone torn from his arm; damages of £1,115 were awarded.

In the context of detaining the insane, Bramwell B in *Scott* v. *Wakem* directed the jury that: 'if the defendant had made out that the plaintiff was, at the time of the original restraint, a dangerous lunatic, in such a state that it was likely that he might do mischief to anyone, the defendant would be justified in putting a restraint upon him, not merely at the moment of the original danger, but until there was reasonable ground to believe that the danger was over.' This might be followed today as an application of the reasonableness principle, but it would be unwise to interpret it as a warrant for the prolonged detention of an informal patient, given that ample statutory procedures with greater safeguards and clearer limits are now provided in Part II of the Mental Health Act 1983. Lanham (1974) supports this conclusion; and it is noteworthy that in the one recent reported case in which the authorities exceeded what is expressly permitted by the Act (*Townley* v. *Rushworth*), Lord Parker CJ showed no disposition to enquire whether the common law might have sanctioned what was done.

A further reason for limiting the use of common law powers to detain the insane to the minimum necessary to meet the need of the moment lies in the second element in 'reasonableness'. The degree of force used, however necessary, must be in proportion to the harm threatened. This is an evaluative or moral question. It is designed, for example, to inhibit the police in shooting to kill, even if there is no other way of preventing a person from riding in a motor vehicle without wearing a seat belt. Complete congruence between the threatened harm and the force used to prevent it is not required, but the imbalance must not be too great. In particular, if a person defending himself against a serious attack only does what he honestly and instinctively thinks is necessary, this is 'potent evidence' that what was done, however drastic, was reasonable (see *R*. v. *Shannon*). In such circumstances, the requirement of proportionality may almost have disappeared. In the hospital context, however, there is an obvious distinction between restraining and segregating a patient while he cools off after a violent episode, on the one hand, and continuing that segregation as a type of preventive detention, on the other. It is neither necessary nor reasonable to rely upon common law powers for anything approaching the latter.

But what if a nurse makes a mistake, and no harm is in fact being threatened at all? Where the justification relied upon is the prevention of crime or private defence, the nurse will be protected if he makes a genuine mistake of fact, at least if that mistake is based upon reasonable grounds. Some would argue that even an unreasonable mistake should protect him from a criminal charge (Glanville Williams 1978: 452–55; Criminal Law Revision Committee, 1980: paras 283, 287); but the weight of authority (extensively, but eventually needlessly, canvassed by the Divisional Court in *Albert* v. *Lavin*) favours the objective test; and certainly there is no good reason why a nurse should not be liable in *tort* for an unlawful restraint imposed as a result of an honest but careless mistake.

However, where the *only* justification claimed is the common law power to detain the insane, there is no defence unless the patient is actually insane (*Fletcher* v. *Fletcher*; *Sinclair* v. *Broughton*). Lanham (1974: 516) states that: 'It is not clear whether the plaintiff must actually be dangerous or whether reasonable belief that the plaintiff is dangerous is sufficient to render the detention lawful.' The cases do not distinguish the question of dangerousness from the question of insanity, but as in each the patient was not even insane, the point did not arise. Lanham also suggests that it would be difficult to prove that a person who was in fact insane and who appeared to be dangerous was not in fact dangerous. The burden of proving justification would lie upon the person imposing the restraint and a nurse might be expected to display special skill in deciding whether a patient constituted an imminent danger to himself or others: but if a nurse were to convince a court that he did reasonably believe the patient dangerous, it would indeed be difficult to prove him wrong. (Where the act is covered by section 139 of the Mental Health Act 1983, discussed earlier, reasonable care would certainly be a defence – but this probably only applies to detained patients.)

It will be seen that there is nothing in the foregoing to justify the use of confinement or restraint upon informal patients simply in order to secure their compliance with hospital routine. The essential

criterion is the prevention of harm. The 'reasonableness' requirement would also support a system such as that described by Faulk
(1979; see also Chapter 2), which may be thought sound psychiatric
practice in all hospital contexts. In this, the appropriate response to
each type of incident which may be anticipated on the ward is
worked out in detail and in advance by the professional team but
preferably with the co-operation and agreement of the patients
themselves. In this way it should be possible to restrict intervention
to the minimum necessary to prevent the harm which is threatened;
to prescribe maxima beyond which responses to certain incidents
must not go; to minimize the risks of misunderstandings between
patients and staff leading to mistaken beliefs as to a patient's
intentions in an incident; to reduce the problem of over-prediction of
dangerousness; and to avoid the risk that any incident, however
trivial, is met with a standard and often unnecessary over-reaction.

Powers under the Mental Health Acts

Everything which has previously been said applies also to detained
patients, but two further justifications for restraint and confinement
may exist in their case. One lies in the statutory power to detain
under the Mental Health Act 1983, and the other lies in the power to
impose treatment without the patient's consent, under Part IV of that
Act. The very fact that the legislation now distinguishes the concepts
of detention and treatment, and makes some attempt to define what
may be done with a patient in hospital, makes it imperative to
consider precisely what may be included in each.

DETENTION

The 1983 Act (in sections 6 and 40) provides that a completed
application under Part II, or hospital order, or equivalent under Part
III, shall be sufficient authority for the hospital managers to detain
the patient in hospital 'in accordance with the provisions of this Act'.
The Act's provisions, however, do not define detention, nor do they
refer in any way to the types of confinement or restraint which may
be employed. They are concerned solely with the mechanics of
beginning, continuing, and ending the power to detain: the nearest
they get to the mechanics of detention itself is when they provide for
transfers, for leave of absence, and for the retaking of patients who
go absent without leave. The overwhelming impression created by
the Act is that it is empowering the managers of a particular hospital

to keep the patient inside that hospital until the authority to do so lapses or is otherwise brought to an end. No express authority is given for measures over and above that, for example, of placing a patient in a straitjacket, or segregating him from his fellows and keeping him in solitary confinement for a prolonged period, as happened in the case of *A. v. United Kingdom.*

That the power to detain does involve some power to control the patient over and above that supplied by the common law discussed earlier is undeniable. But there are several arguments against implying into the concept of detention a general power to impose whatever measures of confinement or restraint the hospital managers see fit.

The first lies in the ordinary principles of statutory construction. Ordinary words of the English language are to be given their natural and ordinary meaning: solitary confinement in the conditions described in *A. v. United Kingdom* is no more a natural and ordinary meaning of the power to detain in a hospital than is the use of obsolete mechanical means of restraint. There is nothing in the context of the Act itself, as has already been shown, to indicate such a wide meaning. Further, it is trite law that statutes dealing with the liberty of the subject are to be strictly construed, so that if more than one meaning is possible, that which is more favourable to liberty is to be chosen.

The second point is that deprivation of general liberty is not to be equated with deprivation of all ordinary legal rights. Even a prisoner serving a sentence of imprisonment remains 'invested with residuary rights appertaining to the nature and conduct of his incarceration' (*per* Shaw LJ in *R. v. Hull Prison Board of Visitors, ex parte St Germain and Others* at p. 716). If a prisoner is unlawfully assaulted by prison officers, his imprisonment remains lawful but he is nonetheless entitled to prosecute or sue for the trespass to his person. Before the Mental Health (Amendment) Act 1982 attempted to clarify the matter, there was a respectable and growing body of opinion to the effect that deprivation under the Mental Health Act of the right to leave hospital did not involve deprivation of the ordinary legal right to give or withhold consent to treatment (see particularly Jacob 1976, and Gostin 1979; see also Butler Committee 1975 and DHSS 1978). That view, like this, was founded upon the Act's failure to give express authority to anything other than the detention of the patient in the hospital. The present argument is perhaps strengthened now that the 1983 Act does define what may be done in the name of treatment, while giving no further powers in the name of detention; as will be seen later, it has probably placed limits on the use of medication *for either purpose*.

The comparison with prisoners highlights the startling results which an implied general discretion would produce. Section 47(1) of the Prison Act 1952 empowers the Home Secretary to make rules for the regulation and management of prisons and for the discipline and control of prisoners. There is no equivalent in the Mental Health Act, for it is impossible to read the regulation-making power in section 32 in that light: it deals with the detailed conduct of the statutory processes laid down in Part II and no more.

The Prison Rules prescribe procedures and punishments in cases of alleged offences against prison discipline. These in themselves import basic notions of substantive and procedural fairness into the conduct of prisons. It was also held in the *St Germain* case that boards of visitors have a duty to observe the rules of natural justice when hearing such cases. However, the courts have so far held that the Prison Rules themselves confer no substantive rights (over and above the ordinary legal rights retained despite imprisonment) for breach of which a prisoner might sue (*Arbon* v. *Anderson*; *Becker* v. *Home Office*). In *Williams* v. *Home Office (No. 2)* however, Cumming-Bruce LJ at least accepted that there would be an arguable case to put to the House of Lords for such an action in respect of a breach of rule 43 (see Zellick 1981 and 1982). Rule 43 places limits upon the power to deprive a prisoner of association with his fellows.

The old lunacy legislation made complex provision for regulating the internal conduct of the various institutions covered; and section 40 of the Lunacy Act 1890 placed limits upon the use of mechanical means of bodily restraint. It would be startling indeed if the Mental Health Act 1959, in sweeping away all these controls and replacing them with a simple power to detain, were to be read as granting a general discretion to confine and restrain, without any equivalent to the substantive and procedural safeguards laid down for prisoners, and without any power to prescribe them. Such a discretion could only be controlled through the general principle of administrative law that administrative bodies must act 'reasonably'. This is quite different from the 'reasonableness' concept discussed in the preceding section, for it is not for the court to decide what was reasonable in the circumstances: the court can only declare the exercise of such a discretion unlawful if it was so obviously wrong that no reasonable body could have so decided (*Associated Provincial Picture Houses Ltd* v. *Wednesbury Corpor-*

ation). For example, the court decides whether a police officer has 'reasonable cause' for an arrest without warrant, but if he has, his decision to make the arrest can only be challenged on *Wednesbury* principles (*Holgate-Mohammed* v. *Duke*).

It is submitted that the extent of the power to confine and restrain ought in principle to be determined by the law and not by administrative discretion. If, therefore, a sensible middle course may be deduced from the legislation, Parliament, it is submitted, may be assumed to have intended it. In *Pountney* v. *Griffiths* at p. 888, Lord Edmund-Davies observed that: 'Section 60 orders are made where the mental disorder of the named person "warrants the detention of the patient in a hospital for medical treatment," and that necessarily involves the exercise of control and discipline.' The obvious inference is that the Act permits the exercise of such control and discipline as is incidental to the express purposes of the legislation and no more.

Thus there is obviously power to keep the patient within the named hospital. In a hospital or unit which is itself secure, this is in fact an easier concept to apply in practice than it is when a patient is liable to be detained in a hospital where most patients are free to come and go as they please. Seclusion may on occasions be the only practicable means of keeping the patient within the hospital without prejudicing the other patients there, and to that extent it may be justified as the more general security is justified in places where all the patients are liable to be detained.

Some control and discipline may also be incidental to the purpose of treating patients to the extent that this is permitted by the 1983 Act. In *Pountney* v. *Griffiths* itself, visiting time was regarded as an obvious aspect of the patient's treatment, and thus the act of inducing him to return to his ward when it was over was incidental to it. In a hospital such as Broadmoor, where the secure and highly disciplined environment is itself regarded as 'milieu therapy', the distinction between control for the purposes of treatment and control for other purposes may be particularly difficult to draw. But that is not to say that such a distinction is impossible, still less that any regime, hower arbitrary or oppressive, could be justified on the ground that it is 'treatment'.

Finally, some control and discipline may be incidental to enabling the institution to function as a hospital at all. Informal patients who disrupt hospital life may be asked to conform or to leave. Compulsory patients may not be so willing to conform and may not always be asked to leave. The analogy of the ship or aircraft put forward by Glanville Williams (1983: 484) is particularly relevant here. But this is limited to taking reasonable steps to restrain those who are endangering the vessel or those aboard, or who are seriously disrupting life aboard: 'it no longer means lashing or putting in irons.' Nevertheless, some control for the purposes of hospital routine may be warranted under this head.

It is suggested that all these powers should be governed by the Criminal Law Act concept of 'reasonableness' – in other words whether the force used was necessary to the purpose permitted and proportionate to the danger presented. The nurse in *Pountney* v. *Griffiths* was granted the procedural protection of section 141(2) of the 1959 Act (now section 139(2) of the 1983 Act), and in properly instituted proceedings *might* have established the substantive defence of reasonable care in section 141(1). But there is no suggestion, for example, that he would have been entitled to beat the patient senseless in order to carry him back to the ward, or even that the degree of force needed was a matter which the law left to his discretion. The limits of reasonableness should be inherent in these powers, just as the police must observe them in the use of their powers to use force in the pursuit of law and order. This is a quite different principle from that in *Wednesbury*. It sets defined limits to what can be done in any given set of facts, rather than leaving it to the authorities' discretion within the very broad ambit of what a 'reasonable' authority might be expected to do in the circumstances. Whether the courts would have the will to impose the tighter control on hospital authorities, no one can know, but it is suggested that they should.

TREATMENT

Part IV of the Mental Health Act 1983 has, for the first time, attempted to define the circumstances in which treatment for mental disorder may be given. These vary according to the nature of the treatment and the legal category to which the patient belongs.

The provision which is most likely to be relevant for our purposes is that laid down in section 63. This provides that, unless a particular form of treatment is brought within the safeguards laid down in either section 57 or section 58, it may be given to a detained patient without his consent. By section 56, this applies to a patient detained for assessment (s. 2), treatment (s. 3), or any of the other longer-term powers in the Act (e.g. s. 37); but it does *not* apply to patients held under the various 'place of safety' powers in the Act (e.g. s. 136) or under the short-term holding powers for in-patients (s. 5), or under emergency admission (s. 4) until the second medical recommendation needed to convert it into a full admission for assessment has been received, or to those conditionally discharged under a restriction order (s. 42), or remanded to hospital by the courts for reports (s. 35).

As the measures which we are discussing (apart from medication) have not been brought within sections 57 or 58, it is crucial to examine the inherent limiting factors in this power to impose treatment without consent. The first is that it must be 'medical treatment'. This is not comprehensively defined, but under section 145(1) it 'includes nursing, and also includes care, habilitation and rehabilitation under medical supervision'. A token economy system of rewards and punishments designed to modify behaviour is obviously capable of falling within this definition. Equally, however, it could not be used to justify any and every means of dealing with detained patients in a hospital, however harsh the punishments and exiguous the rewards, or however arbitrarily each is decided upon or imposed. The object of 'habilitation and rehabilitation' must be to teach the patient normal patterns of behaviour, so as to make good the deficiencies of his earlier socialization and training, and to enable him so far as is possible to take his place in the community without danger to himself or others. The 1972 statement of the aims of Rampton Hospital (quoted in Boynton 1980: 163) observes that: 'present knowledge suggests that the most effective methods of changing behaviour are those which emphasise positive and consistent rewards for appropriate or desirable behaviour, and which deny the individual rewards for inappropriate behaviour.' This, however, begs two questions.

Firstly, who is to define appropriate behaviour for this purpose? The Rampton review team (Boynton 1980: 38) observed that much emphasis was placed, at case conferences to assess the patient's progress through the Rampton system, upon whether or not the patient 'has conformed with the high or artificial norms of behaviour which are expected under the nursing regime on the block wards'. 'Habilitation and rehabilitation' must, however, be carried out under medical supervision; and section 63 of the 1983 Act specifically applies only to treatment given 'by or under the direction of the responsible medical officer'. The appropriate norms should be determined by the clinical team under the ultimate direction of the responsible medical officer, and with the aim of treating the patient rather than serving the system for its own sake.

Secondly, therefore, to what extent must the treatment be adapted to the needs of the individual patient? Once again, the Rampton review team (Boynton 1980: 36 and 38) observed that: 'In practice however it often seems more a question of fitting the patient into the system than of devising ways to suit the patient's needs.' Further: 'in the case of patients who have been convicted in the courts it appears that the nursing staff ... will often relate the time a patient should spend on a block ward, or in Rampton, to the severity of the original offence as much as to his current clinical needs.' Cohen (1981) makes a similar point in relation to Broadmoor, when he argues that the system of strict discipline (which may be termed 'milieu therapy') seems an appropriate method of treating the 'under-controlled' offender, but is unlikely to assist those who are capable of a high degree of conformity in an institutional setting, but who have not learned to control their sudden outbursts of aggression in reaction to certain stimuli which may be encountered outside hospital. The difficulty here is that a token economy may lose its efficacy with the under-controlled patient if he thinks it unjust because it is not applied equally to all patients. Nevertheless, there are obviously ways of grouping patients to avoid this difficulty; and it must be inherent in the concept of 'treatment' that the particular therapy in question is clinically indicated for the particular patient. Section 63 again reinforces this by referring to 'any medical treatment given to him *for the mental disorder from which he is suffering*' (emphasis supplied).

Thus, to be justified under section 63 as treatment without consent (as opposed, for example, to harm-prevention or detention), measures of confinement or restraint must be medically determined and clinically indicated as treatment for the particular disorder suffered by the individual patient, and not simply part of a 'system' devised to meet the needs of the institution itself.

Section 58 lays down extra safeguards which must be observed for certain types of treatment: these are the administration of medicine by any means if three months have elapsed since the first time in that period when the patient was given medicine for his mental disorder, and electroconvulsive therapy. The section would thus be irrelevant for our purposes unless certain measures of behaviour-modification, milieu therapy or individual restraint are prescribed in future regulations, were it not that the administration of medicine is one of the prime measures of restraint employed in psychiatric hospitals. The section provides that the treatments concerned may only be imposed in two circumstances: first, where the patient consents, and the responsible medical officer or an independent doctor appointed for the purpose (in effect by the Mental Health Act Commission) certifies not only that he has consented but also that he is capable of understanding the nature, purpose, and likely effects of the treatment; *or* secondly, where the independent doctor has certified either that he is not so capable or that he has not consented but that the treatment should be given having regard to the likelihood of its alleviating or preventing a deterioration of his condition.

Section 57 lays down even more stringent safeguards which must be observed for psychosurgery and sex hormone implants (Mental Health (Hospital, Guardianship and Consent to Treatment) Regulations 1983, reg. 16(1)). It would therefore only become relevant if the measures under discussion were prescribed, which is unlikely in view of the nature of the safeguards. Not only must an independent doctor certify that the treatment should be given, having regard to the likelihood of its alleviating or preventing a deterioration of the patient's condition, but an independent multi-disciplinary triumvirate must certify that the patient is capable of understanding the treatment and has given his consent to it. Section 57 applies to detained patients and to patients who are not liable to be detained (s. 56). The latter are thus given the benefit of a second opinion in addition to their normal right to give or withhold consent to treatment; detained patients are given the right to give or withhold consent and a second opinion; and incapable patients (perhaps with a higher threshold than at common law) cannot be given the treatments at all.

Various provisions are related to the safeguards laid down in sections 57 and 58. The difficult provision, however, is section 62. Section 62(1) provides that:

'Sections 57 and 58 above shall not apply to any treatment – (a) which is immediately necessary to save the patient's life; or (b) which (not being irreversible) is immediately necessary to prevent a serious deterioration of his condition; or (c) which (not being irreversible or hazardous) is immediately necessary to alleviate serious suffering by the patient; or (d) which (not being irreversible or hazardous) is immediately necessary and represents the minimum interference necessary to prevent the patient from behaving violently or being a danger to himself or others.'

Section 62(2) provides that a withdrawal of consent shall not prevent the continuation of any treatment pending compliance with section 57 or 58 if the responsible medical officer considers that its discontinuance would cause serious suffering to the patient.

This presents obvious problems with the three-month rule. It is clear that the section 58 safeguards do not apply if the *current* administration of medicine is exempted. But what if the *first* administration took place in circumstances described in section 62(1)? It seems that a further administration three months later in non-exempt circumstances *is* covered by the safeguards. However, it could be that any administration of medicine which is given for *other* purposes than the treatment of his mental disorder (for example, to restrain him from harming others or to keep him in the hospital) can be ignored both as a first or as a current administration, because it is not 'treatment for mental disorder' or 'administered ... for his mental disorder'. The alternative view would be that such administrations *do* qualify on both counts, and therefore that, save in the circumstances laid down in section 62(1), medicine can *never* be administered after the three months without the safeguards laid down in section 58. The safe course for the time being would obviously be to observe the latter view, although section 139 would provide some protection in the event of a wrong choice of interpretation.

A further problem is that sections 59, 60, and 62 are applied along with section 57 to informal patients, and it might therefore be thought that section 62 was giving a warrant to impose treatment upon informal patients in those situations without their consent or other common law justification. It is submitted, however, that this is not so. Section 62 is intended merely to *exempt* certain emergencies from the safeguards laid down in sections 57 and 58. The legal justification for treatment must still be found: for detained patients within the meaning of section 56, this includes the power to impose treatment without consent under section 63; for all patients, it includes their consent or the common law prevention of harm discussed earlier; and for incapable informal patients it may include the right 'to use medical procedures to save the life of a patient who lacks understanding' (Butler Committee 1975: 50, probably inspired by Glanville Williams). These justifications, it will be observed, are in some cases wider than section 62: it is permissible at common law to kill a man who is about to kill you, and nothing could be more irreversible than that. In other cases, they are narrower than section 62, for by no means all writers are agreed that the common law permits an incapable informal patient to be treated merely to prevent deterioration, and it is extremely

unlikely that a dissenting informal patient may be treated for that
purpose.

Summary and conclusion

Measures of confinement or restraint are lawful in relation to
individual patients in the following circumstances:

(1) Where a patient with the capacity to do so has given a real
consent to them, but such consent may be revoked at any time unless
perhaps the patient is contractually bound not to do so.

(2) Where the patient is doing, or is about to do, physical harm to
himself, to other persons, or to property, but only to the extent that
the restraint is necessary to prevent that harm and is reasonable in
proportion to the harm which is threatened.

(3) Where a patient is liable to be detained under the Mental
Health Act, but only to the extent that this is reasonably incidental to
the power to keep the patient within the hospital, to the power to
enable the hospital to function properly as a hospital, and to the
power to treat the patient to the extent permitted under (4) below.

(4) Where a patient is liable to be detained under section 2 or any
of the longer-term powers under the Act, to the extent that it has
been medically determined and is clinically indicated for the
treatment of the particular disorder suffered by the patient (and is
not specifically prescribed for the purposes of either section 57 or
section 58).

The administration of medicine to a detained patient, once three
months have elapsed since the first occasion during his current
detention period when medicine was administered, is probably *only*
permissible in the circumstances laid down in sections 58 to 62.

An honest mistake of fact, for which there were reasonable
grounds, will almost invariably provide a good defence where it was
thought that conditions (2), (3), or (4) existed, but not where it was
thought that an informal patient had consented. An honest mistake
of law, for which there are reasonable grounds, will apparently
afford a good defence to individuals when dealing with detained
patients.

It is always possible that the courts would construe the various
powers discussed more liberally than is suggested here, particularly
in relation to the power to detain. However, where hospitals are
anxious to devise guidelines for staff, it is as well to base them upon
those justifications which can clearly be seen to exist, rather than to
take an optimistic view of the law's future development. The practice

commended at the end of section (2)(ii) may be particularly helpful here. It seems clear that the trend is towards greater rather than lesser respect for the rights of the mental patient as an individual and this too should be borne in mind, along with sensitivity to his needs and to those of society.

This trend owes more to the efforts of other bodies than to the courts, and it should not be forgotten that other avenues of redress have in the past proved more fruitful. The Health Service Commissioner has been prepared to consider complaints of unlawful detention, despite the exclusion from his terms of reference of matters which could be taken to a tribunal or a court, and of action taken in the care and treatment of a patient which is taken solely in the exercise of clinical judgement. The European Commission of Human Rights has been prepared to consider conditions in Broadmoor as possible breaches of Article 3 of the Convention, although this has not yet led to a judgement which would oblige the United Kingdom to alter its present law on the subject under discussion. Further challenges to section 139 under Article 6 may be particularly relevant in the future. Also in the future, the Mental Health Act Commission established under the 1983 Act will have the particular function of visiting detained patients in hospitals, interviewing them and investigating their complaints. It remains to be seen how effective this will be, but the very existence of such a body in England is evidence of a new attitude towards patients' rights on the part of all the authorities concerned.

References

Boynton, J. (1980) *Report of the Review of Rampton Hospital*. Cmnd 8073. London: HMSO.

Butler Committee (1975) *Report of the Committee on Mentally Abnormal Offenders*. London: HMSO.

Carson, D. (1982) Detention of the Mentally Disordered. *Local Government Review* 146: 887.

Clerk and Linsell (1982) *Torts*. 15th edition ed. R. W. M. Dias. London: Sweet & Maxwell.

Cohen, D. (1981) *Broadmoor*. London: Psychology News Press.

Criminal Law Revision Committee (1980) 14th Report, *Offences against the Person*. Cmnd 7844. London: HMSO.

DHSS (1978) *Review of the Mental Health Act 1959*. Cmnd 7320. London: HMSO.

Faulk, M. (1979) An Interim Regional Medium Secure Unit. Paper presented at the annual conference of the Social Administration Association, held in Cambridge.

Goldstein, J. (1975) For Harold Lasswell: Some Reflections on Human Dignity, Entrapment, Informed Consent and the Plea Bargain. *Yale Law Journal* 84: 683.

Gostin, L. O. (1979) The Merger of Incompetency and Certification: The Illustration of Unauthorised Medical Contact in the Psychiatric Context. *International Journal of Law and Psychiatry* 2: 127.

Harlow, C. (1974) Self Defence: Public Right or Private Privilege. *Criminal Law Review*: 528.

Jacob, J. (1976) The Right of the Mental Patient to his Psychosis. *Modern Law Review* 39: 17.

Lanham, D. (1974) Arresting the Insane. *Criminal Law Review*: 515.

Robertson, G. (1981) Informed Consent to Medical Treatment. *Law Quarterly Review* 97: 102.

Royal College of Psychiatrists and others (1980) *Report of a Joint Working Party to Formulate Ethical Guide-lines for the Conduct of Programmes of Behaviour Modification in the National Health Service.* London: HMSO.

Skegg, P. D. G. (1974) A Justification for Medical Procedures Performed Without Consent. *Law Quarterly Review* 90: 512.

Williams, Glanville (1978) *Textbook of Criminal Law.* London: Stevens.

—— (1983) *Textbook of Criminal Law.* 2nd edition. London: Stevens.

Winfield and Jolowicz (1984) *Tort.* 12th edition ed. W. V. H. Rogers. London: Sweet & Maxwell.

Zellick, G. (1981) The Prison Rules and the Courts. *Criminal Law Review*: 602.

—— (1982) The Prison Rules and the Courts: A Postscript. *Criminal Law Review*: 575.

Cases

A. v. United Kingdom, European Commission of Human Rights, No. 6840/74 (report adopted 16 July, 1980).

Albert v. Lavin [1981] 1 All E.R. 628 (DC), [1981] 3 All E.R. 878 (HL).

Allen v. Metropolitan Police Commissioner [1980] Crim. L.R. 441.

Arbon v. Anderson [1943] 1 All E.R. 154.

Associated Provincial Picture Houses Ltd v. Wednesbury Corporation [1947] 2 All E.R. 680.

Becker v. Home Office [1972] 2 All E.R. 672.

Bolam v. Friern Hospital Management Committee [1957] 2 All E.R. 118.

Brookshaw v. Hopkins (1772) Lofft 240.

Buckland v. Buckland [1967] 2 All E.R. 300.

Canterbury v. Spence (1972) 464 F. 2d. 772, US App., DC.

Chatterton v. Gerson [1981] 1 All E.R. 257.

Cobbs v. Grant (1972) 104 Cal. Rep. 505, Calif. SC.

Devlin v. Armstrong [1971] N.I. 13.

Fletcher v. Fletcher (1859) 1 El. & El. 420.

Freeman v. Home Office, [1984] 1 All E.R. 1036.

Part IV Dangerousness and Social Control

9 Psychiatry and dangerousness: a counter renaissance?

Paul Bowden

It has been argued that the renewal of interest in the concept of dangerousness can be explained by the apparent failure of the rehabilitative ideal and by the sheer cost of imprisonment which is forcing economies through an isolation of selected groups against whom we wish to take really serious action (Bottoms 1977). These groups include psychiatric offenders, who offend because of individual pathology, and professional criminals. This chapter examines some of the issues raised by the renaissance of dangerousness and it opens by defining its subject matter.

What is dangerousness?

The Roman word *dominium* had two distinct meanings: power of a lord, jurisdiction, dominion; power to dispose of, harm. Its current use can be traced through the old French word *dangier* and Anglo-French da(u)nger. Addition of the suffix -ous to danger forms the adjective with the sense 'abounding in, full of, characterized by, of the nature of'. Adding the suffix -ness to the adjective dangerous forms a substantive noun expressing a state or condition (Oxford English Dictionary). The noun dangerousness is variously qualified as having future activity in terms of potential (Kozol, Bouchier, and Garafalo 1972; Hamilton 1982), tendency (Scott 1977), or risk (Tidmarsh 1982). This anticipated behaviour is usually defined in terms of injury or harm, to persons only, or to people or objects, within a specified period of time. The definition of dangerouness is important because if it is imprecise, judgements and predictions based on it will be inaccurate and most persons labelled as dangerous will, in time, prove not to be.

Some authorities have suggested that it is the fear induced in others which lies at the heart of dangerousness: when the fear is transferred from the behaviour to a person his social identity is transformed into that of a dangerous individual (Hepworth 1982). Sarbin (1967) took this social-interactionist view to the extreme in suggesting that the dangerous offender is in large measure a product of the institutions created to mould him.

Others authors (e.g. Kozol, Bouchier, and Garafalo 1972: 373) consider dangerousness to be an amalgam of behaviours, personality attributes, and traits. No single factor is pre-eminent and each may add to or neutralize the others:

'We can see the dangerous person as one who has actually inflicted or attempted to inflict serious physical injury to another person; harbours anger, hostility and resentment; enjoys witnessing or inflicting suffering; lacks altruistic and compassionate concern for others; sees himself as the victim rather than the aggressor; resents or rejects authority; is primarily concerned with his own satisfaction and with the relief of his own discomfort; is intolerant of frustration or delay of satisfaction; lacks control of his impulses; has immature attitudes towards social responsibility; lacks insight into his own psychological structure; distorts his perception of reality in accordance with his own wishes and needs.'

Similar catalogues of value judgements have been used in an attempt to describe a supposed form of mental abnormality, 'psychopathic disorder' (Cleckley 1976). But as with psychopathic disorder the contingencies or factors which are thought to be associated with dangerousness have proved to be ephemeral so that it is not possible to apply the usual psychological tests of reliability and validity in their investigation. Furthermore, how much and how many of these attributes are necessary for the definition of condition, or whether one in itself is sufficient, is never made clear.

Perhaps more success has been achieved by describing only behavioural abnormalities as having a predictive value, for example, the triad of enuresis, fire-setting, and cruelty to animals (Hellman and Blackman 1966); sadistic sexual fantasies, interests in Nazism, guns, torture, black magic, and bondage (Brittain 1968 and 1970). But the criticisms remain that the degree to which these behaviours occur in the non-dangerous is not apparent, as is the transition from fantasy to violence *in vivo*. It is to avoid these difficulties that dangerousness has been defined in purely political terms, such as usurping by unorthodox or unacceptable means a position of relative power in a role system (Sarbin 1967). Dangerousness, then, is an idiosyncrasy, not an objective concept, and a matter of judgement and opinion.

If the clinical view has any relevance, what is it? Scott (1977) provided a discussion of the concept. He prefaced his remarks by cautioning that as a label dangerousness contributed to its own continuance. To use the concept to legislate for treatment before the nature and effect of that treatment were known demanded a heavy price of both liberty and services. Scott wrote that dangerousness depended on disturbing the often precarious adjustment of others. A dangerous person engendered excess anxiety because he or she had already failed to respond to society's countermeasures. Repeated dangerous acts suggested dangerous intention and their seriousness depended on the ability to organize a defence, the approximation of the threats to the bodily image, and the degree of permanence of damage. Scott emphasized that while some of the factors which were associated with dangerous behaviour acted synergistically, others had a reciprocal effect. Tidmarsh (1982) has rightly criticized Scott's qualification of dangerousness as an 'unpredictable and untreatable tendency' on the grounds that anticipating and modifying a danger does not necessarily reduce the risk.

Psychiatry and dangerousness

Do the scientific base or the tenets of psychiatry help to elucidate dangerousness and do such insights indicate treatment or provide a prognosis? Foucault (1978) has suggested that the link between psychiatry and dangerousness can be traced through shared precarious living conditions of the mad and bad in nineteenth-century Europe. Violence and madness posed a common threat which was to be explained by the doctrines of Lombrosian degeneration and to be eradicated by the application of Galtonian eugenics. Contrary to the medieval English view that the insane suffered enough because of the very existence of their malady, Foucault traces the idea that insanity itself was a crime, and further, that madness could remain hidden until exposed. The stage was set for the alienist to present himself as the expert needed to interpret the barely recognizable signs of madness, and, by foretelling, to prevent the worst explosions. In the guise of therapy, confinement of the mentally ill followed inevitably. Doctors were then called upon both as specialists in motivation and as diviners of the stigmata of the dangerous. Gradually an image was built up of dangerous people who were enemies of society, marked as targets for punitive intervention, and having secured a clientele, interested groups clung to the medical view of dangerousness lest the rationale for their existence be threatened (Bottoms 1977).

Arising from the political and social changes of the nineteenth century psychological theories were used to explain crimes which had no apparent motive or where the perpetrator was driven by a seemingly irresistible force. Suspicions of mental pathology were aroused when there was no reason for an act, insanity being seen as the cause of that which made no sense. Just as today dangerousness is not interpreted as a state or condition of danger but as an explanation of it, so criminal psychiatry developed by providing a pathology both of monstrous behaviour and of insanity with crime as its only manifestation.

Foucault (1978) argued that the borderland of psychiatry and crime offered a modality of power to be secured and justified, and it is clear from the writings of Glover (1960: 347, 348) that this was proposed:

'Many crimes of violence are the result of pathological conditions which ... are nevertheless characteristic forms of mental disorder capable of great improvement, sometimes of cure, by scientific processes of treatment ... Thus the early diagnosis and treatment of potential murders could be dealt with by an adequate service of child psychiatry.'

So psychiatric jargon provided an explanation for dangerous behaviour which otherwise remained a mystery, and once a link was established legislators responded to the public fears and demands about the inability to identify and reduce the rate of habitually violent offenders by relying increasingly on psychiatrists to define dangerousness in the criminal justice system (Steadman and Cocozza 1978).

The contempory use of psychiatric evidence in English law is exampled in the appeal of a convicted man against a sentence of life imprisonment for rape. A sentence of eight years was substituted on the ground that a sentence of life imprisonment would not normally be upheld in the absence of psychiatric evidence that the appellant presented a grave danger to the public in the future (R. v. Hay). Mental abnormality was not an issue and the psychiatrist was clearly seen as the expert in dangerousness.

A power struggle followed the introduction of psychiatric testimony and this led lawyers to assert their ascendancy by insisting on the need for legislative control and the exact definition of terms used. A consequence of this is seen in America where dangerousness is defined in terms of degree of certainty of damage, which must be in the forseeable future, and the probability of substantial injury, which must be high. The dangerousness criteria which form the central component of admissions of mentally ill sectioned patients to hospital in some American states have similar qualifications: violent acts must be recent, the more distant assuming a greater degree of control; the severity of harm must amount to a serious threat to life and limb or a substantial potential for harm; there must also be a substantial likelihood of recurrence.

Radzinowicz and Hood (1981) have suggested that the heart of the dangerousness question is justifiable public alarm, which can be seen essentially as a political process. They argue that although numerically the drunken driver or the neglectful employer represent a far greater risk than the murderer, rapist, or child molester, the former are considered daily risks inseparable from our way of life whereas violent outbursts by the mentally ill are unacceptable. The mad are doubly dangerous because their attacks are considered unprovoked, and they themselves are unpredictable and uncontrollable.

To be in a state of dangerousness is rarely an unconditional thing and is usually situation-specific. To act dangerously is an unusual occurrence and to predict such activity is even more rare.

Assessment and prediction

Judgements regarding dangerousness are important because they can be the sole criterion for detaining people for long periods against their will. The work of Kozol, Bouchier, and Garafalo (1972) provides some empirical evidence in support of the clinicians' skill in assessing dangerousness. These authors found that the recidivism rate of violent sex offenders released by psychiatrists was only 8 per cent, whereas the proportion was 35 per cent for offenders discharged by the courts against psychiatric advice. However,

Kozol's work can be severely criticized on the grounds that the two groups were unmatched on the significant variables. Others are more sanguine in their approach; for example the Report of the Committee on Mentally Abnormal Offenders (1975: 60) states: 'unfortunately subjective judgement, based on however much experience, professional knowledge and available information, and exercised however conscientiously, is inescapably unreliable.'

To examine the precise contribution made by psychiatrists Quinsey and Ambtman (1979) compared clinicians' performance with that of teachers in the prediction of the likelihood and seriousness of re-offending in a group of mentally ill offenders. They found that overall psychiatric ratings were similar to teachers and both groups weighed information similarly in arriving at their judgements. Inter-rater reliability for psychiatrists was no higher than for teachers and for psychiatrists as a group the highest inter-rater correlation was only 0.48. Furthermore, psychiatrists did not make different judgements and they did not employ specialized assessment techniques. These conclusions were ratified by Harding and Montandon (1982) using standardized case histories as the material assessed by 193 participants, comprising psychiatrists and other occupational groups. There was no higher level of agreement amongst clinicians, whose only distinction was that generally they rated patients higher on a scale of dangerousness.

Overall the evidence suggests that when the obfuscations which surround the clinical assessment of dangerousness are penetrated psychiatrists are shown to base their judgements on non-medical information which others are at least as competent to interpret. An example is seen in the work of Steadman and Cocozza (1978), who examined the factors involved in the assessment of dangerousness in a group of such patients confined in maximum-security hospitals in the USA. In this group the most important factor in the release decision was not a clinical issue, which required a high level of skill to be elicited, but a mundane one: the presence of interested families or other persons who kept contact through correspondence and visits.

The actuarial method of prediction depends on measurable factors such as age, sex, criminal record. The purpose of actuarial prediction is to assign individuals to risk groups but the problem arises that with very rare behaviour the relevant factors cannot be weighted even if they can be identified. Many of those who commit the most serious crimes against persons tend to have lived normal lives in the community, and to be without a criminal record. For them the question who might be dangerous cannot be asked.

Despite these qualifications Sawyer (1966) concluded that studies have shown overwhelmingly that actuarial methods of prediction are more accurate than clinical. An illustration of the actuarial method is the work of Steadman and Cocozza (1974), who, using the factors of age and the number of severity of previous convictions, assigned individuals to a scale. Of those with the highest score 36 per cent went on to commit a violent crime within two to three years of release.

At best it is to be hoped that the particular contribution of psychiatry would be an evaluation of mental state on which would be based an estimation of probability that a person will behave dangerously. A second prognostication is the degree of harm that is likely to be caused. However, one is repeatedly faced with evidence that both the history and offence description are more important prognostic indices than the psychiatric assessment (Quinsey and Ambtman 1979). Pfoul (1977), in a study of the assessment procedure in an Ohio maximum-security hospital, observed that assessments led by psychiatrists merely provided patients with a clinical identity which purported to explain why patients were dangerous. Prediction depends on a basic ability to understand human behaviour, but insights are rare and we are usually left with medical explanations which do nothing to clarify the reasons for behaviour. Only nebulous formulations tell anything of the strength of impulses and the control exercised over them but too often such narratives are only applicable to a single case.

Floud and Young (1981) have reviewed predictive assessments of dangerousness and they conclude that, in general, prospective studies, which are correct in 36–46 per cent of cases, are much better than retrospective studies, which have only 14–20 per cent accuracy. In a fifteen-month follow-up of parolees Wenk, Robinson, and Smith (1972) identified subgroups on actuarial data who were three times more likely than other offenders to commit a violent offence while on parole, but even in this high-risk subgroup the possibility of re-offending was only 14 per cent. Wenk went on to select those with the greatest potential for aggression: these latter individuals showed 3.1 actual or potential new crimes of violence per thousand compared with 2.8 for a group considered to be less aggressive. An important British study was part of the 1972 south-east England prison survey where Brody and Tarling (1980) followed up a subgroup of men described in a piecemeal manner as dangerous. They were not those with the most frequent offences or long criminal records but men with histories of serious offences, especially of violence. Of a total sample of 700 there were 77 acts of violence in a two- to five-year follow-up but only 13 were committed by the 52 dangerous offenders free to re-offend. Three categories of anticipated danger, 'serious', 'possible', and 'not serious', could not be distinguished by post-release offence behaviour and inclusion of the variables 'number of previous convictions' and 'age' did not increase predictive accuracy. Follow-up showed that although the dangerous were responsible for a disproportionate number of offences against the person they had fewer convictions overall.

From another group of offenders Walker, Hammond, and Steer (1970) predicted that of those with three or more convictions for violence 50 per cent will have a fourth conviction. Floud and Young (1981) extrapolated from these figures to show that persons with four or more such convictions have a very high probability (0.975) that at least 65 per cent would incur further such convictions. Other studies have offered both contradiction and clarification. Thus Holland, Holt, and Beckett (1982) showed that violence is predictable, but minimally so, and then only by the number of prior non-violent convictions. These latter authors suggest that enduring personality characteristics play an important role in the creation and selection of the milieu in which there is an increased likelihood of violence (for example, carrying a weapon or using certain drugs) but, overall, violent conduct is more frequently dependent on unanticipated events, some of which are idiosyncratic to the point of randomness.

Some psychiatrists maintain that the significant criteria are clinical ones such as the traits of impulsivity, irritability, and arrogance, in combination with a rigidity of personality (Shepherd 1982). The psychological approach offers a plethora of inestimables:

'The expression of remorse is favourable, but this does not preclude risk ... [and] passive-dependent and hysterical personalities who have no prior history of assaultative behaviour give slight reason for concern.'

(Macdonald 1976: 129 and 131)

'Temper tantrums in an adult, a vengeful attitude and a facility with weapons are bad signs.'

(Loucas 1982: 67)

Scott (1977) viewed dangerousness as a process to which the victim might contribute by engendering a state of uncertainty in the assailant. Sometimes there is a resonance of provocation with previous infantile experiences where violence itself serves to allay a basic anxiety. Mental illness, severe personality disorder, and a high degree of childhood deprivation are associated with a type of violence which is both excessive and qualitatively different. Disinhibiting factors include fatigue, the presence of companions, and the use of depressant drugs, for example alcohol. Scott's attempts to provide a psychiatric profile of dangerousness do nothing to counter the penetrating criticisms of such writers as Meehan (1968), who argued that the application of a psychiatric label to the prediction of dangerousness is so conditional that it cannot be verified in advance, or so general as to be wholly non-specific, or so specific as to apply to only one case, or not assertable until the event has occurred. But even the most sceptical find the temptation to identify the important clinical factors irresistible. Thus Steadman and Cocozza (1974) recommended that attention be paid to three factors: behaviour since arrest; evidence of antisocial behaviour before arrest, excluding previous convictions; a description of illness behaviour. But these writers failed to warn that psychiatric predictions of dangerousness can only have a validity in clinical environments, where labelling can exert a self-fulfilling effect, rather than in the community where this influence is less.

For comparative purposes Sawyer (1966) examined clinical and statistical methods of measurement and prediction. In this context measurement was either a mechanical process or a matter of judgement, and prediction either a statistical exercise or a clinical one. If prediction is clinically based its accuracy will depend on the validity of the input data and its relationship with the clinician's judgement. Sawyer compared forty-five clinical and statistical studies and found that in all instances statistical methods of prediction were equal or superior to clinical methods. However, the best method combined clinical judgement as an input source with both measurement and statistical prediction. In terms of judgement, good judges were those with broad-based normative values, with both general and social intelligence, motivationally free to make their decisions, and it follows that both rater bias and reliance on stereotypes affect judgement. Sawyer found no general trait of judgemental accuracy. Clinical skills, developed from both training and experience and leading to an ability to integrate large amounts of data to a pattern, do not make the clinician's judgement superior to the layman's.

How is actuarial prediction undertaken? Probability estimates of criterion status (for example dangerousness rated on a scale, or categorically as present or absent) are derived from contingency tables rating predictor variables, such as age or sex, and criterion variables. If the predictor variables are continuous, as in a scale, the multiple regression equation allows these measures to be used to forecast continuous criterion measures (for example, number of convictions). To increase definition predictor variables must be common enough to provide a large pool from which subclasses of sufficient size for further analysis can be drawn. Input predictor variables should be solely evaluated on the extent to which they differentiate criterion groups. Where actuarial methods are applied to psychiatry, problems are raised with regard to the status of the input data which should ideally be available by being present in all subjects; objective in being quantifiable with a minimum of human judgement; reliable in that the assessments are repeatable; multi-dimensional so that ratings are independent of each other; valid in being a true measurement of what is purported to be measured; and, lastly, theoretically relevant to criterion data. The contribution which psychiatry makes to the assessment of dangerousness is apparent when the personality and clinical profiles summarized earlier in this chapter are judged as input data on the above criteria. A further point is that members of a criterion group (e.g. dangerous) can only be homogeneous with respect to the defining characteristics of the criterion class. Thus groups formed by social criteria are highly heterogeneous and membership will tell us little about the group's psychological characteristics (Wiggins 1973).

Inevitably some individuals will be recognized as an immediate public danger but because they are incarcerated for a long time, it is not possible to test the assumptions made about them. In this vein, repeated decisions not to release a prisoner or patient are a series of judgements whose validity is never tested because the subject is not at liberty to justify or refute the judgements made about him. Dangerousness cannot be decided on either scientific or legal criteria and, at their best, judgements are based on limited aspects of the criminal history. Whatever their claims, and however much status is invested in the person of the assessor, few predict more accurately than would be expected by chance. It will be shown later that more detention can reduce the number of offences, by incarcerating individuals who would otherwise be free to offend, but this policy must be tempered by the knowledge that most dangerousness is produced by individuals who could not possibly be identified as such beforehand. Thus prediction of dangerousness in general attempts the impossible – of anticipating behaviour which will only occur after a series of random events. A further problem is that rare behaviours are inevitably associated with false positive predictions and in the end we fall far short of the minimum moral requirement that predictive judgements should only be acted on if they can be applied with the same degree of probability as was used in the conviction for the original offence.

Crime and mental disorder

It would be surprising if the determinants of crime in the mentally abnormal were different from those personal and social characteristics which are related to crime in those who are not mentally abnormal. If the term mental abnormality is used to include disorders of personality, the addictions, and sexual deviations, there is an association with crime, but with mental illness and impairment of intellectual functioning the link is by no means clear. Furthermore, great difficulties are caused by multiple diagnoses in a single individual, for example schizophrenia, alcoholism, and a disorder of personality may coexist and be in varying relationship with each other. The association between the mental abnormality and the crime may also vary from bearing a direct casual relationship to being only slight or even inverse. Added to these complexities are issues of treatability and accessibility to treatment and the sometimes misguided expectation that treatment will influence re-offending.

The question whether a mentally disordered person carries a greater risk of conviction for an offence is fundamental, but quite distinct from the issue of dangerousness. As early as 1938 Pollock suggested that the rates of arrest in the general adult population for both sexes was over fourteen times as high as that in formerly hospitalized mental patients. Despite the incomparability of former in-patients and the general population they continued to be used as controls. Thus Rappeport and Lassen (1965) compared the convictions of the in-patient population of Maryland psychiatric hospitals in the years 1947 and 1957 with the equivalent rates in the general population of the state. Arrest rates in the five years prior to and following admission were examined and psychiatric patients were said to have higher arrest rates for the offence categories of rape and robbery and for aggravated assault (Rappeport and Lassen 1966). Giovannoni and Gurel (1967) also used the general population as a control group in their four-year follow-up of 'functional psychotics' released from Veteran Administration hospitals. Offences against the person were said to be more common in ex-patients and of those convicted two-thirds were found to have problems with alcohol.

A study of Häfner and Böker published in 1973 has been reviewed by Gibbens (1977). The work is outstanding not least because of the care with which control groups were chosen. It examined all offenders in the German Federal Republic who committed an act of serious violence (murder, manslaughter, assault resulting in death) between the years 1955 and 1964. The authors argue that the high rate of detection of these crimes together with the routine psychiatric assessment which offences of this gravity attract resulted in the accurate ascertainment of mental abnormality in each case. The observed rate of mental disorder was nearly 3 per cent in these crimes compared with an expected rate of 3–4 per cent in the population as a whole. Thus the proportion of mentally abnormal convicted after homicidal attacks equalled the proportion of mentally abnormal in the general population, but the value of such a comparison is lessened by the exclusion of those responsible for homicidal attacks who commit suicide and who are known to have a high degree of psychiatric morbidity. Häfner and Böker (1973) found the largest diagnostic categories were schizophrenia, affective psychosis, and mental retardation. Schizophrenics were over-represented among both the violent and the suicides and at the time of the offence most had been ill for at least one year, and more than one-half for five years. Sixty per cent of the schizophrenics' victims were friends or acquaintances. When violent psychotics were compared with non-violent psychotics the former group were largely untreated or unsupervised after discharge from hospital and significantly more schizophrenics became violent offenders than other diagnostic groups. Mentally disordered offenders were compared with both mentally disordered non-offenders and the general population: men and the age group 20–40 were strongly over-represented amongst mentally disordered offenders, suggesting that age and maleness, rather than mental illness, are the important associates of violence. Furthermore, violence begins when the risk for violence is high in terms of age, rather than at the peak age for the onset of mental disorder. A comparison was also made of violent schizophrenics and subnormals with their non-violent counterparts and it was found that the backgrounds of the schizophrenics were more like other violent offenders rather than other schizophrenics or subnormals. A comparison of mentally ill offenders and mentally ill non-offenders suggested that only the presence of alcoholism and sociopathic behaviour differentiated significantly between the groups. Among the schizophrenics, relationships which were full of tension played a role in the delusions, and threats preceded violence. In contrast, those with affective disorders showed no conflict in their relationships; the violent acts were carefully planned and were directed at close relatives; suicide was also contemplated. The mentally retarded were from broken homes and an antisocial milieu and they had a history of behavioural disturbances which antedated any offences.

Inasmuch as alcoholism and disorders of personality are mental abnormalities they are over-represented in criminal populations; mental illness and subnormality are not (Gulevich and Bourne 1970). With regard to dangerousness the work of Häfner and Böker (1973) suggests that the dangerous mentally ill have more in common with criminals than their mentally ill non-dangerous counterparts. We are left with an attempt to understand the position which psychiatry holds with regard to the issue of dangerousness. It is an important exercise because of the contrast between the relatively minor contribution which psychiatry makes to providing an explanation of dangerousness and its importance in its alleged ascertainment and treatment.

Mental disorder and dangerousness

Perhaps it suits the institutions of society to allow the psychiatrist to practise in the field of dangerousness because he can be relied upon to act conservatively in his deliberations. For the profession the concept supports a position of power although we have seen that its ministrators have unproven skills (Steadman 1972). Dealing with dangerousness carries with it an aura of competence which enables the psychiatrist to contribute to the allocation of legal responsibility, that is, liability to punishment. In these circumstances it is a label which is used tautologically as both an explanation for behaviour and a means of avoiding the despair invoked by the absence of an explanation. Walker (1977) has suggested that explanations which carry predictions have an enhanced value and this must be true of the label 'dangerous'. If the prediction turns out to be false, the truth of the explanation is obviously in question, but predictive utility is not tested because individuals assigned as dangerous are then not free to behave dangerously or not.

Another function of the label 'dangerous' is as a way of selecting and rejecting people for services and resources and as such is useful in demarcation disputes where individual services want to renege on their responsibility to provide care. Besides its use as a criterion for dispensing the benefits of the welfare state, dangerousness has quite distinct legal and moral connotations with regard to responsibility. When dangerous behaviour is associated with mental illness liability to punishment may be diminished or abrogated. However, with every behaviour other than the criminal act people are expected to exercise control over voluntary actions because they cannot be managed for long periods of time without the licence and constraints implicit in the notion that they are responsible for what they do. Thus a person found not liable for punishment for a criminal act may find himself in an institution where individual responsibility is the touchstone of the reward/punishment model on which the system operates. For those labelled as dangerous, powerful forces act in a way to validate the original prediction. In addition to this self-reinforcing quality the label allows for the continuing detention of those who have to be absolved from punishment on medical grounds but who could be considered to represent a continuing risk. In other cases, when treatment and rehabilitation are shown to be insupportable as grounds for continuing detention, the spectre of dangerousness can be invoked as a means of justifying the need for further incarceration.

Walker (1977) has argued that mental disorder is not an explanation of dangerousness since the latter is not a logical consequence of the former. It is only a possible consequence rather than an inevitable one. Neither does the concept of mental disorder carry general laws which must be required for the derivation of dangerousness. It follows that the psychiatrist is at his best working at the level of understanding, not of attempting to provide explanations, even less conjuring up reasons or causes. By understanding dangerousness the psychiatrist apprehends its meaning, character, and nature: it is a process of interpretation and carries an element of empathy.

Dangerousness and maximum security hospitals

Although Radzinowicz and King (1977) say that the concept of dangerousness is so insidious that it should not be introduced into legislation, it is used in section 4 of the National Health Service Act 1977 which provides for the special hospitals. A review of patients discharged from the special hospitals emphasized the difficulty in comparing discharge cohorts dissimilar in age, criminal careers, diagnosis, and legal status (Bowden 1981). Obviously reconviction rates will vary with the length of follow-up but published studies suggest that overall up to 50 per cent of those released will subsequently be convicted. The new offences are, however, mainly trivial and directed at property. About one in five of those discharged are returned to a special hospital and one in ten will be involved in homicidal or other serious acts of violence. When assessing the result of follow-up studies it is important to bear in mind that the criteria for relapse or failure, of readmission or conviction perhaps, are not necessarily the same as the indicators of dangerousness. Patients who are the best risk are those who have been diagnosed as mentally ill, have committed homicide, and are subject to supervision when conditionally discharged into the community. The poor-risk patients have diagnoses of psychopathic disorder and mental handicap, have more previous admissions to mental hospitals, and have more extensive criminal careers. The way in which different diagnostic groups were distributed between special hospitals and the discharge policies which they operated meant that psychopaths and the mentally handicapped were often released by tribunals so that after discharge they were less often subject to the statutory supervision. This summary confirms the work of Pruesse and Quinsey (1977), who examined discharges from a maximum-security hospital in Ontario. Within four years nearly one-half of the Canadian discharges had re-offended, usually having been involved in minor property offences; 17 per cent had at least one minor offence against the person. The younger and the personality disordered were most likely to fail. The suggestion that diagnosis is itself a prognostic indicator is open to doubt. Among a group of hospital-order patients admitted to both secure and non-secure hospitals Robertson and Gibbens (1978) have shown that the mentally ill are older than psychopaths at the time of making orders, have fewer previous convictions, and are older at first conviction. Therefore, it seems likely that it is psychopaths' demographic characteristics, their comparative youth, and the facts that they have more juvenile convictions and are younger at first conviction, rather than any psychological characteristics, which point to a poorer prognosis.

The patients described by Walker and McCabe (1973) were different in two important respects from special-hospital discharge cohorts: first, they were all patients who were involved in criminal proceedings; second, the majority were admitted to ordinary psychiatric hospitals. Walker and McCabe's group comprised 351 men and 105 women, who were studied following their discharge from hospital after a section 60 order had been made between April 1963 and May 1964. Subjects were allocated points depending on the number of previous convictions and custodial sentences, and the diagnoses subnormality and psychopathic disorder. Within one year of discharge 20 per cent of the males with a score of nil were reconvicted compared with 70 per cent of those with the highest scores. Furthermore, these authors showed that after-care was associated with a lower probability of reconviction even in the high-risk groups who are less suitable for, or responsive to, follow-up. In a one- to two-year follow-up of 673 hospital-order discharges 23 were convicted of a serious offence. Serious violence occurred mainly in ex-patients with no record of assaultative behaviour.

Using Walker and McCabe's (1973) criterion of dangerousness as violence involving injury or lasting psychological harm, Soothill, Way, and Gibbens (1980) followed up 220 persons after the hospital order was made by a court. The three-year conviction figures for serious sexual offences and violence were similar to Walker and McCabe's (5 per cent) but the proportion reached 17 per cent by the eighth year. One half of those with the highest prediction score were reconvicted of offences involving serious harm at five years.

Robertson and Gibbens (1978) completed a fifteen-year follow-up of Walker and McCabe's cohort. Among the 600 men they found that there was a very high correlation between the number of court appearances preceding the 1963/4 order and the number subsequent to it. Sexual and other serious violence was very rare on follow-up, and post-order serious offences were not represented in the 152 women. Among the subnormal, post-order sexual offending was quite rare despite the fact that one-quarter of the orders were for sexual offences. Most psychopaths re-offended, usually within a short time of discharge from hospital, but even in this group serious violence was very rare. Post-order differences could not be accounted for by diagnosis but by the fact that psychopaths began their criminal careers at an earlier age, had more convictions, were nearly a decade younger than other diagnostic groups at the time of the order, and spent less time in hospital (although they were readmitted more frequently). These differences of age and criminal record were also found in a group who re-offended dangerously in the post-order follow-up. An analysis of pre-order offences revealed that only one category of offence, arson, distinguished the dangerous re-offender on follow-up. Robertson performed a multiple-regression analysis using post-order dangerous offences as the dependent variable. He found that only age made a significant and independent contribution to the prediction of the dependent variable's distribution.

Some authors (e.g. Zitrin *et al.* 1976) suggest that there has been an increase in recent years in the reconviction of ex-patients. This can be explained partially by longer periods at risk in the community due to the policy of shorter periods of in-patient treatment consequent on the reduction in the total number of in-patient beds. There could also be a trend for those admitted to be more likely to have previous convictions (Rubin 1972) and therefore to be a greater risk after discharge. Some support for this last suggestion is to be found in the work of Robertson and Gibbens (1978) who demonstrated that the mean number of previous convictions in persons subject to restriction orders has nearly doubled between 1962 and 1975 to more than five. These authors also showed that restriction orders were increasingly made for violence and sexual offences rather than other categories of crime. Finally, it can be argued that the practice of informing the police of the whereabouts of restricted patients after discharge results in a higher detection rate of offences in this group.

Killing after release from a special hospital is a very rare occurrence. Thus Tidmarsh (1982) showed that of the 1,946 discharges from one special hospital over a period of eighteen years, 20 committed homicide and in only 4 was it a second killing. However, the rarity of seriously violent behaviour is not reflected by the publicity it attracts. Opinion is moulded by an exaggerated response and so the public interest, insofar as it exists, may be unmoved by the plight of those wrongly labelled as dangerous.

Dangerousness in the criminal justice system

In 1975 the Scottish Council on Crime recommended that a new public protection order should be available to secure the continuing detention of violence-prone offenders. In the same year the Report of the Committee on Mentally Abnormal Offenders (Butler Committee 1975) made a case for an indeterminate but reviewable sentence. This would be served on a small number of very dangerous mentally disordered men for whom release would be dependent entirely on the issue of dangerousness and not on the circumstances of the offence. These two proposals were foreshadowed by the several earlier attempts to identify and provide an exemplary sentence for selected prisoners. The Butler Committee wished to impose its indeterminate sentence on men not eligible or suitable for a life sentence, of which the committee was critical. Even after release subjects would be on licence and liable to recall.

Professor Walker was a member of the committee and his influence is clear. Later (Walker 1982) he argued that in the absence of the achievement of the ideals of treatment, or denunciation, or retribution, or deterrence as grounds of detention it must be justified on the basis of protecting others by doing so. Walker advocated that detention should only be used to prevent serious and lasting hardship to others, and the label 'dangerous' should not be applied to single, out-of-character, episodes. Furthermore, detention solely on the ground of dangerousness should only be in conditions which were tolerable.

But however humane the conditions of containment, disciples of the exemplary-sentence principle, while eager to provide moral and political justifications for their judgements, fail habitually to quantify the benefits and the cost of protectionist policies. Furthermore, it is difficult to understand why the Butler Committee should propose that the mentally abnormal be dealt with in terms of an indefinite but reviewable sentence unless this exemplary disposal was intended as a special measure which could be used against psychopaths. The terms 'mentally abnormal dangerous men' and 'psychopath' would come to be synonymous, both reflecting the circular process by which mental abnormality is inferred from antisocial behaviour while antisocial behaviour is explained by the mental abnormality (Wootton 1959). Although most often inaccurate, the label 'dangerous' when applied to mental abnormality provides the basis for prolonged protective confinement.

In the penal system preventive detention was introduced in the Prevention of Crime Act 1908. It allowed persistent offenders, who had already served sentences of penal servitude, to be detained for several years more in order to protect the public. The Act was intended for hardened violent offenders but in practice it was applied to inadequate recidivists. Like the Criminal Justice Act 1948, which gave corrective training for the young recidivist and preventive detention for those confirmed criminals leading a persistently dishonest life, the distinction between persistent and dangerous was not drawn and those two were interpreted similarly (Hammond and Chayene 1963). In 1967 extended sentences were made available but the law failed again to provide criteria of dangerousness. Consequently, the system was open to abuse, as were indefinite sentences in the USA for so-called 'sexual psychopaths' and other habitual offenders. In Britain, the popularity of the indeterminate sentence is shown by the increasing use of life sentences for offences other than homicide, accounting for 3 per cent of all life sentences in 1962 and 30 per cent in 1979. The protectionist position, which in effect argues that it is right to incarcerate two or three individuals to prevent one from committing serious and lasting harm, is gaining popularity. The denouement of this movement is the argument that special sentences should be applied to both mentally abnormal offenders, unstable characters, and those with abnormal sexual proclivities, not solely on the basis of the gravity of the offence but also according to the likelihood of recurrence in terms of threat, risk, or attempt (Floud and Young 1981).

The principle of containment, or incapacitation, has been reviewed by Brody and Tarling (1980). The principle is that, by imprisoning the relatively small number who are responsible for a disproportionate amount of crime, they are effectively prevented from carrying out those crimes that they would otherwise be free to commit. The authors showed that increasing the length of sentence of all those imprisoned to at least eighteen months would be at the cost of a sevenfold increase in the amount of time offenders spend in custody for the benefit of a 20 per cent overall reduction in the number of convictions. Similarly, by decreasing the time spent in prison by 17 and 25 per cent respectively, convictions are increased by 1.2 and 1.6 per cent. These findings suggest that a large change either way in the amount of imprisonment would have little effect on the amount of crime. Brody and Rarling (1980: 37) conclude that the infrequency of really serious crimes of violence, their apparently random quality, and the rarity of anything like 'a dangerous type' offer little encouragement for a policy which aims to reduce serious assaults by selective incapacitation of those with violent records. 'The public is already as well protected as it can expect from serious danger.'

The expectation that confinement would serve a utilitarian function has not been fulfilled. For example, if its purpose is to bring about a reduction in a particular offence category, that would only happen if a significant number of those responsible were detected and incapacitated by confinement. Furthermore, incapacitation studies depend on convictions as a measure of criminal behaviour, and the limitations of this criterion were shown in a study of undetected crime in California: categorization into the most and the least active criminal groups depending on convictions gave 40 per cent false positives and a similar proportion of false negatives because of undetected criminal activity (Peterson, Braiker, and Polich 1980). These authors also showed that the most active criminals do not confine themselves to a single offence category but engage in a wide variety of crime. Despite these criticisms, it seems that the trend to extend the use of preventive custody will continue with fewer safeguards for the detained person. Factors which were indicative of dangerousness in one environment will be superseded by ones which relate only to custody, and all that will be required to start the process is a justification of the appropriateness of protective custody at the time of sentencing, irrespective of any preventive or incapacitating functions (Floud and Young 1981).

As part of the habilitative or treatment approach to crime psychiatrists make a major contribution to the ascertainment of dangerousness by virtue of their status as medical practitioners. But the weight of evidence suggests that even when dangerousness and severe mental disorder coexist the important factors appear to be associated with the generality of crime rather than the generality of mental illness. A reawakening of interest in dangerousness might well be part of the vanguard of the justice or deserts approach to crime but psychiatrists should resist the temptation to cling on to the apparition of dangerousness as a sinecure. Psychiatrists should confine themselves to understanding rather than being arbiters of politics and morality.

References

Bottoms, A. (1977) Reflections on the Renaissance of Dangerousness. *The Howard Journal of Penology and Crime Prevention* 16: 70–96.

Bowden, P. (1981) What Happens to Patients Released from the Special Hospitals? *British Journal of Psychiatry* 138: 340–45.

Brittain, R. (1968) The Sexual Asphyxias. In F. Camps (ed.) *Gradwhol's Legal Medicine*. Bristol: Wright.

—— (1970) The Sadistic Murderer. *Medicine, Science and the Law* 10: 198–207.

Brody, S. and Tarling, R. (1980) *Taking Offenders out of Circulation*. Home Office Research Studies No. 64. London: HMSO.

Butler Committee (1975) Report of the Committee on Mentally Abnormal Offenders. Cmnd 6244. London: HMSO.

Cleckley, H. (1976) *The Mask of Sanity*. St Louis, Miss.: Mosby.

Floud, J. and Young W. (1981) *Dangerousness and Criminal Justice*. London: Heinemann.

Foucault, M. (1978) About the Concept of the 'Dangerous Individual' in 19th Century Legal Psychiatry. *International Journal of Law and Psychiatry* 1: 1–18.

Gibbens, T. (1977) Review of W. Böker and H. Häfner, *Crimes of Violence by Mentally Disordered Offenders in Germany*. Berlin: Springer Verlag, 1973. *Psychological Medicine* 7: 731–33.

Giovannoni, J. and Gurel, L. (1967) Socially Disruptive Behaviour of Ex-Mental Patients. *Archives of General Psychiatry* 17: 146–53.

Glover, E. (1960) *The Roots of Crime*. New York: International University Press.

Gulevich, G. and Bourne, P. (1970) Mental Illness and Violence. In D. Daniels, M. Gilula, and F. Ochberg (eds) *Violence and the Struggle for Existence*. Boston: Little Brown.

Häfner, H. and Böker, W. (1973) Mentally Disordered Violent Offenders. *Social Psychiatry* 8: 220–29.

Hamilton, J. (1982) A Quick Look at the Problems. In J. Hamilton and H. Freeman (eds) *Dangerousness: Psychiatric Assessment and Management*. London: Gaskell Books.

Hammond, W. and Chayene, E. (1963) *Persistent Criminals*. Home Office Research Unit. London: HMSO.

Harding, T. and Montandon, C. (1982) Does Dangerousness Travel Well? In J. Hamilton and H. Freeman (eds) *Dangerousness: Psychiatric Assessment and Management*. London: Gaskell Books.

Hellman, D. and Blackman, N. (1966) Enuresis, Fire-setting and Cruelty to Animals: A Triad Predictive of Adult Crime. *American Journal of Psychiatry* 122: 1431–435.

Hepworth, D. (1982) The Influence of the Concept of 'Danger' on the Assessment of 'Danger to Self and Others'. *Medicine, Science and the Law* 22: 245–54.

Hiday, V. and Markell, S. (1980) Legal Standards in Civil Commitment. *International Journal of Law and Psychiatry* 3: 405–19.

Holland, T., Holt, N., and Beckett, G. (1982) Prediction of Violent Versus Non Violent Recidivism from Prior Violent and Non Violent Criminality. *Journal of Abnormal Psychology* 91: 178–82.

Kozol, H., Bouchier, R., and Garafalo, R. (1972) The Diagnosis and Treatment of Dangerousness. *Journal of Crime and Delinquency* 18: 371–92.

Loucas, K. (1982) Assessing Dangerousness in Psychotics. In J. Hamilton and F. Freeman (eds) *Dangerousness: Psychiatric Assessment and Management*. London: Gaskell Books.

Macdonald, J. (1976) *Psychiatry and the Criminal*. 3rd edition. Springfield, Ill: Thomas.

Meehan, E. (1968) *Explanation in Social Science: A System Paradigm*. Homewood, Ill: Dorsey Press.

Peterson, M., Braiker, H., and Polich, S. (1980) *Doing Crime: A Survey of California Prison Inmates*. California: Rand Corporation.

Pfoul, S. (1977) The Psychiatric Assessment of Dangerousness: Practical Problems and Practical Implications. In J. Conrad and S. Dinitz (eds) *Fear of Each Other*. Lexington: Lexington Books.

Pollock, H. (1938) Is the Paroled Patient a Menace to the Community? *Psychiatric Quarterly* 12: 236–44.

Pruesse, M. and Quinsey, V. (1977) The Dangerousness of Patients Released from Maximum Security. *Journal of Psychiatry and the Law* 5: 293–99.

Quinsey, V. and Ambtman, R. (1979) Variables Affecting Psychiatrists' and Teachers' Assessments of Mentally Ill Offenders. *Journal of Consulting and Clinical Psychology* 2: 253–62.

R. v. Hay (1983) *Criminal Law Review* 276.

Radzinowicz, L. and Hood, R. (1981) Dangerousness and Criminal Justice: A Few Reflections. *Criminal Law Review* 756–61.

Radzinowicz, L. and King, J. (1977) *The Growth of Crime*. London: Hamish Hamilton.

Rappeport, J. and Lassen, G. (1965) Dangerousness. Arrest Rate Comparisons of Discharged Patients and the General Population. *American Journal of Psychiatry* 121: 776–83.

—— (1966) The Dangerousness of Female Patients: A Comparison of the Arrest Rate of Discharged Psychiatric Patients and the General Population. *American Journal of Psychiatry* 123: 413–19.

Robertson, G. and Gibbens, T. (1978) The Criminal Careers of Mentally Abnormal Offenders. Unpublished report to the Home Office.

Rubin, B. (1972) Prediction of Dangerousness in Mentally Ill Criminals. *Archives of General Psychiatry* 27: 397–407.

Sarbin, T. (1967) The Dangerous Individual: An Outcome of Social Identity Transformations. *British Journal of Criminology* 7: 285–95.

Sawyer, J. (1966) Measurement and Prediction, Clinical and Statistical. *Psychological Bulletin* 66: 178–200.

Scott, P. (1977) Assessing Dangerousness in Criminals. *British Journal of Psychiatry* 131: 127–42.

Shepherd, E. (1982) Assessing Dangerousness in Mentally Subnormal Patients. In J. Hamilton and H. Freeman (eds) *Dangerousness: Assessment and Management*. London: Gaskell Books.

Soothill, K., Way, C., and Gibbens, T. (1980) Subsequent Dangerousness Among Compuslory Hospital Patients. *British Journal of Criminology* 20: 289–95.

Steadman, H. (1972) The Psychiatrist as a Conservative Agent of Social Control. *Social Problems* 20: 263–71.

Steadman, H. and Cocozza, J. (1974) *Careers of the Criminally Insane: Excessive Social Control of Deviance*. Lexington: Lexington Books.

—— (1978) Psychiatry, Dangerousness and the Repetitively Violent Offender. *Journal of Criminal Law and Criminology* 69: 226–31.

Tidmarsh, D. (1982) Implications from Research Studies. In J. Hamilton and H. Freeman (eds) *Dangerousness: Assessment and Management*. London: Gaskell Books.

Walker, N. (1977) *Behaviour and Misbehaviour: Explanations and Non-Explanations*. Oxford: Blackwell.

—— (1982) Ethical Aspects of Detaining Dangerous People. In J. Hamilton and H. Freeman (eds) *Dangerousness: Assessment and Management*. London: Gaskell Books.

Walker, N. and McCabe, S. (1973) *Crime and Insanity in England*. Vol. 2: *New Solutions and New Problems*. Edinburgh: Edinburgh University Press.

Walker, N., Hammond, W., and Steer, D. (1970) *The Violent Offender – Reality or Illusion?* Oxford University Research Unit. Occasional Paper No. 1. Oxford: Blackwell.

Wenk, E., Robinson, J., and Smith, G. (1972) Can Violence Be Predicted? *Journal of Crime and Delinquency* 18: 393–402.

Wiggins, J. (1973) *Personality and Prediction: Principles of Personality Assessment.* Reading, Mass.: Addison-Wesley.

Wootton, B. (1959) *Social Science and Social Pathology.* London: Allen & Unwin.

Zitrin, A. and Hardesty, A. (1976) Crime and Violence Among Mental Patients. *American Journal of Psychiatry.* 133: 132–39.

10 Social control and social theory in secure accommodation

Philip Bean

Classifications of secure provision for mental patients, as with all classificatory systems, can be made according to different criteria: in terms of the legal distinctions, the socio-demographic nature of the patients, the type of regime provided, the extent of security organizations, or whatever. The classificatory system used depends on the aims of the enquiry, and to some extent determines the conclusions. Here I shall be concerned mainly with the regimes rather than the patients themselves, and by regime I mean not just the type of control exerted but the overlying ethos surrounding and justifying the existence of that control. This can extend beyond the physical boundaries of the organizations.

A general justification for secure accommodation

Secure accommodation involves a form of detention, and as such requires justifications. Various government commissions have grappled with the problem, not always successfully, and often as a prelude to their main recommendations. One such commission was that which preceded the 1959 Mental Health Act (Percy Commission 1957). That commission's arguments require closer consideration, not only because of its influence on the 1959 Mental Health Act, and the 1983 Act, but because current psychiatric practice in secure accommodation stems from that commission.

The Percy Commission, like so many earlier ones, justified the detention of mental patients within the social and political context of the times. The late 1950s were a period of rapid social change; the commission recognized this and felt able to produce a more radical document than its predecessors (see Bean 1980). Its radicalism centred on a belief that psychiatry could and should be more firmly linked to the mainstream of medicine. It began its report along those lines, and set the tone with a statement of intent about future policy when it asserted that 'insanity is a disease like all other diseases.' Now, insanity is not 'a disease like all other diseases'. The commission was of course aware of this and inevitably that assertion had to be modified. So a caveat was added: 'but with distinctive features of its own' (para. 136). Those 'distinctive features' formed in the commission's view their justification for detention.

The commission listed three:

1 'Mental disorder makes many patients incapable of protecting themselves or their interests so that if they are neglected or exploited it may be necessary to have authority to insist on providing them with proper care.
2 In many cases it affects the patient's judgment so that he does not realize that he is ill and the illness can only be treated against his wishes at the time.
3 In many cases too it affects the patient's behaviour in such a way that it is necessary in the interests of other people or of society in general to insist on removing him for treatment even if he is unwilling.'

(Percy Commission 1957: para. 136)

The commission did not expect that compulsory powers would be required for all mental patients – only for a small number, a residual group it called them, whose mental disorder was more extreme. (The commission was of course talking only of the noncriminal or civil patients; mentally abnormal offenders having committed a criminal offence are governed by different requirements.) The commission recognized that civil patients have neither the protection granted by the criminal law nor the usual legal justifications for detention. Their position was more vulnerable; hence the commission's hope that detention would be for a small number of the most severely ill – a hope well borne out by subsequent practice where the numbers detained are less than 10 per cent.

Those 'distinctive features' listed above divide into categories. The first, covered by (1) and (2), can be traced to the ancient concept of *parens patriae*; that there exist in society certain vulnerable groups who cannot protect themselves and require protection by the state – literally, the state as father of its people. Mental disorder therefore may produce 'neglect and exploitation' and may 'affect the patient's judgment so that he does not realize that he is ill'. The state therefore under *parens patriae* operates as a paternalistic instrument able through its agents – in this case the medical profession primarily – to care for those whose disability has placed them at the level at which they cannot protect themselves. The second category is more straightforward and is aimed at protecting 'the interests of other people or of society in general'. It becomes an extension of the powers of the state to control those who cannot be controlled otherwise; again literally, the state as police.

The Royal Commission's justifications for compulsory powers were not new; earlier Royal Commissions had used similar arguments (Macmillan Commission 1926). All such arguments have, in spite of claims to the contrary, tended to fit into general common-sense views about mental illness and the dangers thereof. Some people require protection against themselves or from others who may exploit them, and others require protection from those whose behaviour is likely to harm them. That much is clear. What is less clear is the method of implementing those aims, or rather whether those aims put into practice do not create forms of protection which turn out to be a burden to the patient.

Consider first *parens patriae*. If we accept that some people require protection against themselves we need to know who is to offer that protection and the limits to be imposed. Sadly the commission was less than clear on these matters. Since its recommendations were accepted somewhat uncritically by Parliament and drafted into the 1959 Mental Health Act, as well as being continued in the 1983 Act, the legacy of those shortcomings remains. For the commission recommended, and Parliament agreed, that protection should be offered by the medical profession, backed up of course by social workers or relatives. While members of the medical profession are entirely competent to pronounce on medical matters, protection is altogether different. Protection relates to moral and social questions; it is about vulnerability, neglect, exploitation, etc. In those areas there is no expertise that can be derived from medical training. But if this was not enough the commission added a further confusion. It insisted on making a distinction between a patient's psychiatric condition and his need for protection, for it argued that no form of mental disorder should be by itself a sufficient ground for depriving a person of his liberty. So far so good. Yet having made this important distinction it then proceeded to mix it up again by allowing psychiatrists (and others) to see the claims for treatment and the claims for protection as one and the same. It is curious that it did not realize that, given the psychiatrist's orientation, the one was likely to be defined in terms of the other. So for example a severe psychiatric condition could be defined as an urgent need for protection and vice versa. Protection is thereby reduced again to a psychiatric question (Bean 1980: 98) and the distinction becomes meaningless.

The second problem the commission created relates to limitations or rather the lack of them imposed on the psychiatrist. For while it may be obvious that some people require protection it is less obvious what form that protection should take. The commission left the matter open-ended; that is, it never sought to recommend the precise nature of protection, or define its limitations, or consider that protection as a general principle might be open to abuse. Some critics of current psychiatric practice have not been slow to point this out (Gostin 1975, 1977) and have argued for a more circumscribed form of psychiatric activity, where protection is defined in terms of recent events and not on the basis of clinical impressions. Yet the commission firmly believed that professional judgements would produce their own restraints, and eschewed all attempts to impose anything but the mildest restrictions on those judgements. Questions relating to irreversible treatments (e.g. psychosurgery) were not considered – although they had existed for over two decades when the commission reported – nor were patients given rights to appeal against clinical decisions. The courts' powers to act as the final arbiters were removed on the ground that it was inappropriate for a person not medically qualified to take action on the cure and treatment of a mental patient. Was this naivety that prompted such a set of proposals or a political decision to enhance the reputation of psychiatry? Probably a little of both, mixed with an optimism that social and moral questions could be resolved by reference to psychiatric theory or some such theory within the medical paradigm. Either way an open-ended approach to protection carried within it certain elementary dangers which the commission did not foresee – or perhaps chose to ignore. And it is only in more recent legislation (the Mental Health Act 1983) that attempts have been made to redress some of these imbalances and then only in respect of patients liable to be detained in hospital. The 1983 Act does little to change the patient's vulnerable position prior to hospitalization, or the position of informal patients.

The remaining justification given by the commission, i.e. the state as police, is no less free from difficulty. The commission said that compulsory powers are required if the patient's behaviour is such that it becomes necessary in the interests of other people or society generally. It needs to be remembered that we are concerned here with non-criminal patients whose behaviour has not been against the law – the commission spoke of behaviour which merely annoys. Clearly, this justification provides the state with massive powers, and permits critics such as Thomas Szasz to extract the maximum mileage. For Szasz would see this justification as a means of tidying up social life, i.e. penalize behaviour which is merely disliked. He would see mental health legislation operating as an adjunct to the criminal law and as a catch-all to behaviour which is seen as odd, unpleasant, or perhaps disagreeable. Szasz may be accused of ignoring the essential feature of the legislation; that is that the patient has also to be suffering from a mental disorder before detention can occur. Even so this would still not meet his basic point: that behaviour not covered by the criminal law can be covered by the Mental Health Act. And he would add no doubt that these powers operate and are operated by clinicians using diagnostic categories which are poorly defined: for as long as there remain diagnostic categories like 'reactive depression' or others equally vague but included in the International Classification of Diseases (World Health Organisation 1974) then the state's powers are awesome, and the patient's rights negligible. Had it not been for the commission's eagerness to link psychiatry to the mainstream of medicine some of these more obvious limitations might not have existed. As it is the 1959 Act produced an open-ended paternalism which relied heavily on clinical judgements, and there is little or nothing in the 1983 Act to change this.

And there are other problems which stem from that Royal Commission which are still with us, notably the numbers of mentally ill in prison and the overcrowding in the special hospitals. One can see how these problems were created. Having asserted that insanity was a disease like other diseases – albeit with distinctive features of its own – there was a certain elementary logic to the Royal Commission's argument when it suggested that a patient could be detained in any hospital, not just a mental hospital. Perhaps there was a hope that mental hospitals would become more like general hospitals. If so then the hope has been only partially realized. Some mental hospitals still have locked wards in which they detain informal patients, while some have overtaken general hospitals in the freedom they give to visiting friends and relatives (see Chapter 2). There was also a logic to the commission's argument that the decision to admit should be left to the hospital managers. The effect was surely predictable: more mentally ill people detained in prison and gross overcrowding in the special hospitals. Regional secure units (RSUs) have had to be developed as a result. All this is well known and other contributors have dealt with these matters in greater detail (see Chapters 5 and 6). I only want to show that the presence of the mentally ill in prison and the over-crowding in special hospitals stem from the general justifying aims of the 1954–57 Royal Commission. Or in sociological terms, that the solution has become part of the new problem.

Control and secure provision

Another major defect of the Percy Commission's Report was not so much what it said as what it did not. Detention based on *parens patriae* and police powers tell us little about the position of psychiatry in society generally – except, that is, as a branch of medicine – and little about the nature and form of detention. In fact the commission was concerned only to justify detention, and then in order to justify treatment – the latter regarded as a good in itself. But what is the nature of psychiatric control, and can it be given unqualified approval? The answer seems to me to be complex and many-sided, defying simple solutions or slogans.

To some sociologists, notably Michel Foucault, psychiatry and control are indistinguishable. Foucault regards the classificatory systems of mental disorder as a deliberate rival to legal dominance (Foucault 1978). To Foucault all legal definitions of proscribed behaviour have led to a psychiatric one; kleptomania is made equivalent to theft, pyromania to arson, and so on. (The 'manias' were of course nineteenth-century classifications but more recently, mainly under the influence of Freud, other psychiatric equivalents have been produced, such as infanticide.) In Foucault's terms psychiatry and the law produce alternative control systems so that secure provision for mental patients becomes a mirror image of the prisons in the legal system.

It seems entirely appropriate for sociologists to emphasize the nature of the control system in psychiatry. Secure provision for mental patients *is* a form of control exercised primarily by the psychiatric profession and assisted by paramedical and other professional personnel. And this point is not weakened by emphasizing other considerations, i.e. the provision of psychiatric care to disturbed mentally ill people involving diagnostic, evaluative, therapeutic, and rehabilitative processes, for these remain secondary to the major aim. Detention has to take priority; in an obvious sense there can be no treatment if there is no detention, and this is not forgetting that some patients may have been classified by other bodies such as the courts as requiring maximum security. Ignoring for the moment the hyperbole contained in Foucault's arguments, the sociological emphasis on control has had one notable advantage, it redresses the balance. Too often the literature on secure provision ignores or side-steps the control question, preferring to emphasize more morally appealing features such as the availability of therapeutic facilities, etc. Yet to do so is to be dangerously close to a form of deception which has dogged so much of welfare provisions throughout; a trap pointed out by Francis Allen long ago when he spoke of the delusive simplicity and ambiguity in the notion of treatment (Allen 1964). Secure provision for mental patients may well provide a humane regime, and may be preferable to other organizations on any grounds one wishes to choose, but they remain custodial measures nonetheless and will do so as long as there are barriers to the patient's freedom. To regard the patient's condition otherwise is to be involved in a form of label-swapping which disguises the nature of the enterprise.

Foucault is correct therefore to link psychiatry to control – in the most general sense, that is. He is on less firm ground when he moves to the specific, for not all legal definitions have a corresponding psychiatric one. His argument is more relevant to nineteenth-century psychiatry than to the present, for few modern psychiatrists would defend earlier classificatory systems or see every excess in terms of 'manias'. Yet on the other hand he has at least tried to unravel a particularly difficult knot, trying to assess the place of psychiatry within the legal system. But to say that secure provision for mental patients is a form of control may not of itself be a criticism of psychiatric practice. It only becomes so if control is seen as anti-therapeutic or a crude form of social hygiene.

If we accept that industrial societies pose problems of control whether these problems are created by the division of labour or by whatever sociological perspective one wishes to adopt, then psychiatry is placed ideally to operate those control mechanisms. Who better to explain the motives of the insane than psychiatrists;

who better to manipulate and change those motives, and who better to decide which motives are the more acceptable? And for those patients who are criminal or regarded as dangerous (that is those whose motives are often hidden or who are motiveless in some respects), who better to understand them than psychiatrists whose task it is to examine that confused area where madness and crime coexist? For having become the explainers of such behaviour psychiatrists must live with those explanations in the sense that they are the most appropriate group to exercise control. Foucault's fear is that the psychiatric world-view will dominate, with a corresponding loss of freedom gained by centuries of debate over the rule of law. But if so then it is up to the non-psychiatrists to protest and confine psychiatry to its own area of expertise; a move which I think has already begun after the excesses of the last five or six decades, and developed in some aspects in the 1983 Act.

However, sociologists, in their eagerness to portray psychiatry as the controlling discipline, often tend to concentrate on its influence (e.g. Foucault), or regard it as a competitor for an alternative world-view. The latter sociologists begin to be destructive of psychiatry and of medicine generally. There remains the tendency to ignore the positive side of control, and so fail to ask the important supplementary question: what is good or bad control? If psychiatrists really were the sort of people some sociologists believe them to be, then psychiatry would have less internal validity than even its most severe critics within the profession believe. The extreme sociological picture looks something like this: mental hospitals are full of sane patients, railroaded in by their families (Goffman 1961); detention occurs without consideration of the patient's condition (Scheff 1964); and psychiatric diagnosis is worthless (Scheff 1964). More recently, however, there has been considerable research and debate which has tended to present a more balanced view (Scull 1983), and a growing awareness that American psychiatric practice may differ from elsewhere (Bean 1980).

I do not wish to convey, or create, too much distance between myself and the work of Goffman and Scheff, for both have sensitized us to the more glaring abuses of psychiatric practice. Goffman has shown how the comfortable assertions of the post-welfare-state theorists need to be challenged; that is, that humanizing the mental hospitals does not affect the structural distinction between staff and patients, nor will it ever. Scheff has shown how careless and perfunctory are so many psychiatric interviews. Add to this the study by Rosenham (Rosenham 1975) and support is given to Scheff's and

Goffman's critiques of American psychiatry. The stimulus provided by these sociologists has been invaluable and ought not to be dismissed casually.

Furthermore, the control system these sociologists portray fits easily into the experiences of many patients, and is therefore far removed from the public rhetoric of medicine, of the caring doctor, and the equally caring nurse. It is of a world seen to be inhabited by patients, some of whom are harmed by contact with psychiatrists, most are ignored, and some recover in spite of rather than because of psychiatric contact. It is a world where the psychiatrists have limited contacts with their patients, where drugs are prescribed almost indiscriminately, and where the patients themselves are more knowledgeable about psychiatric conditions than the staff (Rosenham 1975). It may well be that this critique fits neatly into the spirit of the times, where the expert is on the retreat and where criticisms of psychiatry are likely to be more readily accepted. (John Monohan for example notes that 'rarely have research data been as quickly or universally accepted by the scholarly community as those supporting the proposition that mental health professionals are highly inaccurate in predicting violent behaviour' (Monohan 1978). Even so, and in spite of its current appeal, the critique is not without its own difficulties, not the least being that it produces a form of radical non-intervention based on the assumption that intervention in people's lives by experts rarely improves their condition and often makes it worse (Schur 1973). Unfortunately the radical non-intervention argument is weakest at the point where it is most needed; for who then is to exercise control? To assume that 'leaving people alone' will make the problem disappear takes no account of the possibility that alternative control mechanisms will develop which will, or could, be worse. The existing advantage of the present system is that psychiatrists operating the control system have professional obligations and can be censured when they fail in their duties. That they may not always be so censured is almost as much a criticism of the rest of us as it is of the professional bodies. Alternative control systems have no such apparatus and so the patient becomes more vulnerable.

Social theory and psychiatry

Whatever we may think of Foucault's view of psychiatric control he can never be criticized for being non-theoretical. If it seems sometimes that he is more concerned with the history of the ideas in psychiatry than with psychiatric practice he nevertheless places his arguments where they should belong; in society and in social theory. As such Foucault's work stands in striking contrast to the usual self-congratulatory historical accounts of the development of psychiatry from its demonological origins to the rational scientific humanism of the present day, where apart from an unusually dark period in the Middle Ages the development of psychiatry has been seen as one of eradicating errors. The modern asylum, according to Foucault, relies not on specific diagnoses or therapy but on the authority of the psychiatrist; a direct expression of the power structure outside. The asylum is:

'a microcosm in which were symbolized the massive structure of bourgeois society and its values: Family–Child relations centred on the theme of paternal authority: Trangression–Punishment relations centred on the theme of immoderate justice: Madness–Disorder relations centred on the theme of social and moral order. It is from these that the physician derived his power to cure.'

(Foucault 1965: 274)

In contrast, the usual debate about detaining patients in secure accommodation is in the manner of the Royal Commission described earlier, i.e. in terms of *parens patriae* and police powers, plus of course the usual medical requirements based on current strictures of mental illness *qua* illness. We search in vain for any elaborate social theory contained in many modern, and particularly modern official, justifications. The Butler Report for example operated on its own admission within 'the established framework of the existing legal, penal, health and community systems' (Butler Committee 1975: para 1.18). And psychiatric theorists such as Thomas Szasz have little or nothing to say about psychiatry within the social system generally, except as an appeal towards a special type of American libertarianism (not to be confused with European liberalism based on the traditions of Locke and J. S. Mill). Nor has Szasz anything to say about the conditions under which detained patients exist. Similarly those writers concerned with the provision of psychiatric services have demonstrated little or no commitment to social theory, being content to show gaps in services or the failure of past provisions. Yet the purpose of social theory is to go beyond these narrow conceptions; it is to show the nature of the psychiatric enterprise, and the position of detained patients within the social system.

The nearest we get to any social theory – apart from Foucault – is with those writers concerned to restrict or regulate psychiatric power. The practical advances made by these writers are considerable, for they have shown the manner in which secure detention of patients abrogates rights and freedoms in favour of a right more attuned to psychiatric professional training; the right to treatment. These writers are in fact operating within a subdivision of a wider theory of society, which we can call legal theory, a theory which is important not so much for what it says as for the manner in which it allows us to understand the position of those citizens who stand apart from the majority. Legal theory is not simply about the law; it also concerns the presumptions and assumptions about rights, duties, and obligations within the law. Writers concerned with the rights of mental patients tend to operate within legal theory whether they acknowledge it or not, and in so doing demand that psychiatrists do likewise. As a theory of society it has limitations but it has nonetheless provided a framework in which the position of mental patients can be examined. Before dealing with the limitations we can state first what legal theory is, and then show how it has helped our understanding of the position of psychiatry generally.

In general terms legal theory holds that society is comprised of a majority of sane individuals who are presumed responsible for their actions and capable of distinguishing between right and wrong. Whenever members of society choose to behave wrongly they are required to accept legal and social sanctions, the former conducted under requirements of legal justice. The sanctions are justified by traditional theories of punishment, retribution, deterrence, and to some extent rehabilitation; all are based on the assumption that people are responsible for their actions. People who are not responsible for their actions can be called legal marginals, the insane and children being the obvious examples (see further, Handler 1973). To these groups traditional theories of punishment do not apply. A person cannot be said to deserve punishment in the retributive sense if he was not responsible for his actions, nor can he be deterred if there is no prospect of foreseeing consequences. Nor can he be rehabilitated, for this also requires an element of responsibility shown as a commitment on behalf of the person to assist with the rehabilitative process. Legal theory deals with members of marginal groups and emphasizes their need for improvement; for the insane that would be treatment and for children it would be care and encouragement towards maturity. Of course some insane people are dangerous, as are some children, but nothing affecting the main argument follows from this; it means only that improvement must exist under secure conditions. The main argument remains intact.

There are many parallels between the insane and children, and while not wishing to push the argument too far it is interesting to note how within both groups there is recognition that being a legal marginal may be a mixed blessing. Attempts to resist the label are commonplace. Among children there is a growing demand to be reassessed as adults with all the rights of adults and there have been demands among some mental patients to be so classified. i.e. restoration of the right to vote etc. On the other hand there are others who find themselves legal marginals where before they were not: persons who have attempted suicide, for example, under the provisions of the Suicide Act 1961 are no longer regarded as criminal but are instead close to being regarded as insane, because the Act requires them to see a psychiatrist before they can be discharged from hospital. Marginality is not therefore a static label.

Legal theory separates those who are responsible sane individuals from those who are not. The position of legal marginals is therefore a tenuous one, for being detached from the mainstream of legal life their usual rights and freedoms become blurred, or rather merged into other rights dominated by that demand for improvement. Writers operating within legal theory have tried to extend legal thinking into that marginal area, whereas psychiatrists in general have tended to resist this. Hence the clash between the two professional groups, a clash which Foucault would see as being about power and influence. What is interesting for our purposes is that as matters stand at the moment patient control, particularly that which is concerned with secure control, is exercised by occupational groups other than those dominated by legal concerns. Or put another way, control is exercised primarily by psychiatrists, social workers, and others more interested in welfare than legal norms; a logical and inevitable extension of the concern for improvement.

This simple and rather obvious point has enormous repercussions on the status of the mental patients. And with one or two notable exceptions (Gostin 1975, 1977) few lawyers have wished to extend legal theory into matters dealing with the insane. Lawyers, and particularly those in Britain, appear less certain once outside the debate about the logical distinctions between legal rules. When that debate is conducted by other professionals and in a different terminology, or under a different paradigm, the lawyer appears to be at a disadvantage. Yet where lawyers have taken an interest in these matters they find a rich area of legal pickings. The recent spate of decisions against the British government by the European Commission and European Court of Human Rights is sufficient testimony to that (Gostin 1983). It is a matter of some importance to find out why it has taken so long to discover that mental patients dealt with in Britain had certain human rights violated and why most lawyers chose to ignore these questions. I suspect the answer has much to do with the structure of the legal profession, its perceived interests, and the current emphasis placed on legal teaching.

But whatever the reasons, a professional barrier has been produced which has not always been of benefit to the patient. I mentioned earlier that there were advantages in having professional groups such as psychiatrists run the control system, but there is another side as well. For if there is a truism to be extracted from sociology it is simply this: changes in welfare provisions since 1945 are more likely to be accepted if they advance professional interests. Proposals which appear to frustrate or curtail professional interests are likely to be less successful and subject to greater scrutiny, while the proposers themselves are subject occasionally to polemical debate. Conversely those advocating change in a manner which furthers professional interests, whether it be in terms of more resources or an increase in the status of the professionals, are more likely to have their views sympathetically received. The fact that 'more is not always good' (Wilding 1975) and that more resources, more professionals, and more time to do more of the same thing might not lead to benefits for the patient is not always considered. That a better deal for professionals does not automatically produce a better deal for the recipients appears also to have been overlooked (Wilding 1982). It is not a matter of dispute that financial resources for mental patients have been proportionately less than for most other areas of medicine, but it is, and should be, a matter for debate as to how an increase in resources will improve the standard of care. Paul Wilding has argued that increases in resources tend if anything to go towards benefiting the professionals first and the patients afterwards (Wilding 1982). The development of the RSUs is a case in point, for when the history of RSUs is written it will I think show that the desire for the benefit of increased status prompted the individual hospitals' decision to have them in the first place, as much as, if not more than, the desire for improved treatment of patients. And I do not wish to exclude the more obvious restrictive and status-seeking practices of some trade unions from the discussion, as shown for example in the evidence of COHSE to the DHSS Review of the Mental Health Act (DHSS 1978).

The clash between those using legal theory and those claiming to be concerned only with the patients' welfare is one of the intriguing features in modern psychiatry. The 1983 Mental Health Act is a recognition of the value or strength of the legal theorist's position, and as such implies a shift from the values embodied in the 1959 Act. The Mental Health Act Commission developed under that Act may be a resurrection of the old Board of Control albeit in a different form but it has helped implant legal theory in the special hospitals, in the RSUs, and in the mental hospitals generally. Time alone will tell how effective such changes will be, for success depends on the energy of the commissioners and a continuing commitment from the government. But even so it represents a major success for the legal theorists where the requirement of legal values intrude on psychiatric care.

And of course a legal theorist ought not to be willing to leave the matter there. We often tend to speak of secure accommodation as if it involved only formal, by which we mean legal, requirements to detain patients in mental hospitals. But secure accommodation can exist at the informal level too and it remains no different, in a qualitative sense, from the other. Legal theorists have, or should have, something to say on these matters. Two types of informal control can be distinguished: that which operates according to the demands of the psychiatric staff, and that which operates according to the patients.

In the first, Alfred Minto (1983) has argued that the revolution in psychiatry through the introduction of chemical-therapy has enabled greater levels of control of patients. Patients who would otherwise be disruptive, violent, or even dangerous perhaps can now be controlled by sedation. He argues that only through the introduction of such drugs could an open-door policy be maintained. Drugs have become the psychiatrists' alternative to locked wards; but more than that, they have allowed some psychiatrists to maintain a relationship with patients. In Minto's terms, 'one of the main advantages of drug therapy was that it enabled authoritariai psychiatric staff to maintain a hold over patients' (Minto 1983: 167). This is the positive side of the psychiatric revolution; it is a method of informal control which is acceptable, for it is in the nature of things psychiatric that some patients can only be cared for if they are rendered virtually unconscious at certain times. If it helps staff and patients then so much the better. But sedation is only one of the ways in which patients can be secured. Taking away their day clothes is another, so too is the use of locked wards and this for some patients who are officially and legally designated as informal (see Chapter 2). There is also the common practice of patients being told they can be admitted voluntarily or compulsorily, the choice, if that can be the word, is theirs – the ancient Latin term *coactus voluit* (at his will although coerced) sums it up nicely. All are measures used to secure or restrain patients from doing what they wish, and all should be evaluated by legal theorists as providing forms of detention.

Of course, to allow some patients to do what they wish would be disruptive, and would perhaps jeopardize the patient's own long-term treatment. No one denies this: but compliance can only be bought at a price. The current, and doubtful, practice of providing difficult children with sedatives works only as long as the sedation lasts, and at best provides only temporary relief to patients and others. The price is distrust and fear of the institution of psychiatry generally. No one knows the full extent of these informal practices described above but from my experience they are sufficiently widespread to warrant attention.

On the second point, the patients themselves, we can distinguish between those who are aware of their surroundings or position and those who are not. Those who are, and voluntarily submit themselves to restrictions and limitations on their freedoms, are the more difficult group to acknowledge or accept. It has been said that we cannot understand the nature of power and authority unless we understand also why some people freely submit to it. That many people are prepared to accept restrictions on freedoms knowing that those restrictions are designed for the benefits of others, in this case the hospital staff, is an aspect of a wider academic problem usually dealt with in terms of the sociology of knowledge. It relates in part to an acceptance of paternalism, and a belief that superior-status groups are immune from criticisms. There are some patients in mental hospitals who are prepared to accept and even welcome quite severe restrictions, who readily accept treatments which are irreversible, where the outcome is not known (within the reasonable canons of prediction), and who do not ask about the outcome. These patients may not be in secure accommodation in the accepted sense of that term but their self-imposed restrictions are no less valid.

There are other patients, such as handicapped children and the demented elderly, who may not be admitted under a formal order but whose detention is equally real. That they may not require a formal order matters little, for being unaware of their surroundings only makes the order unnecessary – it does not alter their predicament. Lacking the physical and intellectual wherewithal to change their status or situation, secure accommodation exists for them as surely as it does for others. If we are to take seriously the view that all restrictions on freedoms require justifications, handicapped children and the demented elderly patients fall into the same category as those on formal restriction. It is here, as much as in the more formal methods of containment, that legal theory still has much to offer; to patients and ultimately to the psychiatrists.

The limitations of legal theory

Yet for all its strengths the use and application of legal theory can easily become a dead end, being unable to focus therapeutic policy on any question other than that directed toward the misuse of medical power (Sedgwick 1982: 217). Consequently legal theorists are reactive, waiting for psychiatrists to commit excesses so as to rail against them. If not, then their contribution has to be about the correct use of psychiatric power and the desirable legal controls, e.g. where can the law intervene? how should it do so? what are the proper legal controls to regulate certain specified practices? I think the time has come to go beyond this.

If so, going beyond legal theory means recognizing certain elementary facts about what secure accommodation means. First, the legacy of the 1959 Mental Health Act, and the optimisim generated by that legislation, is now being repaid in full. That Act has, I think, to be seen for what it was: a unique piece of legislation at a moment in history reflecting social conditions which are gone forever. That it produced psychiatric excesses is clear, that its intentions were avowedly humanistic is also clear, but so too was the manner in which it overlooked some basic and central aspects of the patient's conditions. Rights were seen to be synonymous with treatment, and the right to the best medical/psychiatric treatment was absolute. The Butler Report noted this when it said, 'The Royal Commission placed considerable emphasis on the desirability of ensuring that patients received treatment or training expected to be beneficial, and although the patient's consent should be sought, they believed that compulsion was generally justifiable to this good end' (Butler Committee 1975: para. 3.53).

Second, it means that the insights gained from legal theory are not forgotten. Consider the restriction order under section 41 of the

1983 Act, which permits detention without limit of time (see further Chapter 7).

The questions about secure accommodation are more subtle now than in 1959 and more searching about psychiatric practices. This is what has led to the changing face of psychiatry. While the sociological contribution has sometimes been overtly destructive, it has, as was said earlier, redressed a balance and asked different questions about what secure accommodation means.

Yet having recognized these aspects the important question now seems to be the role of psychiatry in the social order, and in terms of secure accommodation its part in protecting society. We have Foucault's view that it is a mirror image of the legal system and, while I have tried to show that the mirror image may produce an impure reflection, it is a way in which we can understand some of the current dilemmas affecting secure accommodation and psychiatry's part within that. As long as secure accommodation is required there will be control issues to be faced. But it seems entirely wrong to see psychiatry simply as a carbon copy of the penal/legal system. The focal concerns of psychiatrists are different; they will always be on the welfare of their patients, rather than say a strict demand for legal justice. The psychiatrist's training emphasizes the uniqueness of the patient's experiences where the aim is to assist in the patient's well-being (Bean 1980: 188). It cannot be otherwise, and as we require psychiatrists to run the control machinery, or at least parts of it, that fact, unpalatable though it may be to some people, has to be faced. But at the same time an open-ended view of patients' welfare linked to an open-ended or free rein to operate secure accommodation on terms granted in 1959 is no longer acceptable.

The issues relating to secure accommodation for mental patients have a timeless quality about them and no solutions are ever available; instead there are theories which have to be judged on the basis of providing the least detrimental alternatives. Goffman failed to make the important link between secure accommodation and social order. He was concerned more with the interactions and the rituals established between patients, or between fellow patients and staff. And Scheff fell into the same trap as Szasz has done by comparing what psychiatrists do with what they think other physicians are expected to do, or what other physicians say they do under ideal conditions. Even so, Szasz and Scheff have succeeded in pointing to certain elementary differences between psychiatry and other branches of medicine and have done a valuable service in this respect. But the fact remains that the numbers of people detained in secure accommodation is to increase, the RSUs will contribute to this, and the question is, how are we to respond?

Self-congratulatory views of RSUs based on the likely reduction of the mentally ill in prisons may dominate, but if treatment is to be the same mixture as before (the pills-and-sympathy syndrome, or the pills-and-sympathy-and-limited-social-skills-training-and-moral-exhortation syndrome) little will be achieved. That view of madness carefully ignores the persuasive character of those who manufacture the pills. It ignores too the contradictions which stem from a materialistic view of the mental condition and a Cartesian view of the form of cure ('The illness is caused by physiological changes in your brain but you must pull yourself together'). It also ignores matters of political economy: that is the relationship between wealth-creation and the cost incurred by patients who do not create wealth at all. And it also ignores the professional tensions surrounding those groups who run the secure units and the demands of non-medical professionals for a greater say in diagnosis and treatment. For that is what I mean when I talk of social theory, and if psychiatrists are unable or unwilling to tackle these questions they ought not to complain when others do and shape psychiatry's future accordingly.

Some changes are already being made which suggest a greater interest in social theory. Andrew Scull (1977) has examined the 'Decarceration Movement' which swept large numbers of chronic patients out of mental hospitals to be housed in tawdry boarding-houses in the name of community care; he showed also the economic thrust behind this movement as a cost-cutting exercise. The effect, unintentional but real enough, has been to produce, or recreate, replicas of the private asylums of the nineteenth century (Scull 1983). The parallel ought not to go unnoticed. Others (Sedgwick 1982) link psychiatric theory to a more political exercise than hitherto. And if these types of studies are the shape of things to come they are indeed welcome, and I hope will be so to those inside the psychiatric profession as well as outside. If so, we may begin to see secure accommodation for what it is, that is more than a device for treating the criminally insane or whatever, and part of a total system aimed at controlling its deviant members.

References

Allen, F. A. (1964) *The Borderland of Criminal Justice*. Chicago: University of Chicago Press.

Bean, P. T. (1980) *Compulsory Admissions to Mental Hospitals*. Chichester: Wiley.

Butler Committee (1975) *Report on the Committee of Mentally Disordered Offenders*. Cmnd 6244. London: HMSO.

COHSE (1978) *A Review of Mental Health Act 1959*. Cmnd 7320. London: HMSO.

Foucault, M. (1965) *Madness and Civilization*. London:Tavistock.

—— (1978) About the Concept of the Dangerous Individual in 19th Century Legal Psychiatry. *International Journal of Law and Psychiatry* 1–18.

Goffman, E. (1961) *Asylums*. London: Pelican.

Gostin, L. O. (1975, 1977) *A Human Condition*. 2 vols. London: MIND.

—— (1983) The Ideology of Entitlement. In P. T. Bean (ed.) *Mental Illness: Changes and Trends*. Chichester: Wiley.

Handler, J. (1973) *The Coercive Social Worker*. New York: Rand McNally.

Macmillan Commission (1926) *Royal Commission on Lunacy and Mental Disorder*. Cmnd 2700. London: HMSO.

Minto, A. (1983) Changing Clinical Practice 1950–1980. In P. T. Bean (ed.) *Mental Illness: Changes and Trends*. Chichester: Wiley.

Monahan, J. (1978) Prediction Research and the Emergency Commitment of Dangerously Ill Persons: A Reconsideration. *American Journal of Psychiatry* 135: 198.

Percy Commission (1957) *Royal Commission on the Law Relating to Mental Illness and Mental Deficiency*. London: HMSO.

Rosenham, D. L. (1975) On Being Sane in Insane Places. In T. J. Scheff (ed.) *Labelling Madness*. New York: Prentice-Hall.

Scheff, T. J. (1964) The Societal Reaction to Deviance: Ascriptive Elements in the Psychiatric Screening of Mental Patients in a Mid-Western State. *Social Problems* 11: 401–13.

Schur, E. M. (1973) *Radical Non-Intervention*. New York: Prentice-Hall.

Scull, A. T. (1977) *Decarceration: Community Treatment and the Deviant: A Radical View*. New York: Prentice-Hall.

—— (1983) The Asylum as Community or the Community as Asylum: Paradoxes and Contradictions of Mental Health Care. In P. T. Bean (ed.) *Mental Illness: Changes and Trends*. Chichester: Wiley.

Sedgwick, P. (1982) *Psycho-politics*. London: Pluto Press.

Wilding, P. (1975) More Isn't Always Good. *New Society*, 4 September: 519.

—— (1982) *Professional Power*. London: Routledge & Kegan Paul.

World Health Organisation (1974) *Glossary of Mental Disorders and Guide to Their Classification*. Geneva: WHO.

Name index

Subject index